Advanced Placement*
Test Preparation Guide

to accompany

The American Democracy

7th Edition

by

Thomas E. Patterson

Written by

Stephanie Greco Larson

*Pre-AP, AP, and Advanced Placement programs are registered trademarks of the College Entrance Examination Board, which was not involved in the production of and does not endorse these products.

Mc Graw Hill

Boston Burr Ridge, IL Dubuque, IA Madison, WI New York
San Francisco St. Louis Bangkok Bogotá Caracas Kuala Lumpur
Lisbon London Madrid Mexico City Milan Montreal New Delhi
Santiago Seoul Singapore Sydney Taipei Toronto

Higher Education

This book is printed on acid-free paper.

1 2 3 4 5 6 7 8 9 0   QSR/QSR   0 9 8 7 6

ISBN: 978-0-07-325663-4
MHID: 0-07-325663-3

Publisher: *Emily Barrosse*
Director, Higher Education Sales in Secondary Market: *Jim Lewis*
Development editor: *Michelle Cox*
Production editor: *David Blatty*
Production supervisor: *Louis Swaim*
Compositor: *Eisner/Martin Typographics*
Typeface: *11/13 Palatino*
Printer and binder: *Quebecor short run*

www.mhhe.com

Brief Table of Contents

About the Author

Stephanie Greco Larson

Stephanie Greco Larson (Ph.D., Florida State University, 1987) is Professor and Chair of Political Science at Dickinson College. Her research and teaching focus primarily on media, public opinion, elections, and race and gender in American politics. She is the author of three books: *Media & Minorities: The Politics of Race in News and Entertainment* (2005), *Public Opinion: Using Micro Case ExplorIt* (2002), and *Creating Consent of the Governed: A Member of Congress and the Local Media* (1992).

She works extensively with the College Board helping to prepare high school teachers for AP* U.S. Government and Politics. This includes leading workshops in the Middle States region, serving as Content Advisor to AP Central for three years, and grading AP exams since 1995. Her essays on teaching Introduction to American Government appear in College Board publications and *PS: Political Science and Politics*.

Introduction

The purpose of this book is to help high school AP students who are using *The American Democracy, Seventh Edition* by Thomas E. Patterson prepare for the AP U.S. Government and Politics exam. It is intended to be used in conjunction with the textbook, which is why there are so many page references. Nevertheless, the comprehensive chapter summaries, terminology lists, advice about the test, and sample test questions should be useful for anyone taking the exam.

This introduction chapter includes three sections. The first describes the test, the second describes this book and how it is organized, and the final section includes advice based on my experience teaching the class, grading the test, and training high school teachers.

The AP U.S. Government and Politics Test

The AP U.S. Government and Politics test has two sections, multiple-choice and "free-response," each of which makes up 50 percent of your score. The entire test must be completed in two hours and twenty-five minutes. The test is written by a committee of professors, teachers, and test experts. There is about a two-year lag between writing the test and administering it.

Students have forty-five minutes to complete the first section, which includes sixty multiple-choice questions. The questions each have five potential answers. There are no "none of the above" or "all of the above" answer options. Some of the questions indicate that "all of the following are true EXCEPT:" and students need to find the incorrect statement. Although knowing factual information is essential to doing well on this portion of the test, knowing facts is not enough. Students also must be able to apply ideas, interpret data, and use terminology. The multiple-choice portion of the test is scored by giving one point for every right answer, zero for unanswered questions, and minus one-fourth for wrong answers. This means that if students have no idea what answer to choose, they should leave the question blank. The multiple-choice portion is graded using a scanning device.

That leaves one hundred minutes to answer four "free-response" questions. Each of the four questions is equally weighted, so it is essential to answer all four free-response questions. These are not traditional essay questions in that they are not general or unguided. For example, they do not ask questions like this: "Compare and contrast the three branches of government." They do not require thesis statements or eloquent development of ideas. They are focused questions with multiple parts. They typically ask for political factors or government structures to be identified, described, and explained. Many offer students choices such as providing a short list of interest groups, structures of government, parts of the Constitution, or Court cases to describe and relate to other political actors, causes, or results. Students need to read the questions carefully and answer them in a straightforward way.

Answers to the free-response portion are graded by hundreds of teachers and professors who meet for about a week in June. Most graders will grade answers to only one question all week long after they have been trained on how to score answers. Grading consistency results from requiring all of the graders to apply the same standards to the tests they grade. This is why scoring guidelines ("rubrics") are provided. These rubrics explain how many points the question is worth and what is required to earn each point, and they keep graders from using their own individual standards.

How the Book Is Organized

The book includes this introduction, 17 chapters that follow Patterson's substantive chapters, and two practice tests with answers.

Each of the 17 chapters is organized in three parts: "Summary," "Take Note," and sample test questions and answers. The first sections of each chapter summarize Patterson's chapters. The summaries follow the book closely. Although some parts of the chapters are merged and the discussion is condensed, no major points are omitted and no topics are added. For the few times that something that seems essential to the AP test is missing from Patterson's chapter, it is discussed in the introduction to the "Take Note" section.

The "Take Note" section includes an introduction and four parts: "Observations from Past Exams," "What to Do with the Boxes," "Key Terms," and "Making Connections to Previous Chapters." The introduction starts with an assessment of how important the chapter is to the test. For some chapters, the introduction also includes advice to focus attention on specific topics or an explanation of something missing from the chapter.

The first subsection of "Take Note" describes the part of the AP curriculum that the chapter addresses, how the College Board describes that curriculum, and what percentage of the multiple-choice questions are likely to be drawn from it. The curriculum includes six major content areas: constitutional underpinnings, civil rights and civil liberties, institutions of national government, political beliefs and behaviors, linkage institutions (political parties, interest groups, and mass media), and public policy.

The next section describes questions that have appeared on released AP tests, questions that are related to the material in the chapter. This will give you an idea of the emphasis on the exam—how much attention is placed on that chapter and what parts of the chapter are key. These previous tests are AP tests that currently appear on the AP Central Web Page, accessible to teachers but not to students. There are two multiple-choice tests, from 1999 and 2002, and six free-response tests, from 1999 through 2005. In my experience, many students overlook boxes in introductory texts. This is a mistake. As Patterson says in his Preface (p. xxi), "boxes are not mere fillers or diversions." Yet, reminding you of this is not necessarily helpful because the boxes serve various purposes, some more relevant to the AP test than others. Therefore, I provide some advice about boxes in the second part of the "Take Note" section. I indicate which boxes contain information most essential to the test, which are not relevant to the test, and how you can use the boxes to practice understanding data and thinking about broad issues. At times I am suggesting that you use the boxes in ways that differ from Patterson's goals. He wants to help you see how American politics differs from other countries' (in the "How the United States Compares" boxes) and how it is part of an interdependent world (in the "Global Perspective" boxes). These are not central goals of the AP U.S. Government and Politics curriculum. Nor are state comparisons (featured in the "States in the Nation" boxes) or encouraging you to participate in politics (the goal of the "Citizenship" boxes). However, since some of the information in the boxes of these four types is relevant to the exam, I have chosen to talk about the utility of every box in chapters 1–17.

The "Key Terms" subsection is generally a list of terms with a short reminder to understand what terms mean and how they compare to other concepts and to provide examples of them rather than simply memorize them. Each term includes one or more page numbers so that you can see where it is introduced in the chapter. All of the terms that Patterson puts in bold and defines in the margins are included. Others important terms for which he fails to do this are included on the list. I also identify the constitutional amendments that are discussed in the chapter.

The "Making Connections to Previous Chapters" subsection begins with the review of Chapter 2. It is designed to warn you against thinking of the material in these chapters in isolation. Making connections is essential for doing well on the test. Questions on the test will ask you to relate ideas within and among the six content areas. This section provides examples of how you can do this and questions to stimulate your thinking. This section also alerts you to how material found in the chapter you just reviewed was included (or could easily have been included) in earlier chapters.

Each of the 17 chapters ends with 10 multiple-choice questions, two free-response (or open-ended) questions, and answers to these questions. These follow the same format as those on the AP test. For example, the multiple-choice questions have five answer options and no "all of the above" or "none of the above" options. The free-response questions require both factual information and critical thinking. Most of the chapters include one or two questions that require analysis of a graph, table, figure, or map. These are common in the AP test, appearing in both multiple-choice and the free-response sections. Some of the multiple-choice questions ask about material from the chapter alone, while others require you to remember information from previous chapters.

Advice for Taking the Test

I have taught the college-level course to which the AP test is equivalent since 1985 at three different institutions (Florida State University, George Washington University, and Dickinson College). Since 1995, I have been one of the hundreds of professors and high school teachers who meet to grade the free-response questions. I have written multiple-choice questions for the exam, conducted daylong and weeklong workshops for AP teachers, and served as "content advisor" for AP Central for three years. In this job, I have identified and reviewed resources useful for AP U.S. Government and Politics teachers. These experiences have given me insights into the curriculum, how it is taught in high schools, the test, and how students answer the free-response questions. Here are some insights that should be useful to you:

Don't give up. While this is probably good advice no matter what test you are taking, it is particularly relevant for the free-response portion of the test. These questions can seem as though they are coming from "left field" because they are analytical rather than rote. They ask you to analyze data, apply concepts, and explain how things relate to each other. Lots of students are thrown off by these questions. As a result, some seem to underestimate themselves and give up.

I can think of numerous examples of essays I was grading in which students introduced their answers with "disclaimers" usually saying that they had "no idea" what the question was asking for or blaming their teachers for not covering the material—not a persuasive argument to make to teachers! Often, these tirades precede fairly good answers that earn students enough points to have a shot at a passing score. I wonder how many of the students who didn't answer the question at all could have done as well. Therefore, you should not give up: your answer might be worth more than you think it is.

Another reason to try is because scores on free-response questions are calibrated based on how well all the students taking the test do on them. This means that if you get only four points on an eight-point free-response question, your overall score is not doomed—if most other students got fewer points. Doing marginally well on a question that most students do badly on helps your overall score. Your job is to take the test and give it your best try, not to try to figure out how a particular question will be scored and talk yourself out of trying.

Read the question carefully and answer all of it. Don't waste time answering a question that wasn't asked. The questions are focused, so answers should be focused. Do not rush to answer a question without clarifying what is expected. For example, most students know something about political parties, but when those words appear in a question it will not be sufficient (or an efficient use of your time) to dump everything you can remember about parties on the answer sheet. You need to clarify what the question is asking *about* political parties. Is it asking about factors that influence a specific aspect of parties (for example, how campaign finance laws have influenced parties' influence on campaigns) or is it asking for how parties influence something else (for example, how party realignments influence policymaking)?

While incomplete answers might indicate incomplete knowledge, I suspect that this is often not the case. I have graded many AP exams in which students write extensively and well on part of the question yet fail to address the rest of the question. This has disastrous consequences because of the way that the answers are scored. For example, if a question has three parts (A, B, C) and each part is worth two points, then offering a brilliant answer to part A earns you only two points. Students often provide far more than is needed to nail down a point and then provide nothing that addresses the other parts of the question. Over the years, I've read hundreds of essays that go on for pages and earn few or no points, and I've read many that get all of the points in less than a page. The key is to answer the question that is being asked.

Another common problem is that students misunderstand the question and provide answers that are not on the rubric. If the question asks for a factor that influences how something has changed over time, then the factor also needs to be something that has changed. For example, a question might ask you to identify and explain factors that have contributed to a drop in voter turnout since 1960. If you identify the Electoral College as a structure that discourages voters, describe the process accurately, and explain well why it discourages voters, you would not get any points. This is because the Electoral College was around in 1960, too. Therefore, it hasn't contributed to the decline, even though it might discourage voting. A question that asked about the influence of the "mass public" on the Supreme Court did not include interest-group activities on the rubric. A question that asked for a provision of the Clean Air Act did not accept a description of prohibition of toxic dumping in rivers in the rubric.

U.S. Government and Politics and U.S. History are not the same, nor are their AP tests. Dickinson students sometimes ask me if they have to take the "American Government" class for a political-science major if they passed AP U.S. History. The answer is "Of course." History and political science are different majors, different departments, different topics; they have different approaches to studying the United States. The AP tests for the two subjects are also dissimilar. If you have taken an AP U.S. History course and/or done well on that test, do not think that you are prepared to take the U.S. Government and Politics test, or visa versa.

Many students do not answer the question that is asked and instead provide a lot of historical information that might be accurate but is irrelevant. In fact, you should stay away from examples that are "too historical." Sometimes they will count, but often they will not. It is generally best to stay with the modern era. For example, there was once a question asking about the growth in the federal government's power vis-a-vis the power of the states. Students who went further back than the mid-1930s were unable to get the points that the rubric identified. Think of Franklin D. Roosevelt as starting the era of the modern presidency, and stick to examples from then on (unless the question points you further back, such as asking about the Constitution). Some questions specifically delineate the time period (for example, "since the 1960s"). Be sure to abide by these limits.

Use and show an outline. Sometimes I have graded free-response answers that started with a short outline that was clearer than the essay that followed. In such cases, I have awarded more points for the outline than for the essay. Many high-scoring answers are bullet points with some elaboration rather than traditional essays. There is no need to identify a thesis statement or to underline or highlight what you consider your main point. These markings do not make a difference in the grading, as we are looking for points on the rubric. The rubric is the detailed instructions provided to the graders describing how points will be awarded for various answers. For example, if the first part of a free-response question asks students to identify a trend in a graph, then the rubric indicates how many of the total points for that question are awarded for correctly doing this and it lists the various answers that are acceptable to earn this point (or points). Specific, focused, and relevant examples often help clarify what a student means by a too-general explanation.

Understanding processes and explaining how or why factors influence each other is more important than getting some of the facts right. Factual inaccuracies, such as the name of a court case, candidate, politician, or law, are typically overlooked in the grading rather than counted against students. Hypothetical examples are sometimes given as much credit as "real ones" as long as they are used to illustrate an accurate understanding of politics. This is another reason that you should not give up. A specific detail that you are having trouble remembering might be irrelevant for earning the points.

Pay close attention to the terms used in the question: "Identify," "describe," and "explain" are not the same things. When you are asked to *identify* something (for example, a rule of the U.S. electoral system, the trend in the graph, a way that something affects something else), it can usually be done in a clear sentence or two. This is also true of something you are asked to "list." A *description* requires more than an identification but less than an explanation. If you are asked to describe something, such as litigation, the point of view of a cartoon, or an obstacle to campaign finance reform, be specific and concrete. An example can help make a description clear. Unsatisfactory answers sometimes talk around a point or say what something is "about" or "deals with" rather than saying what it is. For example, litigation isn't "dealing with the court" and the message of a cartoon would not be "about the election."

An *explanation* is usually worth more points and will need to be lengthier and more developed than a "description." Explanations should say how or why something works the way it does. Questions often ask for students to "identify and explain." The explanations need to be relevant to the identifications. For example, you could be asked to "identify a politically relevant factor that affects government benefits for children" and then "explain how the factor affects benefits." Explanations need to make logical sense. A factor that contributes to something cannot have happened after the event it is supposed to have affected.

Don't editorialize or pontificate. Questions are not asking for your personal opinions. You should be prepared to explain different sides of "issues" (such as the strengths and weaknesses of divided government or the arguments used for and against campaign finance reform). The questions are trying to test your understanding of concepts and analytical skills, not your political zeal.

Manage your time. If you have time left after answering the questions, go back and add a fallback to what you have already written. Keep track of time so that you are able to finish all of the questions. You have about forty-five seconds for each multiple-choice question, so you do not have time to get distracted by the tables and graphs. They will have more information on them than you will be asked about. Therefore, you should look at the question-and-answer options before getting lost in the data. You have twenty-five minutes for each free-response question. It is important to answer them all. However, if you have time left after writing all your free-response answers, go back and add "fallback answers." Lots of students manage to get points from the rubric with a sentence or two that they have inserted into their essays (using asterisks or arrows). If a question asks you to "describe a factor," there is a chance that the factor you chose is wrong, confusing, or left off of the rubric. Therefore, it is a good idea to provide a second factor. It might be the one that earns the points. You will not jeopardize any points if the second is wrong and the first one was right. You will not be penalized if both are wrong. This is because points are awarded for answers that are on the rubric; points are not taken off for answers that are incorrect.

Write legibly. This might mean writing larger, darker, or with blank lines between your sentences. Although every effort is made to figure out what you are trying to say, it would behoove you to make the grader's job easier. Identify which section of the question you are answering.

Come to the test in the right frame of mind and physical shape. Try not to be tired, frantic, hungry, thirsty, or sedated. Try to stay focused and calm. Even if you do not get a score on the test that earns you college credit, studies show that you will do better in college because of the experience of completing an AP class and taking the test.

CHAPTER ONE

American Political Culture: Seeking a More Perfect Union

Summary, Take Note, and Test Questions

SUMMARY

The United States is based on ideals that have endured since its origin. Conflict over how to define, prioritize, and realize these ideals is what politics is all about. Politics can be thought of as "rules of the game." In America these rules include *democracy, constitutionalism,* and *capitalism.* There are four theories of who governs. They are: *majoritarianism, pluralism, elitism,* and *bureaucratic rule.* The interrelationship among *inputs,* political institutions, and *outputs* is the American political system (and the organizational structure of the book).

Political Culture: The Core Principles of American Government

Shared ideals characterize a political culture. The American *political culture* has been built on a European heritage. American culture gives priority to three core values that have endured and defined America. They are: *liberty, equality,* and *self-government.*

American Core Values: Liberty, Equality, and Self-Government

In America individuals are thought to have *"unalienable rights,"* or freedoms, that cannot be abridged by government. Instead, government is expected to protect these rights. Therefore, *liberty,* or freedom, is a core value celebrated in American symbols, documents, and rhetoric. The U.S. Constitution protects Americans' *natural right* to liberty from government intrusion. The notion of freedom was expanded after the Industrial Revolution to include the idea that government should protect individuals' freedom from businesses.

    Equality is another core value. It was articulated in the Declaration of Independence as "all men are created equal." The definition of equality and the debate over whom it should apply to has changed over time and is at the heart of the greatest conflicts in American politics: slavery and racial justice. Patterson defines equality in America as the idea that all people have equal worth and should be treated the same by law. It does not mean that people are inherently alike—for example, having equal skills—or that they should have the same rewards—for example, wealth or property).

    The third core value is *self-government.* In the United States, government's power comes from the "consent of the governed." This consent is expressed through free elections. Other American values are individualism, unity, and diversity.

The Power of Ideals

Core values identify what is ideal and what are reasonable goals to work toward. Considering the values in combination helps explain public opinion and public policy. For example, commitment to both equality and individualism results in a more limited welfare policy than exists in Europe and a greater commitment to educational opportunity.

The Limits of Ideals

Ideals are not always fulfilled. Slavery, racial segregation, and restrictive immigration laws are examples of the United States' failure to act on the principle of equality. Some values conflict with other values. For example, affirmative action is an issue in which equality and freedom are at odds. Even though values can be hard to define precisely, may be in conflict with each other, and may not be fully realized, they inspire political action.

Politics: The Resolution of Conflict

Conflict is at the heart of politics because resources are scarce and people disagree over which values take priority and who should get what (and when). *Politics* is a process that seeks to resolve these conflicts in a society. This process has agreed-upon rules, with different political systems having different rules.

The Social Contract

The fundamental "rule" is that a government's legitimacy rests on the assumption that the people have entered into a contract with their rulers. In a contract, both sides agree to "do something" (or "give something up") in order to "get something." In the American *social contract*, the people give up their unlimited freedom and agree to defer to a government that they have a say in creating. The government agrees to protect people's lives, rights, and property.

The Rules of American Politics

The three major rules in the American political process are: *democracy, constitutionalism,* and *capitalism. Democracy* gives people a say in governing through elections. In the United States, majorities select representatives in different branches and levels of government. This fragments authority and makes it harder for one interest to dominate. The power of the majority is further limited by *constitutionalism*. The Constitution formally sets limits on government power to protect the rights of individuals and minorities, who would otherwise be at the mercy of majorities. *Constitutionalism* gives the courts the power to resolve conflicts by applying the Constitution and its principles to disputes. *Capitalism* is the economic system used in the United States. It requires limited government intervention in the economy and businesses.

Political Power: The Control of Policy

Unlike other societies that have *authoritarian* or *totalitarian* governments, power in the United States is checked, limited, and changes hands. Competition for power is a central characteristic of democracy. It results in compromises between groups to determine public policy. Ultimately, government has authority to require, even to coerce, compliance with these laws.

Theories of Power

There are four dominant theories about who governs in America. They are: *majoritarianism,*
pluralism, elitism, and *bureaucratic rule.* Patterson argues that they are each valid and that all four
help explain how political power is exerted on some issues at some times. He believes that each
should be considered for what it contributes to understanding specific policy outcomes.

Majoritarianism is the idea that majorities rule. It assumes that the policy reflects the preferences of the majority of Americans. For this theory to hold true, the public needs to be paying
attention to an issue and to care about it. This infrequently occurs.

Pluralism holds that policy is the result of competition among groups that represent the
great diversity of interests in the country. It assumes that the special interests of groups collectively represent the general interest. Critics challenge this assumption, arguing that some interests are poorly represented by groups, that a few economically privileged groups dominate, and
that the public interest can be compromised rather than realized through interest group politics.

Elitism contends that a small group of people, in positions of power inside and outside of
the government, determines public policy. Scholars disagree over whether elites do this for
narrowly self-serving motivations or out of regard for their obligation to serve the public.

Bureaucratic rule theory sees bureaucrats, the people who administer large-scale organizations within government, as being the most powerful. Because these individuals are unelected
experts, they can make decisions that reflect substantive knowledge rather than uninformed
public opinion. This, and their permanent status in government, is inherently counter to the
notion of democratic governance.

The Concept of a Political System

The *political system* is made up of interrelated parts that together show how government works
and what affects its decisions. The system approach also helps organize the sections of the book.
The first section examines the *constitutional framework* within which political actors operate. The
second section looks at *inputs* (what the public, parties, and interest groups demand that government do). The third covers *political institutions* (the three branches of government) and the
last explores *outputs* (the decisions made by the government organized in policy areas). The
important thing to understand is that change in one area of the model affects another. For
example, if the public demands change (input) and expresses those demands through polls,
elections, interest groups, and parties, then government institutions will respond to those
demands and create policy decisions (outputs).

TAKE NOTE

Most of the material in this introductory chapter is unlikely to show up directly on the AP U.S.
Government and Politics test. However, understanding it will help organize information that is
essential to the test because it provides "the big picture." It is useful to think about politics as a
conflict over values and to look at the connections among inputs, institutions, and outputs.

Observations from Past Exams

This chapter falls under topics found in two sections of the AP U.S. Government and Politics
curriculum. Because Chapter 1 deals with theories of democratic government, it is part of
the "Constitutional Underpinnings of the U.S. Government" section. This section makes up

5 percent to 15 percent of the multiple-choice test questions. It also fits under the "Political Beliefs and Behaviors" section, which makes up 10 percent to 20 percent of the objective questions, because it addresses beliefs that citizens hold about their government and leaders. There was only one question on the two most recently released multiple-choice exams about information in this chapter. The 2002 exam asked a question about America's core values.

What to Do with the Boxes

The chapter includes two helpful summaries. One is the box on America's three core values (p. 11) and the other is the table outlining theories of power (p. 28). The visual representation of the system model (p. 32) helps illustrate this approach to seeing how political actors relate to each other.

A useful preparation for the illustration-based questions on the test is to try to write a summary for Figure 1-2 (p. 16), Figure 1-3 (p. 16), and Table 1-1 (p. 17) before you read (or review) the one provided under the title. Try to come up with arguments for why the information looks the way it does.

"Debating the Issues: Should English Be Made America's Official Language?" and "Liberty, Equality & Self-Government: Liberty and Security" are good illustrations of how values can clash on specific issues. Being able to analyze issues for their underlying values is a useful skill. It also helps to be familiar with some specific policies so that answers to free-response questions can include good examples.

Because of the focus of the AP test, you do not need to concentrate on the biographical sketch of Thomas Jefferson (p. 10), the state comparison (p. 14), or the international comparisons (p. 12 and p. 25). Also of little use for the AP test are Figure 1-1 (p. 8), "Why Should I Care?" (p. 21), and "Political Culture" (p. 29).

Key Terms

Don't just memorize these terms. Understand what they mean and how they compare to other concepts. Be able to give examples of each.

Political culture (p. 7)
Liberty (p. 9)
Equality (p. 10)
Self-government (p. 10)
Individualism (p. 11)
Unity (p. 11)
Diversity (p. 11)
Equal opportunity (p. 13)
Politics (p. 18)
Social contract (p. 19)
Democracy (p. 21)
Oligarchy (p. 21)
Autocracy (p. 21)
Majority rule (p. 22)
Fragmentation of authority (p. 22)
Constitutionalism (p. 22)
Socialism (p. 23)

Communism (p. 23)
Capitalism (p. 24)
Power (p. 25)
Public policy (p. 25)
Totalitarian governments (p. 25)
Authoritarian governments (p. 26)
Federalist No. 10 (p. 26; this will be discussed more fully in later chapters)
Authority (p. 27)
Majoritarianism (p. 28)
Pluralism (p. 29)
Elitism (p. 30)
Bureaucratic rule (p. 31)
Political system (p. 31)
"Iron law of oligarchy" (p. 31)
Inputs (p. 32)
Outputs (p. 32)

SAMPLE QUESTIONS

Multiple-Choice Questions

1. In the United States, individual liberty is:
   a. the right to be treated similarly regardless of race
   b. the right to vote
   c. survival of the fittest
   d. undermined by rugged individualism
   e. limited by the liberty of others

2. Where are American core values found?
   I. historical documents
   II. public-opinion poll responses
   III. political leaders' speeches
   IV. national symbols (such as the Statue of Liberty and the bald eagle)

   a. I
   b. I and II
   c. I and III
   d. I and IV
   e. I, II, III, and IV

3. In the United States, equality is:
   I. defined as all people (regardless of their nationality) being of equal moral worth
   II. defined as all people being entitled to the same treatment under the law
   III. defined as all people deserving the same quality of life

   a. only I
   b. only II
   c. only III
   d. only I and II
   e. only II and III

4. The United States has more poverty than many other developed nations. What American value best explains why this is the case?
   a. individualism
   b. unity
   c. equality
   d. idealism
   e. diversity

5. In the United States, the social contract results in:
   a. scarcity
   b. voluntary cooperation
   c. binding arbitration
   d. protection of rights and property
   e. tyranny

6. Politics is defined as:
   a. shared beliefs in a society
   b. a process through which society governs itself
   c. voluntary agreement among individuals in a society
   d. power of the few over the many
   e. majority rule with minority rights

7. Fragmentation of government authority:
   a. is by design a dominant characteristic of the American political system
   b. is by design a dominant characteristic of oligarchy
   c. is by design a dominant characteristic of socialism
   d. is a dominant characteristic of the American political system, but not by design
   e. is a dominant characteristic of autocracy, but not by design

8. Competition among many different interests and groups for power:
   a. is a danger to individual rights
   b. was what Madison warned against in *Federalist* No. 10
   c. results in government using coercive authority
   d. is a characteristic of democracy
   e. is a characteristic of constitutionalism

9. The power of the National Rifle Association to influence gun-control legislation best illustrates:
   a. majoritarianism
   b. capitalism
   c. pluralism
   d. elitism
   e. bureaucratic rule

10. The political-system model demonstrates which of the following relationships?
    a. Institutions influence inputs, which influence outputs.
    b. Outputs influence institutions, which influence inputs.
    c. Inputs influence outputs, which influence institutions.
    d. Institutions and inputs simultaneously influence outputs.
    e. Inputs influence institutions, which influence outputs.

Multiple-Choice Answers

1. E; 2. E; 3. D; 4. A; 5. D; 6. B; 7. A; 8. D; 9. C; and 10. E

Free-Response Questions

1. The systems-model approach looks at the interconnection among three major components. These are inputs, political institutions, and outputs.

    a. Describe what each of these three components looks like in the American political system. (3 points)

    b. Describe how inputs relate to institutions. Provide an example that illustrates this relationship. (2 points)

    c. Describe how institutions relate to outputs. Provide an example that illustrates this relationship. (2 points)

    This answer is worth seven points.

    Part "a" is worth three points. One point is awarded for correctly describing each component.

    Part "b" is worth two points. One point is awarded for correctly describing the relationship between these components. The second point is awarded for providing an accurate example. A hypothetical example is sufficient.

    Part "c" is worth two points. One point is awarded for correctly describing the relationship between these components. The second point is awarded for providing an accurate example. A hypothetical example is sufficient.

2. Scholars disagree over who has power in the United States.

    a. Select two of these theories: pluralism, elitism, and majoritarianism. For each, describe who has power. (1 point)

    b. Identify and explain which of these theories you think is most consistent with a specific core value in American political culture. Be sure to describe that value. (2 points)

    c. Identify and explain which of these theories you think is least consistent with another core value (different from the one you selected for "b") in American political culture. Be sure to describe that value. (2 points)

    This question is worth five points.

    Part "a" is worth two points. Who has power according to two of the theories needs to be correctly identified to get the point.

    Part "b" is worth two points. One is for identifying and accurately describing a core value (liberty, equality, or self-government). The second is for correctly explaining how the theory is consistent with it.

    Part "c" is worth two points. One is for identifying and accurately describing a core value (liberty, equality, or self-government). The second is for correctly explaining how the theory is inconsistent with it.

CHAPTER TWO

Constitutional Democracy: Promoting Liberty and Self-Government

In *Federalist* No. 51, James Madison wrote that men are not angels and therefore cannot be trusted to govern without mechanisms that control them. The Constitution established these mechanisms to protect freedom from abuses within and outside of government. The Framers designed a system with *limited government* and *self-government*.

Limited government is a government that operates within a set of strict limits on its lawful powers. *Self-government* is a government that abides by the preferences of the majority. The Constitution, valuing both principles, respects the power of the majority and tries to restrain it. Chapter 2 describes these two principles, how they are negotiated in the Constitution, and how they have changed over time.

Before the Constitution: The Colonial and Revolutionary Experiences

Pages 39–45 describe how American ideals are based on English legal traditions, such as common law (which guarantees the right to a trial by jury and other due process safeguards) and freedom of expression.

"The Rights of Englishmen"

The Stamp Tax Act of 1765, which imposed a tax on newspapers and other documents, and the Townshend Act, which imposed taxes on other goods after the repeal of the Stamp Tax Act, were attempts by the English government to raise revenues from the colonies. Because the colonists were not used to paying these taxes and had not been represented in the Parliament that levied them, the colonists protested. The First Continental Congress met in Philadelphia in 1774 and issued demands to the King for such things as freedom of assembly, jury trials, an end to military occupation, and no more "taxation without representation." The American Revolution followed Britain's rejection of these demands.

The Declaration of Independence

Based on the beliefs of John Locke, the Declaration of Independence established a justification for the revolution and a new form of government. Locke's belief that people have *inalienable* (*natural*) *rights* and that they have the right to oppose a ruler who does not respect those rights was central to this document, which was written by Thomas Jefferson. The Declaration of Independence did not describe the structure of a new government; rather, it urged the colonists to rebel against England. The ideals it described were eventually used in the Constitution of the United States.

The Articles of Confederation

Before the Constitution, the first United States government was based on the Articles of Confederation. The Articles designed a national government that was intentionally weak and subject to the will of the states. For example, any state could nullify changes to the Articles proposed by the national government, and amendments could be adopted only by unanimous approval of the states. The national government lacked the powers to tax and to defend.

Shays's Rebellion: A Nation Dissolving

In 1786, farmers in Massachusetts violently resisted bank foreclosures during *Shays's Rebellion.* When the state's governor called on the national government to send troops to control the problem, it lacked the power to do so. People—particularly those with property—feared anarchy would spread unless the system was reformed. Therefore, they proposed a constitutional convention to revise the Articles of Confederation.

Negotiating toward a Constitution

The convention of 1787 was charged with revising the Articles of Confederation, but the delegates decided to create a new form of government instead. They believed that a stronger national government was essential, but they disagreed over how to protect the rights and power of people and the states. This resulted in a number of compromises.

The Great Compromise: A Two-Chamber Congress

Two plans for the structure of the new national government were proposed during the Constitutional Convention of 1787. The *Virginia Plan (large-state plan)* provided for a two-chamber congress, with representation based on the population of each state. The *New Jersey Plan (small-state plan)* proposed a single-chamber congress with each state having one representative. After much debate, these plans were combined in *The Great Compromise,* which called for a two-chamber congress, with one chamber having representation based on state population and the other having equal representation by state (two senators from each state).

The North-South Compromise: The Issue of Slavery

A second agreement, the *North-South Compromise,* arose over economic differences between the southern and northern states. The agriculturally based South feared unfair tax policies from the North, which was more industrial. The compromise resulted in Congress being prohibited from taxing exports but allowed to tax imports.

Another compromise between the North and South was the *"Three-Fifths Compromise,"* which allowed slaves to be counted as three-fifths of a person for taxing purposes and for determining the number of seats each state would get in the House of Representatives. Because the South's economy depended on slavery, this accommodation was needed to unite the states under a federal government. This was a particularly difficult compromise for delegates who saw that slavery was at odds with a belief in inalienable equal rights.

A Strategy for Ratification

The Articles of Confederation had required that any changes be approved unanimously by the thirteen states. This would have made ratification of the new Constitution impossible because some states objected to portions of the document, and Rhode Island had even refused to participate in the convention. Recognizing this, the Framers decided to submit the Constitution to the states directly and require only nine of the thirteen states to ratify it in special constitutional conventions. Delegates to these state conventions were to be elected by the people.

The Ratification Debate

Anti-Federalists, as opponents of ratification were called, had a number of concerns about the Constitution. They worried that the national government would be too powerful. They were suspicious of the office of the president and how he would be chosen. They feared that without a bill of rights, freedoms would be trampled. They were suspicious of the motives of the Framers (would the new government be a tool for the wealthy?) and of the national government's new powers of taxation (who would bear the burden?). Anti-Federalists agreed that there were problems with the Articles of Confederation because the national government could not regulate commerce or defend the nation, but they favored revising the system rather than instituting a new form of government.

    Federalists, the supporters of ratification, thought that the Constitution would correct the Articles' defects and secure the new union. They also believed that the new government would not endanger the freedoms of states or individuals because of the separation of powers. Three Federalists—James Madison, Alexander Hamilton, and John Jay—wrote essays explaining the rationale for ratification. They appeared in a New York newspaper and are referred to today as *The Federalist Papers.*

    Public opinion tended to be against ratification, but wealthy interests won out in state ratifying conventions. Nine states ratified before the biggest states, Virginia and New York, did. Only when the Federalists promised to support the introduction of a bill of rights once the new Congress convened, did these two states ratify the Constitution, and a stable union of states was assured.

The Framers' Goals

The Framers of the Constitution had four major goals. They desired a government strong enough to meet the monetary needs of the nation. They wanted a system of government (federalism) that allowed states and a national government to coexist. They also wanted a system of checks and balances, to provide for a limited government that would not threaten liberty, and a system of self-government that would provide for the direct and indirect election of officials.

Protecting Liberty: Limited Government

The Framers of the Constitution wanted a government that was strong enough to defend national interests but not so strong as to deny personal freedoms. In other words, they desired a government that was limited in its use of force but still able to prevent lawlessness. The concept of limited government is integrated into the Constitution through the explicit grants and denials of power, the separation of power with checks and balances, which result in institutions sharing power, the Bill of Rights, and judicial review.

Grants and Denials of Power

Government's powers are detailed specifically in Article I of the Constitution through both *grants of power* and *denials of power. Grants of power* are specific powers given to the government, such as regulating commerce and the power to tax. Grants of power serve as a means of limiting the national government, because the national government does not have power in areas not enumerated in the Constitution. *Denials of power* are those listed in the Constitution that that are specifically denied to the national government (such as the prohibition of passing *ex post facto laws*).

The difficulty in amending the Constitution is another way in which the power of the national government is limited. Amendments must be proposed by a two-thirds majority of Congress or by a national constitutional convention authorized by two-thirds of the states. Three-quarters of state legislatures or state conventions must ratify an amendment before it can become law. The Constitution allows Congress to determine whether the process of approving amendments should be completed by state legislatures or state conventions.

Using Power to Offset Power

The Framers divided powers among the three branches of government to make it difficult for one branch to dominate the others (*separation of powers*). In *Federalist* No. 10, Madison described *factions* (groups of people with a self-interest that may be adverse to others) as being inevitable but potentially oppressive if they gain too much power. To deal with this problem, the Framers decided to use *separation of power* with overlapping authority. This was to prevent one faction from gaining control of a branch of government and having too much political power.

Separated Institutions Sharing Power: Checks and Balances

Checks and balances in the Constitution give each branch of government powers that check those of the other branches. This is different from most democracies where executive and legislative powers are combined rather than separated. The Constitution grants shared powers to all three branches of government. Congress has the power to legislate, the president has the power to veto laws, and the Court has the power to nullify laws of Congress through the process of judicial review (*shared legislative powers*). The president has executive powers, such as the power to make treaties, but these are subject to congressional approval, and the Court can declare a presidential action unlawful (*shared executive powers*). Finally, the courts have judicial power, but Congress can control the size of the court system and rewrite legislation the court finds unlawful, while the president (with Senate approval) can appoint federal judges and can alone pardon criminals (*shared judicial powers*).

The Bill of Rights

Federalists argued that the reason a list of individual rights was not included in the Constitution was because the government could not act in any area not specifically allowed by the Constitution (*doctrine of expressed powers*). For example, because suppression of speech is not a power given to the government by the Constitution, the government cannot act to stifle free speech. Another argument against the Bill of Rights was that listing rights could lead the government to disregard rights not specifically identified. Nevertheless, as promised during the ratification process, the first ten amendments (referred to as the *Bill of Rights*) were introduced during the First Congress. They were approved using the rules for ratifying amendments spelled out in the Constitution.

Judicial Review

Judicial review, which is the power of the judiciary to decide whether officials or institutions have acted within the authority granted to them by the Constitution, was not explicitly included in the Constitution. The judiciary established this principle through case law in the decision of *Marbury v. Madison* (1803). In this decision, the Supreme Court declared that a law passed by Congress giving the Court a new power was invalid because the Constitution did not grant Congress power to expand the Supreme Court's authority. In doing this, the Justices established their right to rule on the constitutionality of actions of other government officials.

Providing for Self-Government

The Framers wanted to provide for self-government, but they also feared popular government. They did not want the public to use power to limit the rights of others (*tyranny of the majority*). To limit the risks of self-government, the Constitution places limits on popular rule through establishing a republic rather than a democracy. Over time, the system has become more democratic.

Democracy versus Republic

The Framers of the Constitution thought of *democracy* as popular government, subject to direct influence by the public. Since they found this worrisome, they instead instituted a republic. A *republic* is a *representative democracy* in which representatives of the people, rather than the people themselves, make decisions. These officials represent the public and promote the public's needs while still acting according to their own conscience. The Framers thought of representatives as public *trustees*, representing the interests of those they serve by determining for themselves what is good for the public.

Limited Popular Rule

The Constitution limited popular rule by providing only one institution, the House of Representatives, that would be elected directly by the public. The full House of Representatives would be elected every other year and would, in theory, be more in touch with popular opinion and better able to express the will of popular majorities. Senators would be selected by state legislatures and have six-year terms of office, with one-third of the body selected every other year. The longer terms and method of election was to balance the House and check the power of the popular majorities.

The Constitution also provided for indirect election of the president. The president would be chosen by the *Electoral College* (a body made up of electors chosen by the states). Each state would get the same number of *electoral votes* as its number of seats in Congress. Federal judges would be appointed rather than elected. By constructing methods of electing and appointing officials in this way, the Framers limited the opportunity of factions to gain control in a single election.

Altering the Constitution: More Power to the People

Provisions for self-government have changed over time. In fact, changes were instituted soon after the Constitution was written. The general trend of change has been towards more direct democracy.

John Adams, the second president, felt that the government was for the wealthy elite, and his administration favored the interests of the rich. In contrast, Jefferson saw government as belonging to all people, not just the wealthy. He also founded the first political party, which united leaders with the same interests in different branches and levels of government. Andrew Jackson convinced states to determine presidential electors by popular vote, effectively giving the public more direct control of the election of the president.

The Progressive era of the early twentieth century spawned reforms in state and local governments, including *initiatives and referendums* (giving the public a direct vote on legislative issues) and the *recall election* (requiring an elected public official to "submit to reelection" before the term of office is over). Progressives viewed representatives as *delegates* (rather than trustees) who were required to directly respond to the opinions of the people who elected them. Federal reforms instituted by Progressives include direct election of U.S. Senators and *primary elections,* which give the public the opportunity to select nominees for public office.

Constitutional Democracy Today

The United States government is a *constitutional democracy.* It is a democracy in that elections express the influence of the popular majority. Yet it has constitutional limits within which elected officials must operate. The bounds of law protect individual freedoms that might not be popular or are unpopular when exercised by certain people. In some ways, the United States political system exhibits many qualities of *self-government,* such as the frequent election of the president and primary elections. In other ways, the link between the popular majority and governmental power is less direct than in other democracies. The popular majority has many barriers to overcome to gain power in the government (for instance, staggered terms of office and the divided powers among the three branches of government). These barriers to power were deliberate and a means for the Framers to protect liberty.

TAKE NOTE

This chapter is important for the AP U.S. Government and Politics test. Much of this chapter will be familiar to students who have already taken the AP U.S. History class and/or exam. Do not be misled into thinking that the two tests are similar. They are not. Most of the questions on the U.S. Government and Politics exam are about the contemporary political system. Nevertheless, it is important to understand the roots of the system and the rationale behind its design. In addition to knowing specifics from this chapter, think about how the challenge of balancing self-government and limited government continues today.

Observations from Past Exams

Material in this chapter is part of the "Constitutional Underpinnings of the U.S. Government" section of the AP U.S. Government and Politics curriculum. This section makes up 5 percent to 15 percent of the multiple-choice questions. The test deals with separation of powers and the factors that influenced the writing and adoption of the Constitution. The College Board explains that this section requires knowledge of history surrounding the Constitutional Convention and the philosophies that influenced the Framers. Specifically, it suggests understanding their concerns about factions and the Bill of Rights. Recent exams reveal a need to understand the various checks and balances and the process for amending the Constitution.

The two most recently released multiple-choice exams (1999 and 2002) had nine questions on material from this chapter. These were about the amendment process, checks and balances (specifically, checks on the federal courts, how Congress can respond to the Court's judicial review, how presidents are removed), *Federalist* No. 10 and what it said about factions, the most important effect of replacing the Articles of Confederation with the Constitution, and the important role of Shays's Rebellion.

Two free-response questions from this chapter have appeared on the last seven exams. In 2000, a question asked about problems of decentralization under the Articles of Confederation and how the Constitution dealt with these. A question on the 2001 exam asked about the process of amending the Constitution.

What to Do with the Boxes

The most important boxes in this chapter are the ones that summarize or illustrate essential information and concepts. They are: the goals of the Framers (Table 2-1, p. 50), the system of checks and balances (Figure 2-2, p. 54), the constitutional limits on government (p. 58), the methods of selection and terms of service of federal officials (Table 2-2, p. 60), and developments that have further democratized the system (p. 62).

Being able to recognize and explain patterns on maps of the United States is useful. For that reason, and because you should know what initiatives and referendums are, it is worthwhile to take a look at the "States in the Nation" box (p. 64). There is no need to remember the patterns on the map. Realize, too, that maps appear on the AP test far less frequently than tables and graphs do. The "Citizenship" box (p. 41) reminds you that the U.S. political system provides many opportunities for activists (a point explained further in Chapters 7 through 9). It also reminds you that the *Federalist Papers* were essays designed to persuade people to ratify the Constitution. Now they are viewed as historical documents that reveal the logic behind the system's design. The "Liberty, Equality & Self-Government" box (p. 51) asks you to think about how constitutionalism affects the core values introduced in Chapter 1. The "Why Should I Care?" box (p. 57) reviews the two sides of a debate you should be familiar with regarding the need for a Bill of Rights. The "Debating the Issues" box (p. 65) is more relevant to Chapter 11 than to this one. You should review it after you read that chapter. Because of the focus of the AP test, you do not need to concentrate on the biographical sketches of James Madison (p. 49) or John Marshall (p. 59), Figure 2-1 (p. 48), or the "How the United States Compares" box (p. 55).

Key Terms

Don't just memorize these terms. Understand what they mean and how they compare to other concepts. Be able to give examples of each.

Limited government (p. 38)
Self-government (p. 38)
Declaration of Independence (p. 42)
Inalienable (natural) rights (p. 42)
Articles of Confederation (p. 43)
Virginia (large-state) Plan (p. 45)
New Jersey (small-state) Plan (p. 45)
Great Compromise (p. 45)
North-South Compromise (p. 45)
Anti-Federalists (p. 48)
Federalists (p. 49)
Constitution (p. 50)
Grants of power (p. 51)
Denials of power (p. 51)
Habeas corpus (p. 51)
Ex post facto laws (p. 52)
Factions (p. 53)
Separated institutions sharing power (p. 53)
Checks and balances (p. 53)

Doctrine of expressed powers (p. 56)
Bill of Rights (p. 56)
Judicial review (p. 56)
Writ of mandamus (p. 57)
Democracy (p. 59)
Republic (p. 59)
Representative democracy (p. 59)
Trustees (p. 59)
Electoral College (p. 60)
Electoral votes (p. 60)
Delegates (p. 63)
Initiative (p. 63)
Referendum (p. 63)
Recall election (p. 63)
Primary election (p. 63)

Making Connections to Previous Chapters

Chapter 1 discussed the core American values of liberty, equality, and self-government (pp. 9–11). Chapter 2 makes it easier to see why Patterson calls these values "enduring." The writing of the Constitution and the ratification struggle are wonderful examples of how politics is a process by which values are defined, prioritized, and balanced against each other (discussed in Chapter 1, p. 18). Think about how the desire to "control the mischief of factions" relates to the pluralist and the majoritarian theories of power (pp. 28–29). Anti-Federalists accused the Federalists of being elitist. Review the description of elitism (pp. 30–31) and evaluate that claim.

SAMPLE QUESTIONS

Multiple-Choice Questions

1. In *Federalist* No. 1, Madison argues that men are not angels and therefore:
   a. there needs to be a separation between church and state
   b. a direct democracy would be a bad idea
   c. governments need to have laws to punish wrongdoing
   d. power in government should be spread out among many people
   e. a strong national army is necessary

2. The Stamp Act was a catalyst to the war for independence because:
   a. taxes were unpopular in the colonies
   b. colonists left Britain to avoid taxes
   c. Britain refused to heed the outcry against the Act
   d. taxes on newspapers and business documents were designed to stifle property in the colonies
   e. the colonists had no say in the imposition of the taxes

3. Articles of Confederation could only be amended:
    a. by the founding fathers
    b. by a unanimous vote by states
    c. by a national referendum
    d. by a majority of states
    e. there was no provision in the Articles to allow for amending

4. What was a weakness of the Articles of Confederation?
    a. There was no way for the states to compel each other to do anything.
    b. All states had to agree for federal legislation to pass.
    c. The national government lacked the power to tax.
    d. Neither national nor state governments had the right to tax property.
    e. Large states held more power than small ones in national government.

5. The Great Compromise:
    a. created two chambers in Congress with different apportionment rules
    b. prohibited Congress from taxing exports but allowed for tax imports
    c. established the three-fifths rule, which counted slaves as three-fifths of a person
    d. attached a Bill of Rights to the Constitution so that it could be ratified
    e. established a federal system in which both national and state government had power

6. Judicial review:
    a. allows the Supreme Court to review court cases
    b. allows Congress to review presidential nominations to the Supreme Court
    c. allows the Supreme Court to review bills before they are passed into law
    d. allows the Court to declare government action null and void
    e. is described in the Constitution

7. The Constitution provided that the president would be selected by:
    a. Congress, which was selected by the public
    b. state legislatures, which were selected by the public
    c. electors, which were selected by the public
    d. the public directly
    e. people from each state who did not have to be selected directly by the public

8. The Federalist Papers advocated:
    a. amending the Articles of Confederation
    b. adding a Bill of Rights to the Constitution
    c. creating government institutions with totally separate powers
    d. creating government institutions with overlapping powers
    e. creating an independent judiciary to eliminate factions

9. The Constitution establishes an amendment process that:
    a. has been altered 22 times throughout history
    b. allows either Congress or the president to propose amendments
    c. requires two-thirds of Congress to pass an amendment
    d. requires a simple majority of legislators to propose change
    e. requires proposals be ratified by either state legislatures or state conventions

10. Which of the methods established by the Constitution for choosing leaders was the most democratic?
    a. president
    b. Supreme Court justices
    c. senators
    d. House of Representatives
    e. governors

Multiple-Choice Answers

1. D; 2. E; 3. B; 4. C; 5. A; 6. D; 7. E; 8. D; 9. E; and 10. D

Free-Response Questions

1. Madison said that liberty was "equally exposed to danger whether the government has too much power or too little power."

    a. Explain how liberty is in danger when government has too much power. Provide an example to illustrate this danger. (2 points)

    b. Explain how liberty is in danger when government has too little power. Provide an example to demonstrate this danger. (2 points)

    c. Identify a feature of the U.S. Constitution designed to address the problem of government having too much power. Explain how it addresses the problem. (2 points)

    d. Identify a feature of the U.S. Constitution designed to address the problem of government having too little power. Explain how it addresses the problem. (2 points)

    The question is worth eight points.

    Part "a" is worth two points. One point is earned for correctly explaining how liberty is in danger if the government has too much power. Acceptable explanations include: ex post facto laws, suppression of free speech, suppression of free press, suppression of property rights, and suppression of free religion. One point is earned for providing an example that illustrates the point. This example may be hypothetical as long as it is illustrative.

    Part "b" is worth two points. One point is earned for correctly explaining how liberty is in danger if the government has too little power. Acceptable explanations include: tyranny of the majority, oppression of minority rights by the majority, threats from abroad, mob rule, and economic instability. One point is earned for providing an example that illustrates the point. This example may be hypothetical as long as it is illustrative.

    Part "c" is worth two points. One point is earned for correctly identifying a feature of the U.S. Constitution that is designed to address the problem. One point is given for explaining how it addresses the problem. Acceptable answers include: specific denials of power, authority not granted is denied, checks and balances, elections, Bill of Rights, specific protections from the Bill of Rights (such as jury trials), and judicial review. The answer does not have to use the correct terminology or identify the precise location of the feature in the Constitution.

Part "d" is worth two points. One point is earned for correctly identifying a feature of the U.S. Constitution that is designed to address the problem. One point is given for explaining how it addresses the problem. Acceptable answers include: Electoral College rather than direct election, appointment of judiciary, life terms of the judiciary, staggered terms for senators, difficulty of amending the Constitution, grants of power to government to tax, punish, and draft. The answer does not have to use the correct terminology or identify the precise location of the feature in the Constitution.

2. The Constitutional Convention created a document without a Bill of Rights.

    a. What is the Bill of Rights? Describe it. (1 point)

    b. Explain the two sides of the debate over whether to include a Bill of Rights in the Constitution. (2 points)

    c. Explain how a Bill of Rights came to be added to the Constitution and how this illustrates a lesson about politics that is still relevant today. (2 points)

    The question is worth five points.

    Part "a" is worth one point for correctly describing what the Bill of Rights is.

    Part "b" is worth two points. One point is awarded for correctly explaining why the Federalists opposed the Bill of Rights. Acceptable answers include: not necessary, doctrine of expressed powers, anything left off the list would be in jeopardy. The second point is awarded for correctly explaining why the Anti-Federalists wanted a Bill of Rights. Acceptable answers include: necessary for protecting individuals from government, necessary for protecting individuals given the increased power to the national government.

    Part "c" is worth two points. One point is earned for describing how the Bill of Rights came to be included. A correct answer must indicate that the Constitution was ratified without the amendments and that there was a struggle between two groups over their inclusion during the ratification process. One point is earned for discussing a lesson about politics revealed in this struggle.

CHAPTER THREE

Federalism: Forging a Nation

SUMMARY

The United States' political system is a *federal* system in which national and state governments share power and both derive their authority from the public. Americans can be said to have "dual citizenship," as they are citizens of both the country and the state in which they live. Federalism was a compromise that resulted from the debate between Federalists and Anti-Federalists. Chapter 3 describes the powers of the national and state governments and explains how these have changed over time because of the Fourteenth Amendment and the Supreme Court's interpretation of it.

Federalism: National and State Sovereignty

Pages 72–79 explain the principles of federalism, discuss issues of national and state sovereignty at the time the Constitution was written, and examine how the Framers ended up dividing authority. Federalism is a unique system developed in America. Divided authority is different from a *confederacy*, which is based on state sovereignty only, and a *unitary system* gives authority solely to the national government.

Proponents of the Constitution pointed to the weak national government under the Articles of Confederation, which lacked the power to enforce laws or raise revenues through taxation. Opponents thought that a weak national government would be the least threatening to individual liberty. Federalism was a political compromise between supporters of a government of the states and supporters of a strong national government that derives its power from the people. This system of *divided authority* between the national and state governments allows states to decide local matters (such as education and law enforcement) and gives the federal government authority over national issues (such as defense and taxation). Some powers are *concurrent*—both federal and state governments have authority in the "same areas of policy." One example of concurrent power is taxation.

The Argument for Federalism

Patterson identifies three arguments for federalism: the protection of individual freedoms, the "moderating power" of a large republic, and the creation of a strong union.

To protect liberty, the Constitution creates competing centers of power in the states and national governments. As Hamilton argued in *Federalist* No. 28, this dual authority helps the people control both governments from infringing on their liberties. Citizens can "shift loyalties" between the two levels of government.

Madison argues in *Federalist* No. 10 that, contrary to the Anti-Federalists' belief, a large republic was preferable to a small one because the "range of interests" that compete for power, not the size of the republic, is what keeps a single powerful *faction* from forcing its self-interest on the rest of the people. He believed that a large republic would make it necessary for groups with competing interests to work together.

The need for a strong union to overcome the weaknesses of the Articles of Confederation was the third argument for federalism. The economic, social-order, and defense needs of the people would be better served by a stronger national government.

The Powers of the Nation

The national government is given authority by the Constitution through *enumerated* and *implied powers. Enumerated powers* are listed in Article I of the Constitution. They give the federal government seventeen powers, including taxation and the power to create military forces. States are prohibited from interfering with the national government exercising these powers. In addition, Article VI says that national law prevails over state law (*supremacy clause*). *Implied powers* are given to the federal government through the *necessary and proper clause*, also known as the *elastic clause*, of Article I. This allows Congress to make laws necessary to carry out its enumerated powers, even when these actions are not explicitly included in the Constitution.

The Powers of the States

The Tenth Amendment addresses Anti-Federalists' concerns that parts of the Constitution, such as the *supremacy clause*, gave the federal government too much power. In this amendment, the states are given *reserved powers*, which are all powers not granted to the national government or prohibited from the states.

Federalism in Historical Perspective

By omitting details of specific provisions, the Constitution was left vague enough to be flexible over time. This section describes the changes the federal system has undergone in three "eras of federalism."

An Indestructible Union (1789–1865)

McCulloch v. Maryland (1819) set the precedent for national authority. The case arose because the state of Maryland tried to tax a branch of the newly created Second Bank of the United States. The Supreme Court ruled in favor of the federal government, saying that is had *implied powers* extending beyond its *enumerated powers*. Another example of the court validating national authority was *Gibbons v. Ogden* (1824), in which Congress's power to regulate interstate commerce was upheld. During the era of national authority, the *Dred Scott* (1857) decision was an example of the Supreme Court advocating states rights. The Court said that slaves were property and could not sue for freedom in federal courts. Since citizens could take property across state lines, Congress could not outlaw slavery in any part of the country.

Dual Federalism and Laissez-Faire Capitalism (1865–1937)

In the second era, states were seen as supreme in race matters, and the federal government was supreme in areas of commerce. The doctrine in which separation of federal and state authority is seen as desirable is called *dual federalism*. For example, the federal government is in charge of national defense and interstate commerce, while state governments are responsible for education and public health.

The Fourteenth Amendment, passed after the Civil War, was intended to protect citizens from having their rights infringed upon by the states. Initially, the Supreme Court interpreted the amendment in a way that allowed states great leeway to define rights of its people. This was evident in the *Plessy v. Ferguson* (1896) decision, which established the "separate but equal" ruling allowing states to segregate the races. The Fourteenth Amendment was also used by the Court to protect businesses. For example, the Court said that businesses were to be treated as people under the Fourteenth Amendment, thus protecting them from government regulation. The Supreme Court defined the *commerce clause* narrowly during this time, giving the federal government control over the transportation but not the manufacture of goods. At the same time, it prevented states from regulating the manufacture of goods because these powers were restricted by the Fourteenth Amendment. *Hammer v. Dagenhart* (1918) and *Lochner v. New York* (1905) are examples of conflicting Supreme Court decisions. *Hammer* prevented the federal government from regulating child labor, saying that this was an area of state control. However, *Lochner* barred states from regulating labor. Things changed in the late 1930s shortly after the Court invalidated the National Industry Recovery Act in *Schecter v. United States* (1935), saying that the act seized power reserved to the states. This prevented President Franklin D. Roosevelt from implementing a major public-works program to counter the effects of the Great Depression. In response, Roosevelt proposed a "court packing" plan to Congress. This plan would allow the president, with Senate approval, to appoint additional Supreme Court justices to the Court when justices reached the age of seventy. In the decisions that followed this threat, the Court upheld legislation that gave Congress broad authority to regulate commerce in a time of an emerging national industrial economy that was not bound by state lines. This heralded the third era of federalism—national supremacy. First in the area of commerce powers and later in the areas of civil rights and civil liberties, the Court upheld *national citizenship*, the idea that rights and opportunities are not bound by where a person lives.

Federalism Today

Two trends have emerged since the 1930s: the expansion of national authority and *devolution* (authority passed down from the national to the state governments). *Dual federalism* is no longer a correct description of the American political system. National and state governments share power and work together in a system of *cooperative federalism*. The expansion of federal authority is the result of increased interdependence in modern life and the greater taxing ability of the national government.

Interdependency and Intergovernmental Relations

Interdependency occurs when "developments in one area affect what happens elsewhere" (p. 90). It has both increased national authority and encouraged the national and state governments to work together. Today, many policy programs are jointly determined, funded, and administered by national and state governments. States still retain traditional authority, but federal influence has increased the consistency of policies among states. This is *cooperative federalism*. It can be thought of as being like a marble cake, in which the layers flow together, whereas dual federalism was like a layer cake with distinct and separate layers.

Government Revenues and Intergovernmental Relations

The federal government is able to raise tax revenues more easily than state and local governments. Money has become the way in which the federal and state governments relate, with the federal government allocating funds to programs run by the states. This is *fiscal federalism*. It is another example of *cooperative federalism*.

The national government provides money through *grants-in-aid*, money allocated to states for programs that will be run by the state governments. The federal government gives money through two types of grants: *categorical* and *block*. *Categorical grants* are more restrictive, as they explicitly state what money can be used for. *Block grants,* because they are given for a general area such as health care rather than a specific program, are preferred by states. They give states more latitude in spending money.

A New Federalism: Devolution

What is *devolution?* Devolution can be defined as a delegating of power from national to state and local government. It has created more interdependency between the two levels of government. This change in fiscal and cooperative federalism developed for both political and pragmatic reasons. In the 1970s and 1980s, Republicans advocated devolution, also called *"new federalism."* Once Republicans gained control of Congress in 1994, they acted on the idea, mandating that more responsibility and authority be given to the states. Two examples illustrate this effort. The Unfunded Mandates Reform Act of 1995 reduced *unfunded mandates*, which required states to pay for programs mandated by the federal government. The Welfare Reform Act of 1996 contained Temporary Assistance for Needy Families (TANF) block grants giving states the power to spend money as they chose to regulate aid to the poor.

The Supreme Court has contributed to devolution as well. Although *Garcia v. San Antonio Authority* (1985) gave the federal government the authority to apply minimum-wage standards to state and local government employees, later decisions restricted Congressional authority to enact policies affecting state governments. In two cases related to gun laws, *United States v. Lopez* (1995) and *Printz v. United States* (1997), the Court decided that states had the authority to resist federal gun regulations. In matters of employee rights, the Supreme Court has not spoken consistently. The Court has limited national authority over states in some instances (*Kimel v. Florida Board of Regents*, 2000) and sided with the federal government in others (*Nevada Department of Human Resources v. Hibbs*, 2003).

The Court has continued to apply the principle that the federal government has broad authority over commerce and spending. An example of this is *Reno v. Condon* (2000), in which the Supreme Court upheld a federal law forbidding states from selling databases containing personal information gathered from automobile license applications. The databases were determined to be "articles of commerce" and thus came under federal authority.

The Public's Influence: Setting the Boundaries of Federal-State Power

In conclusion, federal power has both increased and decreased in the twentieth century as public demands and expectations have changed. The New Deal programs from the 1930s, the Great Society programs of the 1960s, and the rollbacks of federal authority in the 1990s were all driven by public demands. This illustrates the flexibility and pragmatism of federalism envisioned by the Framers of the Constitution.

TAKE NOTE

This is an extremely important chapter for the AP exam. The exam tests a broad understanding of federalism rather than focusing on just one or two aspects of this chapter. It is important to understand how the Constitution established federalism (defining which levels of government are responsible for which types of issues), various types of federalism, types of grants and their implication for state power, and changes over time in the power of the federal government.

Observations from Past Exams

Federalism is only part of the "Constitutional Underpinnings of the U.S. Government" section that is supposed to make up 5 percent to 15 percent of the multiple-choice questions. Specifically, the College Board identifies a "familiarity with the Supreme Court's interpretation of key provisions of the Constitution" so that students can show an "understanding of theoretical and practical features of federalism." Yet an examination of the last two released tests reveals a lot of attention to federalism.

The two most recently released multiple-choice exams (1999 and 2002) include eleven questions related to federalism. A general sense of what federalism is would suffice for answering two of the questions (one about federalism resulting in diversity in public policy throughout the country and the other about the division of power between central and regional governments). Questions related to the Constitution asked about the Tenth Amendment, the constitutional clause used to expand national government power, and "reserved powers." Other questions required an understanding of fiscal federalism and cooperative federalism, *McCulloch v. Maryland*, which grants states the most power, and "unfunded mandates." One question provided a table on grants-in-aid for students to interpret. In addition to the multiple-choice questions on federalism, three of the last seven exams had free-response questions related to this topic. Students could choose to answer a 2002 question by writing about how federalism is both an obstacle to and presents opportunities for racial minority groups. The 2003 test included a graph of the number of federal, state, and local government employees over time. Students needed to discuss how block grants and federal mandates contributed to the differences shown in the graph. The 2005 exam asked about the increase in federal power and how constitutional provisions (tax and spend, necessary and proper clause, and commerce clause) contributed to this change.

What to Do with the Boxes

Figure 3-1 (p. 74) is a helpful summary of important information about federalism.

A useful preparation for the illustration-based questions on the test is to try to write a summary for Figure 3-2 (p. 91), Figure 3-3 (p. 92), and Figure 3-4 (p. 93) before you read (or review) the one provided under the title. Try to come up with arguments for why the information looks the way it does. You might also want to do this for the "Federal Grants-in-Aid to the States" box (p. 94). Be sure you understand what grants-in-aid are and their implications for state and federal power.

"Why Should I Care? Federalism: Who Governs Affects You" (p. 79) provides some clear examples of federal laws that do not apply to states. "Liberty, Equality & Self-Government: What's Your Opinion?" (p. 84) reviews and asks you to consider Madison's point about large republics (found in *Federalist* No. 10). It is important to understand and evaluate his argument. "Debating the Issues: Does Congress Have Authority to Prevent States from Legalizing Marijuana Use for Medical Purposes?" (p. 98) presents an interesting debate over the decision in *United States v. Oakland Cannabis Buyers' Cooperative.*

Because of the focus of the AP test, you do not need to concentrate on the biographical sketch of Alexander Hamilton (p. 76), John C. Calhoun (p. 81) and William H. Rehnquist (p. 97) or international comparisons (p. 75, 89).

Key Terms

Don't just memorize these terms. Understand what they mean and how they are relevant to federalism and the powers of the national and state governments. Be able to give examples of each.

Federalism (p. 73)
Sovereignty (p. 73)
Concurrent powers (p. 74). Be able to give and recognize examples of these.
National powers (p. 74). Be able to give and recognize examples of these.
State powers (p. 74). Be able to give and recognize examples of these.
Confederacy (p. 74)
Unitary system (p. 74)
Federalist No. 28 (p. 75). Be sure you understand what "shifting loyalties" means.
Federalist No. 10 (p. 76). Be sure to understand the mischiefs of factions and how a federal
    government helps do this.
Implied powers (pp. 77, 78)
Enumerated (expressed) powers (p. 77)
Reserved powers (pp. 77, 78–9)
Supremacy clause (p. 78)
"Necessary and proper" clause (elastic clause) (p. 78)
Interstate commerce (p. 79)
Intrastate commerce (p. 79)
Dual federalism (pp. 82, 88, 90)
Fourteenth Amendment (p. 83)
Commerce clause (p. 85)
Court packing (p. 87)
Devolution (pp. 89, 95)
Cooperative federalism (new federalism) (p. 90)
Interdependency (p. 90)
Fiscal federalism (p. 92)
Grants-in-aid (p. 92)
Categorical grants (p. 93)
Block grants (p. 93)
Unfunded mandates (p. 96)

Making Connections to Previous Chapters

Realize how federalism promotes and protects some of the core American values discussed in Chapter 1. The idea of national citizenship promotes unity while state rights can protect regional diversity. Think about how important federalism is in the continuing challenge of balancing the two core values of equality and liberty.

Chapter 2 introduced federalism as one of the constitutional limits on government (p. 58). Understand that many of the issues upon which Federalists and Anti-Federalists disagreed during the ratification debate continue today. A central concern was, and continues to be, how best to balance national and state interests.

SAMPLE QUESTIONS

Multiple-Choice Questions

1. Which of the following is true of the federal system of the United States?
   a. State governments get their power from the national government, which gets its power from the people.
   b. Both the national and state governments derive authority directly from the people.
   c. Throughout history which government is supreme, the federal or the states, has shifted back and forth.
   d. It is a unitary system.
   e. The national government holds all but the concurrent powers of the states.

2. Which of the following is a concurrent power?
   a. the post office
   b. interstate commerce
   c. education
   d. law enforcement
   e. registration and voting

3. Which of the following is true according to *Federalist* No. 10?
   a. Sacrificing states' power to the nation is unnecessary and unwise.
   b. A small republic is more likely than a large one to respect people's rights.
   c. A large republic would better impede a special-interest group from gaining control of government.
   d. Factions could be destroyed by a federalist system.
   e. "The government is best which governs least."

4. Enumerated powers:
   a. are the powers that the Constitution explicitly gives to the national government
   b. are the powers that the Constitution explicitly gives to the state governments
   c. are the powers that the Constitution explicitly retains for citizens
   d. are the powers that the Constitution does not talk about explicitly, which are the national government's
   e. are not found in the Constitution

5. Which of the following clauses found in Article IV of the Constitution provides a rule for resolving conflicts between state and federal laws?
   a. the reserved powers clause
   b. the supremacy clause
   c. the necessary and proper clause
   d. the elastic clause
   e. the sovereignty clause

6. Which of the following is given "reserved powers" by the Constitution?
   a. national government
   b. state governments
   c. local governments
   d. the people
   e. both national and state governments

7. Which of the following enhanced (or enhances) national authority?
   a. the *McCulloch v. Maryland* decision
   b. the *Dred Scott* decision
   c. the decision in *Schechter v. United States*
   d. block grants
   e. devolution

8. The commerce clause:
   a. gives federal government the right to regulate intrastate commerce
   b. gives states the right to regulate intrastate commerce
   c. was interpreted narrowly by the Supreme Court until the mid-1930s
   d. was invalidated by the Supreme Court in the name of laissez-faire capitalism
   e. had no impact on states until the Fourteenth Amendment was passed

9. Which of the following best characterizes federalism today?
   a. a system in which there is a precise separation of national and state power
   b. a system in which state power is supreme
   c. a system in which national, state, and local governments work together to solve problems
   d. a system in which local power is supreme
   e. "dual federalism," also known as the "layer cake" model

10. Which of the following best supports the idea of devolution?
    a. federal regulatory policy
    b. unfunded federal mandates
    c. categorical grants
    d. block grants
    e. taxing capacity

Multiple-Choice Answers

1. B; 2.D; 3.C; 4.A; 5.B; 6.B; 7.A; 8.C; 9. C; 10. D

Free-Response Questions

1. Dual federalism and cooperative federalism are two different models of federalism.

    a. Describe both of these models. (2 points)

    b. Which of these characterizes today's system? Explain how or why federalism has changed from one of these to the other. (2 points)

    c. Describe one of the following and explain how it is an example of dual federalism OR cooperative federalism. (2 points)

    > The *Plessy v. Ferguson* decision
    > Medicaid
    > Grants-in-aid

    The question is worth six points.

    Part "a" is worth two points. One point is given for correctly describing dual federalism. Merely identifying it as the "layer cake" type is not enough. The answer must describe how power and responsibilities are separate. A well-explained example may serve to correctly describe. One point is given for correctly describing cooperative federalism. Merely identifying it as the "marble cake" type is not enough. The answer must describe how the power and responsibilities are shared. A well-explained example may serve to correctly describe.

    Part "b" is worth two points. One point is for identifying a factor that contributes to the change. The second point is for explaining how or why the factor changed. Factors include: economic crisis of the 1930s, leadership of Franklin Roosevelt, changes in Supreme Court opinions, changing notions of national citizenship among the public, interdependency (in transportation, commerce, communication), federal government's superior taxing capacity. No points are awarded unless the answer specifies that cooperative federalism is the current model.

    Part "c" is worth two points. One point is for correctly describing one of the three choices and one point for explaining how it is an example of either dual or cooperative federalism. To get the second point, the correct type of federalism needs to be identified.

    > *Plessy v. Ferguson* needs to be identified as an example of dual federalism because it allowed states authority in racial segregation despite the Fourteenth Amendment.

    > Medicaid needs to be identified as an example of cooperative federalism because it demonstrates how states and federal government work together to provide health care to poor people. It is jointly funded, with national eligibility standards and gives states latitude in developing regulations.

    > Grants-in-aid should be identified as an example of cooperative federalism because it demonstrates how states and federal government work together. Federal money is provided to states, which administer programs.

2. Using the federal grants to state and local governments graph below:

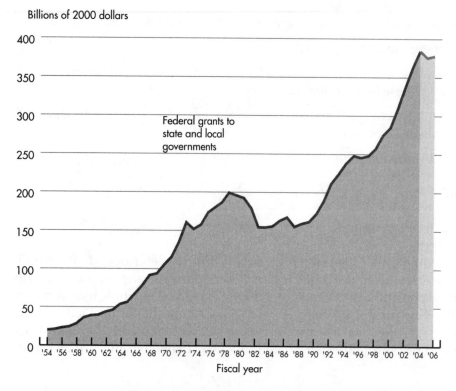

Billions of 2000 dollars

Federal grants to
state and local
governments

Fiscal year

a. Identify two trends in the figure. (1 point)

b. Identify a factor that has contributed to one of these trends and explain how it has contributed. (2 points)

c. There are two different types of federal grants—categorical and block. Describe each and explain which of the two state and local governments prefer. (3 points)

The question is worth six points.

Part "a" is worth one point. The answer needs to indicate two correct trends. Indicating only one correct trend earns no points. Trends include: increase from 1954 to 2004 in federal grants, increase from 1954 to 1979 in federal grants, increase from 1990 to 2004 in federal grants, decrease in federal grants from 1979 to 1983, and stable amount of federal grants from 1983 to 1990.

Part "b" is worth two points. One point is awarded for identifying a reasonable factor. The second point is for explaining it. Factors include: interdependency (in transportation, commerce, or communication), federal government's superior taxing capacity, more activist federal government (for example, Great Society programs), increased need (area of law enforcement, transportation, education, health care), and devolution.

Part "c" is worth three points. One point is for correctly describing "categorical grants" as those that must be spent for designated projects. One point is for correctly describing "block grants" as those permitting the states and local governments to decide how to spend money. One point is awarded for correctly identifying "block grants" and explaining why they are preferred by state and local governments.

CHAPTER FOUR

Civil Liberties:
Protecting Individual Rights

SUMMARY

Chapter 4 discusses civil liberties, specific individual rights that are constitutionally protected against infringement by the government. The Bill of Rights specifies individual rights that the national government is obliged to protect, including freedom of speech, freedom of religion, and due process. The Fourteenth Amendment became the basis for protection of rights against actions by state and local governments once the Court interpreted it as doing so. Although laws and Court decisions have expanded individual rights in the past fifty years, these rights have limits. Understanding these limits and the rationale behind them is important.

Freedom of Expression

Pages 107–17 discuss freedom of expression. Patterson makes the point that freedom of expression is not absolute and government limits on it have changed over time. Free expression can be denied if it "endangers national security, wrongly damages the reputation of others, or deprives others of their basic freedoms" (p. 108).

The Early Period: The Uncertain Status of the Right of Free Expression

During the early period of the country, laws (such as the *Sedition Act of 1798*, Civil War laws, and *Espionage Act of 1917*) prohibited criticism of the government. The Supreme Court finally ruled on the question in the case of *Schenck v. United States* (1919). This decision upheld restrictions on free expression when it presented a *clear and present danger* to national security.

The Modern Period: Protecting Free Expression

Since World War II, free expression has been defined in terms of national security. The Supreme Court has ruled that the government must show that security is directly imperiled before restricting the freedoms of expression and assembly. *Symbolic speech* (such as flag burning) is protected as long as it does not interfere with government functioning (such as burning a draft card). With the exception of reporting on wartime operations, *prior restraint* (forbidding speech or press before it occurs) is not permissible. This was established in the *New York Times Co. v. United States* (1971) decision.

Free Expression and State Governments

Barron v. Baltimore (1833) upheld the idea that the Bill of Rights protected individual rights from actions of the federal government but not from the actions of states and local authorities. This eventually changed once the *due process clause of the Fourteenth Amendment* (forbidding states from "depriving any person of life, liberty, or property without due process of law") was interpreted by the Supreme Court as incorporating the Bill of Rights. *Incorporation* was selective, occurring slowly over time. It began with *Gitlow v. New York* (1925). Other groundbreaking selective-incorporation cases in the area of free expression were: *Fiske v. Kansas* (free speech), *Near v. Minnesota* (free press), *Hamilton v. Regents, University of California* (religious freedom), and *DeJonge v. Oregon* (freedom to assemble and petition). *Brandenburg v. Ohio* (1969) established the *imminent lawless action* test, which set a higher standard for government efforts to restrict free expression in a case that challenged a state law.

Libel and Slander/Obscenity

Freedom of speech and of the press can be limited when people's reputations are damaged with false information. However, the standards of proof are high when the subject of the attack is a public official. The case of *New York Times Co. v. Sullivan* (1964) established that individuals must prove "knowing or reckless disregard for the truth" in the material published about them.

The Supreme Court has modified its definitions of obscenity several times. The current test is that material must be "particularly offensive." Standards that were used in the past were, in order: if the material overall appealed to "prurient interest" and had no "redeeming social significance" (*Roth v. United States*); if it was offensive to local community standards (*Miller v. California*); and if it was objectionable to a "reasonable person" and was "particularly offensive." The Court has also made distinctions based on where the material is viewed (in public places and at home) and who is in the images (adults or children). Laws attempting to outlaw the use of the Internet for distribution of sexually explicit materials have been deemed unconstitutional.

Freedom of Religion

Pages 117–20 describe two ways in which freedom of religion is protected. The first is through the *establishment clause* of the First Amendment, which prohibits the federal government from endorsing a religion; this clause was later applied to the states. The "wall of separation" between church and state is a popular understanding of the establishment clause. In the case of *Engel v. Vitale* (1962), the Court held that prayer in public schools violated this clause and was therefore unconstitutional. Private schools have been given more flexibility. The *free-exercise clause* of the First Amendment protects Americans' right to choose their religious beliefs from interference by the federal government; again, the Fourteenth Amendment applies this to the states. The Court sometimes has to balance these two religious-freedom causes in its application to specific cases, such as the question of whether Amish children should be exempt from having to attend school.

The Right of Privacy

Pages 121–23 discuss the right of privacy. Although there is no explicit articulation of this right in the Bill of Rights, the Supreme Court ruled in *Griswold v. Connecticut* (1965) that it was implied there and in the due process clause, and as a result, states could not outlaw the use of birth-control devices. This right has been interpreted as meaning that the government cannot have laws prohibiting abortion (established in *Roe v. Wade*, 1973) or prohibiting consensual sexual relations between people of the same sex (established in *Lawrence and Garner v. Texas*, 2003). The right of privacy does not, however, prohibit laws against doctor-assisted suicide. Much debate continues over the right and its application. Although the *Roe v. Wade* decision has been upheld in subsequent cases, the Court (in *Webster v. Reproductive Health Services*, 1989) has accepted regulations restricting abortion rights as long as the regulations were not seen as overly burdensome.

Rights of Persons Accused of Crimes

Pages 124–34 discuss the rights of people accused of crimes. *Procedural due process* (the procedures that government needs to follow before punishing someone) is defined in the Fourth, Fifth, Sixth, and Eighth Amendments of the U.S. Constitution. The Supreme Court has modified and extended these protections over time.

Selective Incorporation of Procedural Rights

Starting in the 1960s, the Court selectively incorporated the protections outlined in these four amendments using the "due process clause" of the Fourteenth Amendment. This means that state and local government authorities had to stop violating the *Fourth, Fifth, Sixth,* and *Eighth Amendment* protections. Important cases of incorporation of procedural rights are: the *search and seizure* (Fourth Amendment) case of *Mapp v. Ohio* (1961); the *right to counsel* (Sixth Amendment) case of *Gideon v. Wainwright* (1963); and the *self-incrimination/right to counsel* (Fifth and Sixth Amendments) case of *Miranda v. Arizona* (1966).

Limits on Defendants' Rights

The Fourth Amendment protects people in their homes and vehicles from "unreasonable search and seizure." What constitutes "unreasonable" is up to the Court and has changed since the exclusionary rule was established in 1914. The *exclusionary rule* prohibits the use of evidence in trials when the evidence has been obtained in violation of a person's constitutional rights. The rule thereby serves to discourage unlawful searches. Recent actions have weakened the rule while still maintaining limits on police. A 1962 precedent concerning *habeas corpus* appeals established that prisoners have the right to have their appeals heard in federal court. Recent decisions have limited this right in an effort to limit frivolous appeals and undue burdens on federal courts.

Crime, Punishment, and Police Practices

The reality of police practices can fall short of the promise of constitutional procedural guarantees. One example is *racial profiling*. When police assume that certain types of people (typically racial minorities and the poor) are more likely to be criminals, they become unfair targets of scrutiny. Punishment is another area in which critics see inequality and injustice. Although the *Eighth Amendment* protects prisoners from "cruel and unusual punishment," the Court has made it difficult for prisoners to sue over prison conditions, allows the use of "three strikes" laws, permits the death penalty (although not in the case of the mentally retarded), and imprisonment rather than treatment for drug users.

Rights and the War on Terrorism

Pages 134–37 discuss the issue of rights and the war on terrorism. Just as free expression has been limited in wartime, protection for other civil liberties has taken a back seat to national security during the post-September 11, 2001 "war on terrorism."

Detention of Enemy Combatants

The Bush administration's policies on handling *enemy combatants* during the war on terrorism have severely limited the rights of prisoners suspected of engaging in terrorist actions. Those who are suspected for terrorism can be held without legal representation and without their families being notified. Noncitizens can be deported without due process. The Court has permitted prisoners to be held at Guantanamo Bay but found that they had the right to use federal courts to challenge their detention.

Surveillance of Suspected Terrorists

The *USA Patriot Act* reduced constitutional protections by expanding the government's surveillance powers. For example, it became easier for the government to wiretap, search property, and review records. The rationale is that additional authority and flexibility are needed to fight the war on terrorism. Critics have argued that the loss of liberty is too extensive to be justified. The Supreme Court has not yet ruled on aspects of the USA Patriot Act, but lower court rulings have been mixed.

The Courts and a Free Society

This section makes the point that Americans support the idea of rights and freedoms but are less supportive of these rights when they are applied. In fact, elites are more supportive of civil liberties in practice. Federal judges are more protected from public opinion than elected officials; hence, one of their primary responsibilities is to uphold civil liberties even when it is unpopular to do so.

TAKE NOTE

This is an extremely important chapter. It is essential to understand that freedom is defined as something that people had prior to the formation of the American government. The Bill of Rights identifies those freedoms the federal government cannot take away. The Supreme Court interprets what those freedoms mean in concrete incidents, and this interpretation has changed over time. The most important change is how the *due process clause* of the *Fourteenth Amendment* was used to apply the Bill of Rights protections to state and local governments. It is essential to know that this "incorporation" of the Bill of Rights did not occur immediately after the Civil War amendments were added, did not happen all at once, and did not happen at the same time for procedural guarantees and freedom of expression. Do not merely memorize case names and decisions. Understand the logic used in deciding each case, why it is important, and what it tells us about politics.

Observations from Past Exams

Information from this chapter is part of the "Civil Rights and Civil Liberties" section of the test, which is supposed to make up 5 percent to 15 percent of the multiple-choice questions. Specifically, the test deals with the development of civil liberties by Court decisions, substantive liberties, and the impact of the Fourteenth Amendment on liberties.

The two most recently released multiple-choice exams (1999 and 2002) had nine questions about material from this chapter. These questions reveal the importance of understanding incorporation, terminology, and how the Court interprets civil liberties. The cases included in these multiple-choice questions were *Miranda v. Arizona, Roe v. Wade,* and *Griswold v. Connecticut.* However, it is not enough to memorize cases. For example, a student could know that *Roe v. Wade* legalized abortion but still miss the multiple-choice questions because they required an understanding of the legal reasoning behind the case: the right of privacy implied in the Bill of Rights.

The multiple-choice questions from the 1999 exam did not refer to specific cases but asked about the Court's current interpretation of the right of free speech, what the Court interpreted to make the Bill of Rights apply to states, what the purpose of "*Miranda* warnings" are, and what the *establishment clause* "does." The 2002 multiple-choice test asked what the central concern of the First Amendment was, what the "wall of separation" doctrine applied to, what *Miranda v. Arizona* held, what the incorporation doctrine is, what the basis of the *Roe v. Wade* decision was and where in the Constitution it appears.

In addition to the multiple-choice questions on civil liberties, two of the last seven exams had free-response questions that required an understanding of civil liberties, incorporation, and relevant Court decisions. The 2005 test specifically asked students to define selective incorporation and to describe two appropriate cases and explain how a provision of the Bill of Rights was incorporated. The 2001 exam asked students to choose one of three civil liberties cases (*Mapp v. Ohio, Gideon v. Wainwright,* and *Miranda v. Arizona*) and explain its significance. They also had to say which provision of the Fourteenth Amendment was applied to the case.

What to Do with the Boxes

Helpful summaries of important information about civil liberties are Table 4-1 (p. 113), Table 4-2 (p. 126), and "The Bill of Rights" definitions (p. 127).

A useful preparation for the illustration-based questions is to try to write a summary for Figure 4-1 (p. 123) and Figure 4-2 (p. 138) before you read (or review) the one provided under the title. Try to come up with arguments for why the information looks the way it does.

"Why Should I Care? Civil Liberties and National Security" (p. 109) does a good job of illustrating the political issues that arise when core values such as security and freedom come into conflict. "Debating the Issues: Should 'Under God' Be Removed from the Pledge of Allegiance?" (p.118) presents a useful application of the "establishment clause" to a contemporary issue to illustrate the concept. "Liberty, Equality & Self-Government: What's Your Opinion?" (p. 125) reinforces the lesson in the "Crime, Punishment, and Police Practices" section. Because of the focus of the AP test, you do not need to concentrate on the biographical sketch of Oliver Wendell Holmes Jr. (p. 108), the state comparisons (p. 131), or the international comparisons (pp. 120, 133).

Key Terms

Don't just memorize these terms. Understand what they mean and how they compare to other concepts. Be able to give examples of each.

Civil liberties (p. 106)
Bill of Rights (p. 106)
Freedom of expression (p. 107)
Clear-and-present-danger test (p. 108)
Symbolic speech (p. 110)
Prior restraint (p. 111)
Due process clause (of the Fourteenth Amendment) (p. 112)

Selective incorporation (p. 112)
Imminent-lawless-action test (p. 113)
Libel (p. 115)
Slander (p. 115)
Obscenity (p. 115)
Establishment clause (p. 117)
Free-exercise clause (p. 119)
Right of privacy (p. 121)
Procedural due process (p. 124)
Search and seizure (p. 127)
Exclusionary rule (p. 128)
Habeas corpus (p. 129)
Racial profiling (p. 130)
Cruel and unusual punishment (p. 132)
Enemy combatants (p. 134)

Five constitutional amendments are discussed in this chapter. You should know what rights they protect, why the rights are important, and how and when the amendments were applied. The amendments are:

First Amendment (p. 127)
Fourth Amendment (p. 124, p. 127)
Fifth Amendment (p. 124, p. 127)
Sixth Amendment (p. 124, p. 127)
Eighth Amendment (p. 124, p. 127)

Making Connections to Previous Chapters

Chapter 1 defined liberty as one of the core American values (p. 9) that shapes public policy (p. 12). How this value has been defined over time through legislation and Court decisions is demonstrated in pages 107–23 of Chapter 4. Another value is justice. Justice is promoted through "just procedures." These are the focus of pages 124–37. The chapter demonstrates well how these values come into conflict with others, such as security, unity, and patriotism.

Chapter 2's discussion of the Constitution protecting liberty through putting limits on government (pp. 50–56) is well illustrated in civil liberties. The responsibility of the Court to protect civil liberties and its power of judicial review (pp. 53–54) are illustrated in the cases reviewed in this chapter. This chapter also illustrates the "principle of separated institutions sharing power" (p. 53). Congress passes laws that are evaluated by the Court when disputes over their constitutionality arise. Congress can respond to the Court's decision by passing new legislation, which can also be reviewed by the Court. This is illustrated well by the discussion of the Internet and obscenity (pp. 116–17). After the Court struck down the *Communications Decency Act* of 1996, it passed the *Child Online Protection Act* of 1998 (which was also judged as unconstitutional by the Court).

Federalism (Chapter 3) is also relevant to the discussion of civil liberties. The role of the Fourteenth Amendment in limiting state discretion (pp. 83–84) is illustrated in the incorporation cases in this chapter. National supremacy (p. 78) is evident in the Court's decisions that require states to do certain things, such as read Miranda warnings, and stop doing others, such as allowing prayer in schools.

SAMPLE QUESTIONS

Multiple-Choice Questions

1. Civil liberties:
   a. are rights against government infringement
   b. are enumerated in the Fourteenth Amendment
   c. are rights the government gives people
   d. are all listed in the First Amendment
   e. include the right to vote

2. The "clear-and-present-danger" test:
   a. was established in *Gitlow v. New York*
   b. restricts freedom of the press
   c. was replaced by the imminent-lawless-action test
   d. established the military draft
   e. is an example of the expansion of civil liberties

3. Selective incorporation:
   a. began when the Fourteenth Amendment was ratified
   b. allowed states to establish bills of rights
   c. established due process for those accused of national and state crimes
   d. limited the authority of states to restrict civil liberties
   e. was established in the case of *Barron v. Baltimore*

4. What can the government regulate about the right to assembly?
   a. the types of people allowed at the assembly
   b. the subject matter discussed at the assembly
   c. the time and place of the assembly
   d. the sexual explicitness of the language used at the assembly
   e. there is no aspect of freedom of assembly that can be regulated

5. What is the current content standard used by the Supreme Court to determine if sexual materials are obscene?
   a. whether the material "taken as a whole" appeals to "prurient interest"
   b. whether the material has no "redeeming social significance"
   c. whether the material violates "contemporary standards" of the United States
   d. whether the material violates "contemporary standards" of the locality it appeared in
   e. whether the material is "particularly offensive" to a reasonable person

6. The "establishment clause":
   a. establishes the right of Americans to freely exercise their religions
   b. prohibits government from establishing a state religion
   c. prohibits states from establishing laws that contradict the federal government's
   d. prohibits the government from providing financial support to church-run schools
   e. establishes laws of the federal government as superior to those of states when the two are in conflict

7. The right to get a safe and legal abortion in all 50 states is based on:
   a. the Fourteenth Amendment's "equal protection clause"
   b. a "right to privacy" implied in the Bill of Rights
   c. the notion that government protects "life, liberty, and pursuit of happiness"
   d. the Twenty-seventh Amendment passed after *Roe v. Wade*
   e. The Ninth Amendment, which reserves rights not articulated in the Constitution to the people

8. Selective incorporation of procedural rights can be seen in:
   > I. *Engel v. Vitale* decision
   > II. *Gideon v Wainwright* decision
   > III. *Mapp v. Ohio* decision

   a. I
   b. I and II
   c. I and III
   d. II and III
   e. I, II, and III

9. The figure demonstrates that:

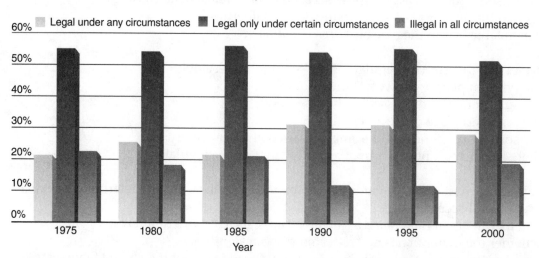

Americans' Opinions on Abortion

a. in all years, a greater percentage of people support legalizing abortion under all circumstances than making it illegal in all circumstances
b. public opinion changed dramatically after the *Roe v. Wade* decision
c. the most popular response is that abortion should be legal under certain circumstances
d. opinions on abortion are more polarized in 1985 than in the other years in the figure
e. many Americans allow their religious beliefs to influence their political attitudes

A Multiple-Choice Question That Links Chapter 4 to Lessons in Earlier Chapters

10. In the *Schenck v. U.S.* decision, the Supreme Court unanimously held that the Espionage Act was constitutional.
     I.   This is an example of the Court using judicial review.
    II.   This is an example of the Court using the "supremacy clause" to decide a federalism issue.
    III. This is an example of limited government.
    IV. This is an example of the Supreme Court prioritizing one American value over the other.

   a. I and II
   b. III and IV
   c. II, III, and IV
   d. I, II, and III
   e. I and IV

Multiple-Choice Answers

1. A; 2. C; 3. D; 4. C; 5. E; 6. B; 7. B; 8. D; 9. C; and 10. E

Free-Response Questions

1.   The First Amendment includes the freedom of expression. Like all rights, it is not absolute.

   a. Describe two ways in which the freedom of expression is currently restricted in a way deemed constitutional by the Supreme Court. (4 points)

   b. Describe the rationale for one of these restrictions and an interest group that would support this decision. Explain why that group would support it. (2 points)

   c. Describe the rationale for the other restriction and describe an interest group that would oppose this decision. Explain why that group would oppose it. (2 points)

   The question is worth eight points.

   Part "a" is worth four points. One point is earned by correctly identifying a restriction. The second point is for correctly describing it. The third point is earned for correctly identifying a second restriction. The fourth point is earned for correctly describing it. The two must be different. For example, libel and slander cannot count as two separate restrictions.

   Restrictions include:

   1. Censorship of battlefront reporting.
   2. Speech aimed at producing an imminent lawless action. A discussion that uses the term "clear and present danger" or applies that test is not correct unless it talks about the standard being changed.
   3. Slander/Libel. This needs to be described as something false and damaging to a person's reputation. If the person is identified as a public figure (by name or type), the description needs to refer to malice or "reckless disregard for the truth" must be present.

4. Obscenity. The answer needs to describe obscenity today as offensive to a reasonable person. A discussion of "community standards," "prurient interest," or "no redeeming social value" will not suffice unless provided as being changed to a less-restrictive definition. Any reference to materials involving adults on the Internet or in homes does not count.

Part "b" is worth two points. The rationale for the restriction is worth one point. Describing an interest group that would support this decision and why is worth one point. Note that the interest group does not need to be properly named. It can be hypothetical as long as it is described in a way that is appropriate to the issue.

Part "c" is worth two points. The rationale for the restriction is worth one point. Describing an interest group that would oppose it and explaining why is worth one point.

Again, the interest group does not need to be properly named. It can be hypothetical as long as it is described in a way that is appropriate to the issue.

2. There are limitations on how police can treat suspects and on how the Court can treat individuals charged with or convicted of a crime. There are also limits on the rights of defendants.

    a. Describe one limitation on police. Explain how the Supreme Court has interpreted a constitutional amendment to justify this limitation on police. Be sure to specify what amendment you are referring to. (3 points)

    b. Describe one limitation on courts. Explain how the Supreme Court has interpreted a constitutional amendment to justify this limitation on judges. Be sure to specify what amendment you are referring to. (3 points)

    c. Describe one limitation on a criminal defendant's rights. Explain how the Supreme Court has interpreted a provision of the Bill of Rights to justify this limitation on criminal defendants' rights. Be sure to specify what amendment you are referring to. (3 points)

This question is worth nine points.

Each part is worth three points. One is for accurately describing a limitation. One is for correctly identifying the amendment. One is for explaining how the amendment is used to justify the limitation. Note that a specific Supreme Court case need not be named.

Limitations for "a" include:

*   No unreasonable search and seizures unless waived (Fourth Amendment)
*   Must alert suspects of their right to a lawyer (Sixth Amendment)
*   Must alert suspects of their right to avoid self-incrimination (Fifth Amendment)
*   No arrest without probable cause (Fourth Amendment)

Limitations for "b" include:

*   No double jeopardy (Fifth Amendment)
*   No forced self-incrimination (Fifth Amendment)
*   No denial of right to grand jury (Fifth Amendment)
*   No loss of life, liberty, or property without due process (Fifth Amendment)
*   No denial of right to counsel (Sixth Amendment)
*   No denial of right to confront witnesses (Sixth Amendment)

- No denial of right to speedy trial (Sixth Amendment)
- No denial of right to trial by jury in criminal case (Sixth Amendment)
- No imposition of cruel and unusual punishment (Eighth Amendment)
- Cannot execute mentally ill (Eighth Amendment)
- Cannot sentence in death-penalty cases (Sixth Amendment)

Limitations for "c" include:

- Can be stopped for roadside check for intoxication as long as not arbitrary (Fourth Amendment)
- Can be stopped and searched if the decision to stop meets a "reasonable" standard (Fourth Amendment)
- Can be searched and have materials seized and used in court without correct warrant if the error was inadvertent (Fourth Amendment)
- Can be given long terms in overcrowded prisons and executed (Eighth Amendment)

CHAPTER FIVE

Equal Rights:
Struggling toward Fairness

SUMMARY

Chapter 5 is about civil rights. It focuses on what civil rights are (how extensive and how limited), the role and limitations of each branch of federal and state governments in determining civil rights, and how and why civil rights have changed over time.

Defining Civil Rights

Civil liberties and civil rights are not the same thing, and the terms should not be used interchangeably. Civil liberties deal with freedom and individual rights. Civil rights deal with equality and members of groups. Another way you can think about this is that civil liberties are thought of as rights that we are born with that the government should not take away from us (for example, freedom of speech). Cases that enhance civil liberties put limits or requirements on government. Civil rights are rights that the government must intervene to protect. Cases that enhance civil rights are those that put restrictions on governments, organizations, or individuals seeking to limit the opportunities of others.

The Struggle for Equality

On pages 144–61, Patterson describes "the struggle for equality." This discussion is organized by group (African Americans, women, Native Americans, Hispanic Americans, Asian Americans, and others) rather than by topic or chronology. It is important to realize that decisions and laws brought about by one group's struggle often apply to other groups. Obviously, people can fit into more than one of these categories because some people are multiracial and all of us fall into categories of race, sex, age, and sexual orientation.

Each part of this section emphasizes the long-term struggle of specific groups to achieve equal rights under the law, their successes, and the fact that inequality remains despite these laws and Court decisions. Specific lessons about each group's struggle are:

African Americans—Even though the Supreme Court decision in *Plessy v. Ferguson* (1896) occurred after the Civil War, it endorses racial discrimination. This ruling established the "separate but equal" doctrine, which determined that segregation by race was constitutional as long as facilities were "equal." Although more progressive decisions about segregation came out of the Court starting in the 1930s, the precedent was not reversed until *Brown v. Board of Education of Topeka* (1954). This case predated the mass movement for civil rights and the major congressional acts for equal rights. Inequality remains, particularly in the area of criminal sentencing.

Women—Women gained the right to vote in 1920 when the Nineteenth Amendment to the Constitution was ratified. Soon afterward, they started efforts to get an *Equal Rights Amendment* (ERA). Renewed efforts to get the ERA passed in the 1970s failed. However, many laws were passed to prohibit sex discrimination in employment, education, and banking. Inequality remains in terms of job opportunities and pay. Traditional values, sexual harassment, and child-care responsibilities contribute to this inequality.

Native Americans—Native Americans have a long history of oppression by the U.S. government. It was not until 1924 that they were given official citizenship. In 1968, an *Indian Bill of Rights* was passed by Congress to give Native Americans living on reservations constitutional rights. In 1974, after the American Indian Movement took over Wounded Knee, Native Americans were given more control over federal programs that affected them. Today, the federal government's policy toward Native Americans encourages self-government and economic self-sufficiency and protects cultural diversity.

Hispanic Americans—Hispanics are the largest racial minority group in the United States and the fastest growing. Their geographic concentration in California, Texas, New Mexico, Arizona, and southern Florida makes them a political force in these places. Examples of this influence can be seen in the farm workers' strikes of the late 1960s and electoral politics today. Non-English-speaking Hispanics have been aided by the 1968 amendment to the *Civil Rights Act of 1964*, which required funding for language instruction. Although the Supreme Court ruled that it was constitutional to deny jobs to illegal aliens, it nullified many of the provisions of California's *Proposition 187* that barred illegal aliens from receiving public services and public schooling. How to deal with the large number of illegal aliens is a major contemporary issue, as we can see from the debate set off by President Bush's proposal for a guest worker program.

Asian Americans—Discrimination against Asian Americans was eased by changes in immigration restrictions against them in 1965 and civil rights laws that apply to racial minorities and non-English speakers. The case of *Lau v. Nichols* (1974) declared that placing a Chinese American child into a regular public school class without special assistance violated the Fourteenth Amendment's equal-protection clause. Although the Court did not define what kind of assistance was necessary, many schools have created bilingual instruction. There is much debate over how much bilingual instruction should be provided and how and when it should be taught.

Other Groups—The *Civil Rights Act of 1964* explicitly prohibited discrimination against people based on their sex, race, and national origin. Therefore, laws could still deny equality to people based on their age, disabilities, and sexual orientations. Other laws were passed later to prohibit job discrimination against older workers. The *Americans with Disabilities Act* (1990) gave the disabled employment protections previously granted to other disadvantaged groups. There are limitations to these laws' application. For example, some jobs can have mandatory retirement ages, and state governments do not have to comply with federal laws against age and disability discrimination in the workplace.

Supreme Court decisions and state laws rather than federal legislation have defined the rights of gays and lesbians. Both vary greatly. Whereas Vermont and Massachusetts passed laws legally recognizing same-sex unions, Colorado passed a constitutional amendment prohibiting legal protections for homosexuals. The Supreme Court overturned this law in *Romer v. Evans* (1996). The Court also invalidated a state law that made homosexual sex illegal in *Lawrence v. Texas* (2003). On the other hand, the Court allowed the Boy Scouts to ban gays from the organization.

Equality under the Law

Pages 162–66 interpret laws and Court decisions that deal with "equality under the law." This section is divided into three parts. The first looks at how the equal-protection clause has been interpreted. The second discusses laws dealing with access to private accommodations, jobs, and housing. The third examines voting rights as a civil right.

Equal Protection—What is meant by "*equal protection under the law*," the phrase found in the Fourteenth Amendment? The clause says that no state can deny equal protection to people in its jurisdiction. This does not mean that all laws must treat all people the same. The Court has devised various tests that it applies to laws that treat people differently to determine whether these laws are unconstitutional. The Court has decided that it is much harder to justify discrimination based on race or ethnicity (using the "*strict-scrutiny test*"), than discrimination based on sex (using the "*intermediate scrutiny test*"), or other categories such as age or income (using the "*reasonable-basis* test"). The "reasonable-basis test" says that if the law has a sound basis, such as requiring people be a certain age to drink, then it is acceptable. The "strict-scrutiny test" assumes that laws discriminating against race and national origin are suspect because they are classifying people in order to discriminate. The "intermediate-scrutiny test" was introduced in the decision of *Craig v. Boren* (1976), when the Court argued that sex may be a permissible classification for discrimination. There is much confusion over how the Court will apply this test; however, most recent decisions find laws that differentiate by sex unconstitutional.

Equal Access—The Fourteenth Amendment did not require equal access to private (nongovernmental) places and organizations. This was the focus of the Civil Rights Act of 1964 that sought, successfully, to bar discrimination in public places and, less successfully, to eliminate job discrimination. Housing discrimination was prohibited in the *Civil Rights Act of 1968*. However, segregated housing continues as a result of previous discrimination actions, such as *redlining* (banks refusing to give mortgage loans in some neighborhoods).

Equal Ballots—Despite the Fifteenth Amendment, which gave blacks the right to vote after the Civil War, African Americans were prevented from voting in the South until the Voting Rights Act of 1965 was enacted. This act prohibited discrimination in voting and registration and allowed federal agents to register voters and oversee elections. Although barriers such as the all-white primary and the poll tax had already been outlawed, it was not until the Voting Rights Act did away with literacy tests and protected blacks from intimidation that black voting substantially increased. Congress renewed the act and required that changes in election laws be pre-approved by the federal government. One goal was to prevent state legislatures from drawing electoral district lines in a ways that diluted minority votes. The Supreme Court has ruled that drawing lines to create districts with a majority of racial minorities in them, thereby virtually assuring racial representation in elected offices, is unconstitutional. Race could not be the "deciding factor" in creating districts, but partisanship could be.

Equality of Result

Pages 167–75 describe discrimination that results not from discriminatory laws (*de jure discrimination*), but from biases and socioeconomic conditions (*de facto discrimination*). It examines policies such as affirmative action and busing that have tried to address de facto discrimination and bring about *equality of results*. Many of these policies are unpopular because they are seen as infringing on liberty, unfairly burdensome, and creating reverse discrimination.

Affirmative Action—Affirmative action programs were designed to provide equal education and employment opportunities to groups that had previously been discriminated against. The assumption was that banning overt discrimination was not enough because "unwritten preferences" still gave advantages to white men. Affirmative action requires that employers and schools demonstrate that they are not privileging white men in their decision-making processes in areas such as selection, retention, and advancement.

What types of affirmative action programs are constitutional? The Supreme Court has ruled on affirmative action numerous times and is likely to do so again. The first time was in *University of California Regents v. Bakke* (1978) when the Court decided that an affirmative action plan that used rigid racial quotas was not permissible. In *Fullilove v. Klutnick* (1980), the Court found acceptable a quota system requiring that 10 percent of federal public works funds be saved for minority-owned firms. Next, the Court narrowed the scope of affirmative action policies to protect white employees' rights. In *Adarand v. Pena*, they found that preferential treatment of minorities had to be in response to specific past discrimination rather than general historical discrimination. This decision reversed the precedent set in *Fullilove* by establishing the expectation that programs be "narrowly tailored." In 2003, the Court handed down two more decisions on affirmative action. It decided in *Gratz v. Bollinger* that awarding specific points for race in a college admissions policy was unconstitutional but ruled in *Grutter v. Bollinger* that considering race in admissions decisions was acceptable.

Busing—The *Brown v. Board of Education of Topeka* case had limited success in overcoming school segregation because much of the segregation was based on where students lived rather than students' being forced to attend a segregated school farther from their homes. In 1971, the Supreme Court in *Swann v. Charlotte-Mecklenburg County Board of Education* found busing an acceptable remedy for school segregation. The Court later found that busing needed to be within a school district, as long as that district was not drawn in order to discriminate. In the 1990s, the Court found that busing was intended to be a temporary solution, and other solutions needed to be created. Although busing had been unpopular in the North as well as the South and contributed to whites departing from public schools and city neighborhoods, it had achieved some of its goals: to integrate schools, improve racial attitudes among children, and raise blacks' test scores. School desegregation reached its high point in the late 1980s.

Persistent Discrimination

The main point of this short section is that "true equality for all Americans has remained elusive" (p. 175). It also reminds us that racial equality is not just about blacks and whites by pointing out recent attitudes and discrimination against Middle Easterners.

TAKE NOTE

A complete understanding of Chapter 5 requires knowing the correct terminology and being able to provide accurate and appropriate examples. Although all groups' struggles for equality are important, it is imperative that you understand the struggles and successes of African Americans for equal rights. It is also important to be familiar with the *Civil Rights Act of 1964*, the *Voting Rights Act of 1965*, and Court cases dealing with desegregation, especially *Brown v. Board of Education of Topeka* (1954).

It is also important to understand that the *Brown* decision did not result from the civil rights movement. It was a success achieved through a litigation strategy of the *National Association for the Advancement of Colored People* (NAACP) that came before the civil rights movement began. The *Brown* case was only one of many cases the interest group had brought to the Court.

Another important case not mentioned in the textbook was *Sweatt v. Painter*, a case that preceded Brown. In this case, a black man wanted to attend the all-white University of Texas Law School rather than the law school created for him in the basement across from the capitol building. Although the Supreme Court did not overrule *Plessy v. Ferguson*, the Justices did decide that the alternative school was not equal to the University of Texas and that Herman Sweatt was unconstitutionally being denied an equal education because of his race.

Observations from Past Exams

Material in this chapter falls under the "Civil Rights and Civil Liberties" section of the AP U.S. Government and Politics test. Questions from this section are supposed to make up 5 percent to 15 percent of the multiple-choice questions on the test. Specifically, the test focuses on the development of civil rights by Court decisions, substantive rights, and the impact of the Fourteenth Amendment on rights.

A review of AP U.S. Government and Politics exams released by the College Board helps identify some key elements of this chapter. The specific Court cases and laws that were included on the last two released multiple-choice tests (1999 and 2004) were the *Dred Scott* case, *Plessy v. Ferguson, Brown v. Board of Education of Topeka, Sweatt v. Painter, Civil Rights Act of 1964, Voting Rights Act of 1965, Civil Rights Act of 1968,* and the Emancipation Proclamation. Specifically, the 1999 multiple-choice test asked what expanded civil rights in the 1950s and what made discrimination in public accommodations illegal. The 2002 multiple-choice test asked what the Fourteenth Amendment was designed to overturn.

Information from this chapter was also useful for answering one of the free-response questions from the 2005 exam and another from 2004. On the 2004 test, students could select (from a list of four) the National Association for the Advancement of Colored People as an interest group they wanted to discuss. They were to explain which technique (litigation, campaign contributions, or grass roots lobbying) the group uses and why. On the 2005 test, students could select the *Civil Rights Act of 1964* (from a list of three laws) and use it to explain how the federal government's power has increased over time compared to state governments'. For this question, it was necessary to be able to describe a provision of the bill.

What to Do with the Boxes

Table 5-1 (p. 162) provides a nice summary of important information in the text.

"Liberty, Equality & Self-Government: What's Your Opinion?" (p. 164) provides some relevant information on private discrimination and gives a recent case as an example. Knowing this is more relevant for the test than determining your own opinion. Table 5-2 (p. 170) provides a succinct summary of key decisions in the history of affirmative action. The dates are less important to remember than the chronology and how the decisions changed over time.

A useful preparation for the illustration-based questions on the test is to try to write a summary for Figure 5-1 (p. 147), Figure 5-2 (p. 150), Figure 5-4 (p. 156), Figure 5-6 (p. 166), Figure 5-7 (p. 167), Figure 5-8 (p. 169), and Figure 5-9 (p. 173) before you read (or review) the one provided under the title. Try to come up with arguments for why the information looks the way it does.

"Debating the Issues: Should Same-Sex Marriage Be Legalized?" (p. 160) provides you with some contemporary information relevant to the topic of equality. It might serve as a useful example for a free-response question, but because it is a state court decision, it is not material that you are likely to be asked about directly.

Because of the focus of the AP test, you do not need to concentrate on the biographical sketches of Martin Luther King Jr. (p. 146), Susan B. Anthony (p. 149), or Cesar Estrada Chavez (p. 154); the state comparisons (p. 148); the discussion boxes on equality and citizenship (p. 159, p. 174); or the international comparisons (pp. 150, 152, 161).

Key Terms

Don't just memorize these terms. Understand what they mean and how they compare to other concepts. Be able to give examples of each.

Civil rights (p. 144)—be able to contrast this with civil liberties.
Equal Rights Amendment (p. 148)
Gender gap (p. 149)—this is more relevant to public opinion and elections than to civil rights
Comparable worth (p. 151)
Glass ceiling (p. 151)
Equal-protection clause (p. 162)—be able to explain how this was incorporated
Reasonable-basis test (p. 162)
Strict-scrutiny test (p. 162)
Suspect classification (p. 163)
Intermediate-scrutiny test (p. 163)
Civil Rights Act of 1964 (p. 164)
Civil Rights Act of 1968 (p. 164)
Redlining (p. 165)
Voting Rights Act of 1965 (pp. 165–66)
De facto discrimination (p. 167)
De jure discrimination (p. 167)
Equality of result (p. 167)—this is more relevant to understanding American core values and
    how we define equality as "equality of opportunity")
Affirmative action (p. 168)

Four Constitutional amendments are discussed in this chapter. You should know what rights they protect, why the rights are important, and how and when the amendments were applied. The amendments are:

Fourteenth Amendment (p. 162)
Fifteenth Amendment (p. 147)
Nineteenth Amendment (p. 147)
Twenty-fourth Amendment (p. 165)

Making Connections to Previous Chapters

Chapter 1 defined equality as one of the core American values (10–12). Liberty, self-government, unity and diversity were others. Defining, prioritizing, and allocating these values is what politics is all about (p. 18). The information about civil rights in this chapter provides examples of this. For example, affirmative action brings freedom and equality into conflict. Diversity was given less weight than freedom and social order when busing was set aside.

You can apply the theories of power in Chapter 1 to civil rights disputes. To the extent that civil rights policies were developed in response to social movements, the model of pluralism is supported. When elites interpreted the Constitution in opposition to public opinion (as in the case of *Brown v. Board of Education of Topeka*), we see evidence of elitism.

The shared powers that result from checks and balances described in Chapter 2 (pp. 53–56) are illustrated by the *Adarand v. Pena* decision. The Supreme Court exercised judicial review (pp. 56–58) by ruling that federal affirmative action policy went too far. The difficulty of amending the Constitution (p. 52) can be seen in the failure of the ERA.

National supremacy (p. 78) is seen here in the Supreme Court declaring Colorado's constitutional amendment restricting legal protections for homosexuals null and void. An important conflict over states' rights and federalism resulted from the Voting Rights Act of 1965, which empowered federal agents to oversee registration and voting in Southern states. This conflicts with elections being within the "reserved powers" of states (p. 74) but is essential for guaranteeing voting rights and national citizenship (p. 88).

SAMPLE QUESTIONS

Multiple-Choice Questions

1. Women were given the right to vote for president:
   a. by the Fifteenth Amendment
   b. by the Nineteenth Amendment
   c. by the Voting Rights Act
   d. by the Seneca Falls Convention.
   e. gradually by state legislatures across the country

2. The "equal-protection clause":
   I. requires the federal government to treat all groups of people the same way
   II. requires state governments to treat all groups of people the same way
   III. requires private organizations to treat all groups of people the same way
   IV. does not require that the federal or state governments or private organizations treat all groups of people the same way

   a. I
   b. I and II
   c. I and III
   d. I, II, and III
   e. IV

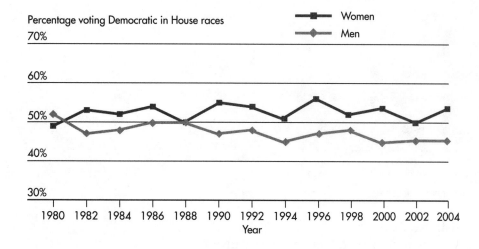

Percentage voting Democratic in House races

3. The figure above demonstrates that:
   a. regardless of the year in question, women are more likely to vote for Democratic House Representatives than men are
   b. the gender gap was larger in 1996 than 1998
   c. men were more likely to vote for George W. Bush than women were
   d. all of the elections included in the figure show a gender gap
   e. Democrats target their campaign communications to women more than Republicans do

4. The Civil Rights Acts of the 1960s did NOT apply to which group?
   a. black Americans
   b. Hispanic Americans
   c. female Americans
   d. Asian Americans
   e. elderly Americans

5. The 1982 amendment to the Voting Rights Act:
   a. limited the scope of the original act
   b. led to the creation of congressional districts in which racial minorities were the majority
   c. was deemed unconstitutional by the Supreme Court because it violated the rights of whites
   d. was deemed unconstitutional by the Supreme Court because it violated states' rights
   e. expanded the original act to include Hispanics

6. The *Brown v. Board of Education of Topeka* case:
   a. ended public school segregation
   b. mandated school integration but was not immediately enforced
   c. was one of the major achievements of the civil rights movement
   d. mandated busing as a solution to public school segregation
   e. did not require that the government take action to integrate schools

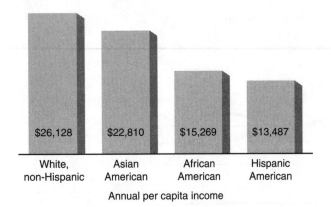

| $26,128 | $22,810 | $15,269 | $13,487 |

White, non-Hispanic   Asian American   African American   Hispanic American

Annual per capita income

7. The figure above illustrates that:
   a. white Americans work harder than racial minority groups
   b. the largest racial minority group in the United States has the lowest average income
   c. equality of opportunity is highly valued in the United States
   d. equality of results is the aim of civil rights policies
   e. African Americans are more likely to be unemployed than whites are

Multiple-Choice Questions That Link Chapter 5 to Lessons in Earlier Chapters

8. Which of these Court decisions protected "reserved rights"?
   a. upholding the Voting Rights Act of 1965
   b. overruling provisions in California's Proposition 187
   c. permitting the Boy Scouts to ban gays
   d. allowing considerable flexibility in the drawing of Congressional district lines.
   e. *Brown v. Board of Education of Topeka.*

9. Which branch of government developed the "reasonable-basis test"?
   a. the executive
   b. the legislature
   c. the judiciary
   d. the federal
   e. the states

10. Which of American's core values was given the highest priority in *Swann v. Charlotte-Mecklenburg County Board of Education?*
    a. freedom
    b. equality
    c. self-government
    d. patriotism
    e. individualism

Multiple-Choice Answers

1. B; 2. E; 3. B; 4. E; 5. B; 6. E; 7. B; 8. D; 9. C; and 10. B

Free-Response Questions

1. Americans have received equality under the law but not de facto equality.

   a. Explain what this statement means. (1 point)

   b. Identify and describe a national law that promoted equality. (2 points)

   c. Identify and describe a Supreme Court case that promoted equality. (2 points)

   d. Identify an area in which there is de facto inequality and explain how it remains. (2 points)

   The question is worth seven points.

   Part "a" is worth one point. It requires that you correctly differentiate between de facto and de jure discrimination.

   Part "b" is worth two points. One is for correctly identifying a national law that promoted equality. One point is for correctly describing how it promotes equality. Government acts from Chapter 5 include the Civil Rights Acts of 1964, 1968, or 1991, the Voting Rights Acts of 1965 or its amendments, the Equal Pay Act of 1963, Title IX of the Education Amendment of 1972, the Equal Credit Act of 1974, the Family and Medical Leave Act of 1993, the Indian Bill of Rights of 1968, the Age Discrimination Act of 1975, the Age Discrimination in Employment Act of 1967, the Americans with Disabilities Act of 1990, the Education for all Handicapped Children Act of 1975, the act making Native Americans official citizens in 1924, the changes in immigration quotas in 1965, and the 1968 civil rights legislation on housing.

   Part "c" is worth two points. One is for correctly identifying a Supreme Court case. One point is for correctly describing how the case promoted equality. If the case did not promote equality it does not count. Supreme Court cases that promote equality from Chapter 5 include: *Brown v. Board of Education of Topeka, Lau v. Nichols, Romer v. Evans, Lawrence v. Texas, United States v. Virginia, Easley v. Cromartie, Fullilove v. Klutnick, Grutter v. Bollinger*, and *Swann v. Charlotte-Mecklenburg County Board of Education*. It is possible that *University v. California Regents v. Bakke, Adarand v. Pena*, and *Gratz v. Bollinger* could count if it talked about protections from reverse discrimination. However, if the description doesn't make this clear, then identifying the case does not earn a point.

   Part "d" is worth two points. One point is for identifying an area in which de facto inequality remains. One point is for correctly describing how it remains. Areas of de facto inequality from Chapter 15 include: criminal sentencing; workplace discrimination in employment, advancement, and sexual harassment; hate crimes; marriage rights; education; and housing.

2. Three different standards, or tests, are used to determine whether a law that treats people differently based on their race, ethnicity, sex, age, or other category is constitutional.

   a. Identify two of these standards (or tests) and identify a group to which they apply. (2 points)

   b. Describe how one of these tests is used to determine what is lawful. (2 points)

   c. Provide an example of how this test has been applied to a specific case. Explain how the test was applied in this case. (2 points)

The question is worth six points.

Part "a" is worth two points. One is for correctly identifying a standard and a group it applies to. One is for correctly identifying a second standard and a group it applies to. The standards and groups are: "reasonable-basis test" applies to categories such as age and income; "intermediate-scrutiny test" applies to sex; "strict-scrutiny test" applies to race, ethnicity, and national origin.

Part "b" is worth two points. Two points are awarded for clearly and accurately describing the test. One point is awarded for a description that contains some accurate information but does not describe the test thoroughly.

Part "c" is worth two points. One point is for correctly identifying an example. The second point is for accurately explaining how the test was applied. Note that examples do not need to contain a specific Supreme Court decision's name to be given points.

CHAPTER SIX

Public Opinion and Political Socialization: Shaping the People's Voice

SUMMARY

This chapter describes how people first acquire their political opinions, how political opinions are measured, what factors influence public opinion, and the impact of public opinion on policy. It begins by noting that despite the theoretical importance that the public plays in a democracy, public opinion influences only the general direction of public policy. This is why Patterson calls public opinion an "inexact force" (p. 184).

The Nature of Public Opinion

Public opinion refers to opinions held and expressed, either verbally or nonverbally, by ordinary citizens. While it might seem as though public opinion refers to a shared opinion of the public, in reality there can be many opinions held by different subgroups with no majority opinion. In other cases, there can be few opinions outside of an informed segment of the population. The general lack of interest in political issues is one of the things that discourage government responsiveness to public opinion. Another is the lack of agreement among the informed or interested public. Not only is there misinformation and inconsistency in attitudes (for example, people wanting lower taxes and more government spending), but also most people pay little attention to government and have little knowledge about it. Of course, people can still hold opinions even if they lack specific information because opinions are derived from values.

Although public opinion can be observed indirectly through votes, media, mass demonstrations, or interest-group activity, it is more systematically and directly measured by *polls*, also called surveys. Because of the laws of probability, polls can ask a random *sample* of people questions and generalize to the opinions of the *population*. A relatively small random sample of about 1,000 people is sufficient to generalize to the population of the nation. Polls are not perfect. All probability surveys have a *sampling error* that is expressed as plus or minus a certain percentage. This indicates how "far off" the sample's estimate of the population is likely to be. There can also be problems with how questions are worded. The wording may lead people to answer in a certain way. When people do not have attitudes, but they answer survey questions anyway, these are called *nonattitudes*.

Political Socialization: How Americans Learn Their Politics

People acquire their political beliefs through *political socialization*. Although this is a lifelong process, childhood learning tends to shape later learning. Therefore, it is important to understand how children come to understand politics. The chapter describes six factors that influence children's political development. These are considered *agents of socialization*.

The most important agent is the family. Children learn most of their beliefs and values from their parents. These include their party identification (whether they consider themselves

Republican or Democrat). Schools are also important in communicating political information and values to children. For example, rituals like saying the Pledge of Allegiance can promote patriotism. The mass media is also important in informing and shaping children's perceptions of politics. Peers and friends tend to reinforce attitudes. Political institutions and leaders, who communicate through the media, can influence opinions. Churches also convey values that have political implications.

Frames of Reference: How Americans Think Politically

Patterson identifies four factors that influence how Americans evaluate politics. The first pushes toward consensus, or agreement. It is cultural thinking that Americans share: ideals such as liberty, equality, and individualism. The other three factors—ideological, group, and partisan thinking—help explain why Americans disagree.

Ideological thinking is "a consistent pattern of opinion on particular issues that stems from a core belief or set of beliefs" (p. 197). About a third of the American public has political ideologies. Others may use ideological terms and have some opinions that fit those terms, but they do not consistently hold *liberal* or *conservative* positions. Although liberal and conservative are the most common ideological terms used in American politics, they are not the only patterns. *Libertarians* and *populists* make up two other ideological types. The difference between these groups arises over their disagreement over what they think that government should do. Should government do more to solve social and economic problems? For the most part, liberals and populists think it should and conservatives and libertarians think it should not. Should government compel people to behave according to traditional moral values? For the most part, populists and conservatives think it should and liberals and libertarians think it should not.

People's positions on political issues can better be understood by looking at what groups they belong to than by asking about their ideology. The groups discussed in this section are religious, class, regional, racial/ethnic, gender, and age. It is important to remember that people are members of different groups that might think about issues differently. These *crosscutting cleavages* can result in moderate opinions. For example, an upper-class black person would be pulled by his or her racial group identification toward being liberal on affirmative action but would be pulled toward a conservative position by his or her economic class. As a result, this person might take a middle-of-the-road position on the issue.

On issues such as abortion or welfare, members of religious groups often share opinions. One of the most politicized religious groups is born-again Christians, who make up the *religious right*. The term *right* is another term for conservative, and *left* is another word for liberal. Although class has less of an influence on Americans' public opinions than on Europeans', its influence can still be seen how people perceive economic issues. Although regional differences are not as stark as they once were, people from southern and mountain states are more likely to be conservative on some issues than people from other states. Race and ethnicity influence attitudes on economic, crime, and race issues. Whites are generally less liberal on these issues than other groups. Positions on the issues tend not to differ by gender. The exceptions are gender gaps on welfare and the use of military force, with women taking more liberal positions on these issues. The impact of age on political opinions has increased over time, with the self-interest of the elderly dictating their positions on government spending, particularly for programs such as social security and Medicare.

Partisan thinking is the fourth frame of reference. The loyalty people feel toward the Democratic or Republican parties is acquired in childhood, tends to be lifelong, and substantially influences their perceptions of events, issues, and candidates.

The Influence of Public Opinion on Policy

Although most people believe that the government is responsive to their opinions, whether this is true is an empirical question that is difficult to answer. Some research indicates that policy decisions reflect public opinion on issues that are visible and salient (important) to people. Other research indicates that the public's opinions are far less influential, and becoming less so over time, than are the opinions of specific groups or elites. Yet politicians seem loath to get too far away from public opinion, and they use it to justify certain actions. Patterson characterizes public opinion as "a boundary on what policymakers can reasonably do" (p. 208).

TAKE NOTE

Although some of the material from this chapter is part of the AP U.S. Government and Politics curriculum, the tests do not seem to draw heavily from this chapter's material. They seem to focus more on behaviors such as voting and other forms of political participation than on beliefs as expressed through public opinion research.

One important lesson to learn from this chapter is the language of causality. The chapter clearly distinguishes between "causes" (what influences public opinion) and "effects" (what are the consequences of public opinion). Many questions on the AP test do as well.

There is also a useful distinction to learn between a "normative question" (p. 208) and an empirical question. Questions that ask you what your opinions are or whether something is good or bad are normative. These are not the kinds of questions that appear on the AP test. Resist expressing your opinion about politics. You might be asked to take a position on a question, but this should not invite an "opinion dump." Instead, you should marshal the evidence needed to support a certain idea (see Free-Response Question No. 2 on p. 58).

Polling methodology is not part of the AP U.S. Government and Politics curriculum. Therefore, it is not important to worry about the intricacies of survey sampling techniques (pp. 189–91) for the test. You should be skeptical about polls but not cynical about them. It is important to realize that sampling size, question wording, and political context can distort poll results and that polls are limited in what they can tell us, especially if the public is uniformed or undecided on an issue. However, these challenges should not lead you to dismiss polls entirely because—when done well—they are the best form of measuring public opinion that we have and are more accurate than inaccurate at demonstrating what the American public is thinking at a particular time.

Observations from Past Exams

The chapter would fall under the "Political Beliefs and Behaviors" section that is supposed to make up between 10 percent and 20 percent of the multiple-choice questions. Specifically, it addresses the focus on "beliefs held about government, processes by which people learn about politics, the nature, sources and consequences of public opinion, ways citizens vote and participate, factors that influence how beliefs and behaviors differ."

Material from this chapter was the focus of only three multiple-choice questions on the last two released exams. Students had to identify the most important agent of socialization on the 2002 exam. They needed to know the definition of political socialization and how to interpret a table about wealth and ideology for the 1999 exam. Similarly, questions about public opinion were rarely asked in the free-response section of the text. An exception was a question on the 2004 exam that asked about causes for the decrease in political participation. Public opinion could be used to address this question; however, the relevant information is found in Chapter 7.

What to Do with the Boxes

Figure 6-1 (p. 186), Figure 6-2 (p. 203), Figure 6-3 (p. 204), and Figure 6-4 (p. 206) are worth trying to summarize without reading the caption under the title. Come up with ideas about the causes or consequences of the predominant attitudes in each of these surveys. Figure out what the pattern is in Table 6-1 (p. 207), but do not worry about remembering specifics from that table.

"Debating the Issues" (p. 188) deals with a central debate. You should be able to defend and critique "rule by public opinion." Be able to inform this discussion with information from Chapters 1 and 2. "Political Culture" (p. 192) and "How the United States Compares" (p. 196) tell you that national pride and religion are important aspects of public opinion. The "States in the Nation" box (p. 199) shows the distribution of conservatives and liberals in the country. Try to come up with ideas about what the causes and the consequences of these patterns are for national elections and the development of government policies. The "Liberty, Equality & Self-Government" box (p. 200) is useful for helping you understand the ideological groups and how they are defined.

The basic idea behind the "Why Should I Care?" box (p. 187) is that Americans are less informed and less interested in global affairs than people in other countries. Be able to analyze why this is or is not a problem.

Key Terms

Don't just memorize these terms. Understand what they mean and how they compare to other concepts. Be able to give examples of each.

Public opinion (p. 185)
Poll (p. 189)
Sample (p. 189)
Population (p. 189)
Sampling error (p. 189)
Probability (p. 190)
Nonattitudes (p 191)
Political socialization (p. 191)
Age-cohort tendency (p. 193) The idea is more important than the term and may be referred to in other ways.
Agents of socialization (p. 193)
Ideology (p. 197)
Liberals (p. 198)
Conservatives (p. 198)
Libertarians (p. 198)
Populists (p. 198)

Religious right (p. 201)
Crosscutting cleavages (p. 203)
Party identification (p. 204)
Partisanship (p. 205)

Making Connections to Previous Chapters

Lessons from Chapter 6 deepen and challenge the understanding of politics and American values described in Chapter 1. For example, self-government was identified as one of the core American values in the first chapter. How does the lack of interest, information, and agreement among the public affect this ideal? Relate the lessons about public opinion and its impact on policymaking to the four competing theories of power described in Chapter 1. Different sections of Chapter 6 provide evidence for majoritarianism, pluralism, and elitism. Chapter 1 helps explain the frame of reference that promotes consensus (cultural thinking, p. 197).

The debate over the role that public opinion should play in politics is central to this chapter and has deep historical roots. These were introduced earlier in the book in the section on the debate between Federalists and Anti-Federalists (pp. 48–49) and the one on the limitations and eventual expansion of popular rule (pp. 58–66). The information from this chapter should help you assess the risk of *tyranny of the majority* (p. 59). The *trustee* approach of government officials discussed on p. 59 is one answer to the normative question posed about how much of an influence public opinion should play in policymaking (posed on p. 208).

Many current political issues were described throughout Part I. You should now be able to identify which positions liberals, conservatives, libertarians, and populists would likely take on these issues.

SAMPLE QUESTIONS

Multiple-Choice Questions

1. The attitudes of the American adult public:
   a. cannot be measured because they change so much
   b. cannot be measured because they contradict each other
   c. cannot be measured because they are misinformed
   d. cannot be measured by surveys because they have sampling errors
   e. can be measured

2. What is a limitation of using an election to interpret public opinion?
   a. Politicians run campaigns to win votes.
   b. Interest groups mobilize voters.
   c. Different voters will vote for the same candidates for different reasons.
   d. Voters express nonattitudes.
   e. People who vote are only a random sample.

3. Which agent of socialization tends to reinforce, rather than change, a child's political attitudes?
   a. schools
   b. churches
   c. peers
   d. family
   e. the FBI

4. Which of the following is true about political ideology?
   a. Most Americans choose a political ideology by the time they are in high school.
   b. Political ideology is the most important influence on voter choice.
   c. Political ideology cannot be measured.
   d. A person's political ideology is based on beliefs about the proper role of government.
   e. Most Americans claim to have either a Republican ideology or a Democratic ideology.

5. Members of which group are most likely to say they believe that government tries to do too much and should stay out of both economic matters and personal lifestyle choices?
   a. liberals
   b. conservatives
   c. free riders
   d. libertarians
   e. populists

6. The impact of age on public opinion:
   a. cannot be measured
   b. is getting stronger over time
   c. is getting weaker over time
   d. is irrelevant once class is taken into consideration
   e. is negligible

7. A person's party identification:
   a. is typically acquired during childhood
   b. is measured by that person's voter registration
   c. is the formal membership in a party organization
   d. typically changes when there is a popular candidate in the other party
   e. is rarely relevant to that person's political behaviors

8. Values shared by the American public:
   a. are impossible to find because of the country's great diversity
   b. are based on extensive information about public affairs
   c. include military intervention in Iraq
   d. are the result of politicians manipulating the media
   e. place boundaries on political action

9. The figure below demonstrates:

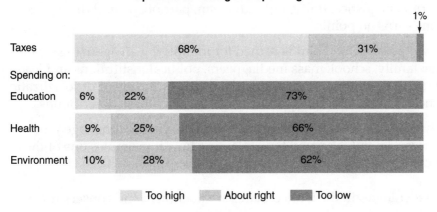

Opinions on Taxing and Spending

Used by permission of National Opinion Research Center, University of Chicago.

    I. people believe taxes are too high
    II. people want more government spending on education, health, and environment
    III. public opinion can be contradictory and inconsistent

a. I
b. I and II
c. II and III
d. I, II, and III
e. I and III

A Multiple-Choice Question That Links Chapter 6 to Lessons in Other Chapters

10. Someone who supports a law mandating comparable worth is most likely to be:
    a. either a liberal or a conservative
    b. either a liberal or a libertarian
    c. either a conservative or a libertarian
    d. a liberal
    e. a conservative

Multiple-Choice Answers

1. E; 2. C; 3. C; 4. D; 5. D; 6. B; 7 A; 8. E; 9. D; and 10. D

Free-Response Questions

1. a. Describe two core values that are part of American political culture. (1 point)

    b. Identify one of the agents of childhood political socialization. Explain how it promotes one of these values. (2 points)

    c. Identify another agent of childhood political socialization. Explain how it promotes the other value. (2 points)

This question is worth five points.

Part "a" is worth one point for describing two core values. These include: equality, freedom, self-government, justice, unity, individualism, patriotism, and diversity. Identifying only one earns no points.

Part "b" is worth two points. One point is earned for identifying an agent of socialization. These include: family, school, mass media, peers, political institutions and leaders, and churches. The second point is earned for explaining how the agent of socialization promotes one of these values. Examples can be used to clarify these descriptions.

Part "c" is worth two points. One point is earned for identifying another agent of socialization. The second point is earned for explaining how it promotes one of these values. Examples can be used to clarify these descriptions.

2. Two common political ideologies in the United States are liberalism and conservatism.

   a. What are the fundamental differences between these two ideologies? (1 point)

   b. Choose a political issue. Describe what position a liberal would take on that issue and how that position illustrates a liberal ideology. (2 points)

   c. What position would a conservative take on raising the minimum wage? Explain how this position reflects the ideology. (2 points)

   d. Identify and describe an ideology other than these two (liberal and conservative). (1 point)

   This question is worth six points.

   Part "a" is worth one point for providing a fundamental difference between the two ideologies. These include: extent of government intervention in the economic marketplace, maintenance of traditional values.

   Part "b" is worth two points. The first point is earned for identifying a political issue and clearly and accurately describing the position that liberals would take on it. The second point is earned for clearly and accurately describing the rationale.

   Part "c" is worth two points. The first point is earned for identifying the correct position (opposition to an increase). The second point is earned for clearly and accurately describing the rationale.

   Part "d" is worth one point for correctly identifying and describing another ideology. The description needs to be accurate for a point to be awarded. These include: socialism, feminism, populism, or libertarianism. Simply identifying the ideology without correctly describing it is worth no points.

CHAPTER SEVEN

Political Participation and Voting: Expressing the Popular Will

SUMMARY

This chapter describes different forms of *political participation* that members of the American public can engage in. It pays particular attention to voting. Citizen participation is key to self-government in a democracy, yet there is limited participation in the United States. The reasons for this and its consequences are explored.

Voter Participation

Over time, *suffrage* has been expanded to groups that were not given the right to vote after the nation's founding. In 1840, white men no longer had to own property to vote. In 1920, the Nineteenth Amendment allowed women to vote. Although the Fifteenth Amendment gave blacks the right to vote after the Civil War, many were unable to exercise the right until the Twenty-fourth Amendment outlawed poll taxes and the Voting Rights Act of 1965 was passed. Voting rights were extended to Americans between the ages of 18 and 21 in 1971 with the Twenty-sixth Amendment. Despite the public's belief that voting is important and effective, millions do not exercise this basic right of citizenship.

Factors in Voter Turnout: The United States in Comparative Perspective

Voter turnout in the United States has averaged about 55 percent since the 1960s and is consistently lower than in other western democracies. It is lower during midterm elections than it is in presidential elections. Patterson identifies three factors that contribute to low turnout in the United States relative to other nations. These are registration requirements, frequent elections, and perceptions of little difference between the major political parties.

To prevent corruption, *registration laws* were passed in the early 1900s. The requirement to register, a process carried out by states, added a burden that individuals needed to overcome in order to vote. Many of them did not do so, and voter turnout declined as a result. States with more lenient registration laws, such as registering at the polling place on election day, have higher rates than states with more restrictive laws such as longer residency requirements or remote registration locations. The national *motor voter* law passed in 1993 tried to make registration easier by mandating that states provide application forms at motor vehicle bureaus and welfare offices. Registration increased after the law was passed, but voter turnout did not.

The frequency with which elections are held in the United States also deflates turnout. In other countries, elections are held less often and on holidays or weekends. In the United States they are typically on Tuesday, a workday.

Logistics are not the only obstacle to turnout; attitudes are another. Many people believe that there is little difference between the political parties and the candidates that they run in elections. This differs from European voters, who have more parties to choose from and see substantial differences among them. Their clear-cut choices make it easier for European voters to decide, and they appear to be more compelled by the options.

Why Some Americans Vote and Others Do Not

Civic attitudes, age, education, and income help explain why some Americans vote and others do not. The single most important factor is education. Educated people have more interest in politics and greater confidence that their vote matters than those who lack education. However, despite an increase in the education level of the nation since the 1950s, voter turnout has gone down. This is because interest in politics and other civic attitudes that encourage voting have gone down over this period.

There are some attitudes (called *civic attitudes*) that encourage people to vote and other attitudes that discourage them. People who believe that Americans have a *civic duty* to vote are more likely to vote than people who do not have this belief. Like many general attitudes about government, civic duty is developed during childhood socialization. Other civic attitudes are trust in government and a feeling that voting makes a difference. People who are *apathetic* (uninterested) or *alienated* (distrustful and/or feeling powerless) are unlikely to vote.

Age also influences voter turnout. Young people vote less frequently than other age groups. This is even more evident today than it was in the 1970s, when 18- to 21-year-olds first got the right to vote. Income also has a substantial influence on voting. Poor people have lower turnout levels than the middle class, and the middle class votes at a lower rate than the upper class.

The Impact of the Vote

Most elections fail to send a clear message that the majority of voters prefer the winning candidate's proposals on the issues; a clear message of this type is called a *policy mandate*. This is because few voters tend to know the candidates' positions. This lack of awareness arises from the public's lack of attention to campaigns, the media's focus on strategies rather than issues, and the candidates' failure to take clear positions on controversial issues.

Some voters are informed on issues. People who look to the future, seeking the candidate whose positions are most similar to theirs, are practicing *prospective voting*. More people exercise *retrospective voting* by supporting or opposing the incumbent based the job he or she has done in office. Retrospective voting is more often based on economic assessments than on foreign-policy issues.

Conventional Forms of Participation Other than Voting

Voting is the most widespread form of political participation, but there are myriad other activities that people alone or in groups can do to try to influence public policy and political leaders. Unlike voting and campaigns, which take place at particular times, community activity and lobbying occur year round.

Campaign activities include acts as easy as wearing a button advertising a candidate's name and those as difficult as volunteering to work for a campaign. More people in the United States participate in campaigns than do citizens in other countries, in part because there are so many elections, including federal, state, and local ones. Still, most Americans are inactive during campaigns; less than 5 percent report having worked for a candidate or party.

Community activities, such as participation in groups and clubs, are more common in the United States than campaigning and more common here than in Europe. About 50 percent of Americans say they volunteer time to groups or their communities. Yet civic participation, sometimes referred to in aggregate as the nation's *social capital,* has declined over time.

Lobbying involves the public trying to influence public officials. Although they can do this by writing, calling, or meeting with politicians, people usually join, and often pay dues to, groups that lobby professionally.

Following politics through the media can be considered a passive form of political participation. Awareness of political issues, events, and politicians is a necessary precursor for more active participation such as campaigning and lobbying. Americans vary in the extent to which they follow the news. A third follow closely, a third do not follow the news, and a third are somewhere in between. More people prefer watching news on television to getting it from other media; however, like newspaper reading, this activity has declined. This is particularly true among young adults. Although the Internet has the potential for reversing the trend away from using media for political news, it is too early to know what impact it will have on passive participation (informing people about politics) and active participation (getting them to communicate their desires to politicians, through sites like MoveOn.org).

Unconventional Activism: Social Movements and Protest Politics

Voting is a form of political participation organized and authorized by government. Elections offer limited options that do not reflect some people's choices. Yet elected officials can claim legitimacy because they were popularly selected. Sometimes when people feel that these officials and institutions are not responsive to them, they protest through mass *social movements.* From the Boston Tea Party to the civil rights movement to the farm workers movement to recent antiwar demonstrations, protest has been an option for people without political connections or conventional resources who want political change. Protests are typically planned and organized rather than spontaneous. This has increasingly become the case. Participants in social movements tend to be young and idealistic. Although protest is legal and usually tolerated, it has often been met with strong public and elite opposition.

Participation and the Potential for Influence

Americans say that political participation is important, but few do more than vote. Even voting comes from a sense of civic duty more than from a deep interest in politics or a sense that voting matters. There is a class bias in political participation, with high-income groups being much more active than lower-income groups. The gap between income groups is bigger in the United States than in other Western democracies. It results in politicians being more responsive to members of the upper class.

TAKE NOTE

This is a moderately important chapter for the AP U.S. Government and Politics test. It is essential to understand the variety of ways that people can participate and that most people do little more than vote—and a great many never do that. Understanding and being able to distinguish among institutional, attitudinal, and demographic factors that influence participation levels is important. It is absolutely essential to understand the "upper class" bias of participation (What does it mean? Why does this bias exist? What are its consequences?).

Observations from Past Exams

The material in this chapter falls under the "Political Beliefs and Behaviors" section of the AP curriculum. This section is supposed to make up between 10 percent and 20 percent of the multiple-choice questions. Its focus is on "beliefs held about government, processes by which people learn about politics, the nature, sources and consequences of public opinion, ways citizens vote and participate, factors that influence how beliefs and behaviors differ." Topics from this chapter were the basis of five multiple-choice questions on the last two released exams and three free-response questions on the last six tests.

The 2002 multiple-choice test asked two questions about factors that influence voter turnout, one question on the relationship between education and activism, and another on provisions of election laws. The 1999 multiple-choice test asked a question on the impact of enfranchisement on turnout.

The 2000 exam included a free-response question that asked students to analyze voting patterns shown on a map of the United States. The 2002 exam asked about factors that influence voter turnout and factors that explain the difference in turnout between midterm and presidential elections. A free-response question on the 2003 exam asked about ways to participate other than voting and about the advantages of each technique.

What to Do with the Boxes

Some boxes include information that might help you on the test, even though it is unlikely that they will be asked about specifically. For example, the debate over Internet voting (p. 232) could be a useful proposal to remember if you are asked for strategies to improve voter turnout. Yet it is unlikely to be asked about directly. It is vital to understand that after suffrage laws change, voting habits do not emerge quickly among the newly enfranchised (from the "Political Culture" box on page 236). The "Ballots Cast but Not Counted" box (p. 220) provides information about an important problem that is relevant to popular sovereignty, civil rights, and federalism. The "Why Should I Care?" box (p. 226) contains useful observations about voter turnout and its consequences.

Because of the focus of the AP test, you do not need to know specific data from the "How the United States Compares" box (p. 217). However, it is important to realize that the United States has a low level of turnout compared with other Western democracies and to be able to explain why this is the case. Information in the box's text is useful for doing this. Another box that addresses this issue is found on p. 224.

A useful preparation for the illustration-based questions on the test is to try to write a summary for Table 7-1 and Figure 7-1 (p. 216), the turnout data on the map (p. 219), Figure 7-2 (p. 221), Table 7-2 (p. 223), Figure 7-3 (p. 225), Figure 7-4 (p. 229), Figure 7-5 (p. 230), and Figure 7-6 (p. 234) before you read or review the one provided under the title. Try to come up with arguments for why the information looks the way it does. Be aware that the title of the box on p. 219 refers to both presidential and midterm elections.

Key Terms

Don't just memorize these terms. Understand what they mean and how they compare to other concepts. Be able to give examples of each.

Political participation (pp. 213, 214)
Suffrage (p. 214)
Voter turnout (p. 215)
Registration (p. 216)
Motor voter (p. 218)
Civic attitudes (pp. 221–22)
Civic duty (p. 221)
Apathy (p. 222)
Alienation (p. 222)
Policy mandate (p. 225)
Prospective voting (p. 226)
Retrospective voting (p. 226)
Conventional participation (p. 227)
Social capital (p. 228)
Lobbying (p. 229)
Unconventional activism (pp. 231–35)
Social movements (p. 233)
Class bias (p. 235)

Constitutional amendments reviewed in this chapter are:

Fifteenth (p. 214)
Nineteenth (p. 214)
Twenty-fourth (p. 214)
Twenty-sixth (p. 214)

Making Connections to Previous Chapters

Political participation is central to the ideas of self-government and popular sovereignty discussed in Chapters 1 and 2. The lack of participation noted in this chapter undermines the majoritarian theory of power discussed in Chapter 1.

Revisit the "Citizenship" box (p. 41) in Chapter 2. Consider how the constitutional mechanisms for providing self-government with limits and their reforms over time (pp. 58–66) have affected political participation.

Chapter 3 explained how registration and voting are "state powers" in the U.S. federal system. The consequences of this can be seen in this chapter.

The struggle for equality described in Chapter 5 included the efforts of various groups to obtain equal access to the ballot. More information on the struggles to amend the Constitution to expand suffrage is provided in this chapter. An important lesson in this chapter is that obtaining a legal right and exercising it are not the same thing (see the box on p. 236).

Chapter 6 discussed how ill-informed the public is, and the consequences of that ignorance are seen in this chapter. Childhood political socialization (discussed in Chapter 6) that emphasizes civic duty and political interest has important implications in adulthood for influencing political participation. You can see how some of the same demographics that influence public opinion also influence participation levels. These are education, income, and age.

SAMPLE QUESTIONS

Multiple-Choice Questions

1. What is the best explanation for why voter turnout in the United States is lower than in most other Western democracies?
   a. The United States measures turnout differently.
   b. The United States has a bigger population.
   c. The United States has political parties that are more combative and divisive.
   d. The United States has fewer people who are highly educated.
   e. The United States has voter registration laws that are more burdensome.

2. People who believe that their vote does not count are:
   a. apathetic
   b. alienated
   c. ideological
   d. retrospective voters
   e. spread equally among all income groups

3. The single best predictor of voter turnout is:
   a. ideology
   b. party identification
   c. race
   d. sex
   e. education

4. Which of the following is a source of "social capital"?
   a. watching television coverage of politics
   b. voting in a local election
   c. donating money to the Red Cross
   d. helping the local garden club plant flowers along Main Street
   e. participating in a political chat room on the Internet

5. Which of the following is true of political participation?
   a. Young people are more likely to vote than old people.
   b. Young people are more likely to participate in social movements than old people.
   c. Young people are more likely to follow politics on television than old people.
   d. Young people are more likely to vote, participate in social movements, and follow politics on television than old people.
   e. Young people are less likely to vote, participate in social movements, and follow politics on television than old people.

6. Which of the following do the fewest Americans do?
   a. vote in presidential elections
   b. vote in midterm elections
   c. work for a party or candidate during a campaign
   d. volunteer time to a group or community cause
   e. read about politics in a newspaper

Multiple-Choice Questions That Link Chapter 7 to Lessons in Earlier Chapters

7. Most Americans are inactive in politics. Which American value is this consistent with?
   a. due process
   b. unity
   c. patriotism
   d. freedom
   e. equality

8. Which of the following is true of voting turnout among women?
   a. Soon after the Nineteenth Amendment was passed, they were voting at the same rates as men.
   b. Soon after the Civil Rights Act of 1964 was passed, they were voting at the same rates as men.
   c. Ever since they received the right to vote, they have voted at a lower rate then men.
   d. Like other newly enfranchised groups, it took a long time for the voting habit to develop and become comparable with previously enfranchised groups.
   e. Unlike other newly enfranchised groups, it took a long time for their voting habit to develop and become comparable with previously enfranchised groups.

9. How does childhood socialization affect whether a person will vote as an adult?
   a. by instilling a sense of civic duty
   b. by developing liberal ideologies in some children and conservative in others
   c. by encouraging obedience to authority through discipline
   d. by creating crosscutting cleavages
   e. by teaching students American history

10. After the 2000 election, Congress passed legislation that provided money and set standards intended to reduce the percentage of uncounted ballots. What is this an example of?
    a. the federal government exercising its constitutionally defined national powers
    b. the federal government exercising its constitutionally defined concurrent powers
    c. the federal government exercising unitary federalism
    d. the federal government exercising fiscal federalism
    e. devolution

Multiple-Choice Answers

1. E; 2. B; 3. E. 4. D; 5. B; 6. C; 7. D; 8. D; 9. A; and 10. D

Free-Response Questions

1. The map below shows voter turnout in different states.

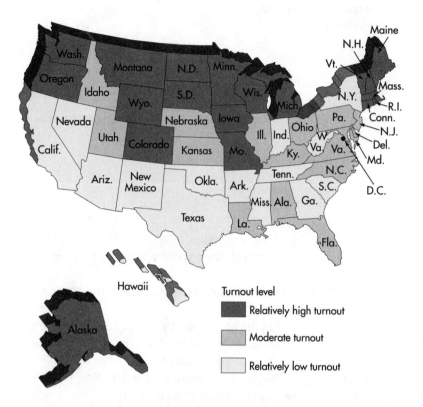

a. Identify a region of the country with low voter turnout. (1 point)

b. Identify a region of the country with high voter turnout. (1 point)

c. Identify a demographic characteristic that contributes to this regional difference. Explain how or why each contributes. (2 points)

d. Identify an attitudinal difference between voters and nonvoters and explain how or why that difference in attitude contributes to differences in turnout. (2 points)

e. Identify a difference between how high-turnout states and low-turnout states might run their elections. Explain how or why this difference contributes to differences in turnout. (2 points)

This question is worth eight points.

Part "a" is worth one point for correctly identifying the Southwest or the South.

Part "b" is worth one point for correctly identifying the Midwest, the Northwest, or the Northeast.

Part "c" is worth two points. One point is earned for identifying one demographic characteristic that contributes to this regional difference. Factors may include: income, occupation, age, or education. The second point is earned for explaining how or why the factor contributes to regional differences.

Part "d" is worth two points. One point is earned for identifying an attitudinal difference that contributes to this regional difference. Factors may include: partisanship, civic duty, alienation, apathy, or interest. The second point is earned for explaining how or why this contributes to regional differences.

Part "e" is worth two points. One point is earned for identifying a structural difference between the states. Differences may include: registration laws (when, where, how, residency requirements), poll hours, registration purge policies, and types of ballots. The second point is earned for explaining how or why it contributes to turnout differences.

NOTE: for c–e, the second point can only be earned if the first point was earned.

2. Patterson writes, "Elections do *not* ordinarily produce a policy mandate for the winning candidate" (p. 225).

   a. Define "policy mandate." (1 point)

   b. Identify a factor having to do with the public and explain how it contributes to the lack of policy mandates. (2 points)

   c. Identify a factor having to do with candidates and their campaigns and explain how it contributes to the lack of policy mandates. (2 points)

   d. Identify another factor that is not about candidates or the public and explain how it contributes to the lack of policy mandates. (2 points)

   This question is worth seven points.

   Part "a" is worth one point for correctly defining "policy mandate."

   Part "b" is worth two points. One point is earned for correctly identifying a factor having to do with the public that helps explain this. Factors may include: lack of interest, lack of knowledge (for example, of issues, parties, or candidates' positions), or lack of policy opinions. The second point is earned for correctly explaining how the factor contributes to the lack of a policy mandate.

   Part "c" is worth two points. One point is earned for correctly identifying a factor that has to do with candidates and their campaigns that helps to explain this. Factors may include: lack of clear positions, changes in positions during the campaign, or no difference between candidates' positions. The second point is earned for explaining how the factor contributes to the lack of policy mandates.

   Part "d" is worth two points. One point is earned for identifying a factor that does not have to do with candidates or the public but contributes to the lack of policy mandates. Factors may include: media coverage, election rules (voting for people rather than policies), or the inability to anticipate the issues that will be relevant in the future. The second point is earned for explaining how the factor contributes to the lack of a policy mandate.

CHAPTER EIGHT

Political Parties, Candidates, and Campaigns: Defining the Voter's Choice

SUMMARY

This chapter examines the role of political parties in American politics. It describes the history of the two-party system, the nature of party organizations, and the candidate-centered campaigns that have replaced party-centered ones.

Party Competition and Majority Rule: The History of U.S. Parties

Political parties provide a vehicle through which like-minded citizens can influence government. People do this by selecting leaders who identify with a particular party and its ideals. Through parties, people who are relatively powerless as individuals become collectively powerful.

Despite skepticism among the elite, who feared that parties would have "baneful effects," parties emerged short after the nation's founding. The earliest parties were the Federalist party, which was led by Alexander Hamilton and advocated strong national government, and the Jeffersonian Republicans. Their disagreements were in keeping with those during the ratification process between the Federalists, who favored a strong national government and propertied interests, and the Anti-Federalists, who preferred equality and a more popular form of government. Although this two-party system has continued, the specific parties competing for power have changed over time. For example, during the 1820s Andrew Jackson's Democratic Party emerged as a more *grassroots* party replacing the Jeffersonian Republican party. The modern Republican party emerged with Abraham Lincoln. Since the Civil War, Republicans and Democrats have been the two major competing parties. They have both adapted, changing what they believe and whom they represent. Major adjustments in the parties come during *party realignments*.

Party realignments are characterized by elections in which new issues emerge that shift voter support from one party's advantage to another's. As a result, major policy change ensues and new party coalitions form. New voters are more likely to identify with the stronger party, allowing it to continue its dominance. Realignments occur infrequently. The three most recent were: the Civil War realignment, resulting in Republican dominance nationally and a Democratic stronghold in the South; the 1896 realignment, in which economic problems further strengthened the Republican party; and the New Deal realignment that resulted from the Great Depression and Franklin D. Roosevelt's expansion of the role of national government. This realignment created a Democratic majority that continued for the rest of the century.

The current Democratic party is not as strong as it was immediately after the realigning election (also referred to as a *critical election*) of 1932. This is natural because as time goes by and new issues emerge, party realignments weaken. For example, in the 1960s the civil rights issue weakened the Democratic party in the South and to some extent weakened the Republican party in the Northeast.

Although voters are split equally between the Republican and Democratic parties today, it is not because there was a Republican realignment. There was no sudden realigning (critical) election or single galvanizing issue or crisis. Instead, party attachments have faded over time. This is called a *dealignment*. While today's prevalence of Independents is evidence of a dealignment, the decrease in *split-ticket voting* (when voters choose some Democrats and some Republicans on the same ballot) and the increase in partisan conflict suggests a move toward party identification. These disparate trends lead party analysts to wonder what is going on and what will happen next.

Electoral and Party Systems

While most countries have multiparty systems, the United States has always had a two-party system. This is mainly because politicians are selected by *pluralities* in *single-member districts:* the candidate who gets the most votes wins. *Plurality* means the largest number of votes when there are more than two choices; a plurality may be less than half the total votes cast. An alternative to this process is *proportional representation*, in which parties get a percentage of the seats in a legislative body based on what percentage of people voted for the party. In other words, these systems do not require that a party comes in "first place" to get its politicians in office.

Because American parties need to by a plurality or majority—in either case, to get the biggest chunk of total votes cast—to get in office, they run moderate campaigns. Rather than appeal to a small ideological minority, they campaign to the center. The election years in which the Republicans or the Democrats failed to do this, they lost (Republican Barry Goldwater in 1964 and Democrat George McGovern in 1972). This means that moderate, rather than ideological, voters are the most powerful in determining the outcome of elections. It also means that American parties are less extreme than those in multiparty systems and less set in their ideas. Instead, they move ideologically in response to changes in public opinion.

Party coalitions (the groups that make up the party) in a two-party system are diverse and overlapping because the parties need to gain pluralities to win. Nevertheless, they differ. They stand for different things and represent certain types of people to a greater or lesser degree. The Democratic Party favors the intervention of the national government to promote the economy and equality. Its coalition includes the less privileged (racial minorities, the poor, women, and city dwellers). White middle-class Protestants form the largest element in the Republican coalition. They promote less government intervention in the economy and support policies that promote traditional values.

Minor Parties

Despite the two-party dominance in American politics, different minor parties offer alternative policies and philosophies. They tend to be short-lived, and all but one, the Republicans, have failed to become a majority party. Yet the minor parties sometimes attract enough supporters to cause the two major parties to change their agendas and be more responsive to the public. There are three types of minor parties: single-issue, factional, and ideological.

As the name says, single-issue parties have narrow concerns. For example, the Prohibition Party pushed for the Eighteenth Amendment, and when it passed, the party disappeared. Factional parties result from unresolved conflicts within a major party. For example, when Governor George Wallace opposed the pro-civil rights direction of the Democratic Party in 1968, he ran for its presidential nomination. When he failed to get the nomination, he ran as the American Independent Party's candidate. Ideological parties promote philosophies that are more extreme than those held by the two major parties. Presidential election years in which ideological parties received a substantial number of votes were: 1892 (the Populist Party), 1992 (the Reform Party), and 2000 (the Green Party).

Party Organizations

Winning elections is the main purpose of political organizations, whether the local, state, or national units. Yet their control over the selection, funding, and policy positions of candidates has decreased over time. The biggest reason that party organizations have weakened is because the way that candidates are selected has changed. These changes have allowed candidates more freedom, and they now run many of the campaign activities that were once controlled by party organizations, including raising and deciding how to spend campaign money. This means that parties now have a *service relationship* with candidates, in which they raise, contribute, and spend money for the candidate's election.

Party organizations were once responsible for choosing candidates. This resulted in candidate loyalty but also allowed for corruption. One of the reforms of the Progressive Movement that gave voters more control of the candidate selection process was the *primary election.* Primaries allow voters to choose the nominee. Most primaries (called *closed primaries*) require that the voters be registered with the political party. Those that do not are called *open primaries*; in open primaries, voters can decide which party's primary they want to vote in on Election Day. Some states have *blanket primaries* in which voters can choose between Republicans and Democrats. In most primaries, the winner is the person who got the most votes. In some there are *runoffs* between the top vote-getters. Many states prohibit primary losers from running as independent candidates.

The decline in patronage is another reason party organizations have lost power. A large number of government jobs that were once given to people who worked for the party of the candidate who won are now earned through a merit system. There are still some jobs that can be filled by appointment, but the people selected for these jobs have the winning candidate, rather than the party, to thank. This means that they will feel more loyalty to the person than to the party.

The Structure and Role of Party Organizations

Party organizations remain as loose associations through which politicians work and voters are organized and brought to the polls. They assist candidates by raising money and by gathering and communicating information. While the national, state, and local party organizations share the same goals and often work together, they cannot compel each other to do or stop doing something.

Most party workers are part of organizations at the local level. Although not nearly as powerful as they were during the days of party machines that compelled voters through rewards and punishments, party organizations in urban areas tend to be more organized and active than others. Urban party organizations come to life during campaigns. Their volunteers and campaign funds can make a difference to a candidate's success.

State party organizations have central committees composed of local party officials who meet irregularly. A chairperson and the state party staff run the daily operations, such as organizing fundraisers and voter-registration drives for statewide races. The Republican National Committee (RNC) and the Democratic National Committee (DNC) are organized similarly with committees, chairs, and staff. They both provide services such as research, campaign management training, funding, and advertising to presidential and congressional candidates and their campaigns. The RNC's role was expanded in the 1970s and the DNC followed its lead in the 1980s. The financial advantage that the Republican organization maintains over the Democratic one has allowed it to be more helpful to its candidates.

Money that candidates receive directly from party organizations, party campaign committees (such as the Democratic Congressional Campaign Committee or the National Republican Senatorial Committee), interest groups, or individuals is called *hard money.* Campaign finance laws passed after the Watergate scandal placed clear limits on the amount of hard money that could be contributed by these groups. This legislation did not limit *soft money*. Soft money is money raised and spent to get a candidate elected but not controlled by the candidate or explicitly advocating that person's election. No limit was placed on the amount of money that individuals could give to parties. The huge amount of soft money spent on "party building"— voter registration drives, advertising for the party, funding for state and local parties—clearly helped party candidates. A 2002 law banned soft money for parties. However, the ban does not apply to "not-for-profit" groups, referred to as *527s*, which can spend unlimited money for *issue advocacy*. Because the line between advocating an issue and attacking a candidate is a thin one, the reform has had limited effectiveness.

The Candidate-Centered Campaign

Candidates today are *self-starters*. Rather than be recruited and have their campaigns controlled by parties, they decide to run on their own and create a personal organization for their campaigns. This means they spend a lot of time trying to raise money. They hire professional campaign managers who, with their teams, determine strategies, raise money using direct mail and other methods, conduct polls and *focus groups* to see what voters want and what they think of the candidates and their messages, produce television advertising and decide when ads should run, organize events to get news coverage, and prepare candidates for debates.

When parties ran the campaigns, the campaigns were *prepackaged*. In other words, the candidates ran on the ideals and issue positions of the party. *Candidate-centered campaigns* entail strategizing over how the candidate should be packaged—that is, how the candidate's experiences, character, values, and issue positions should be presented. This package is presented through television. More than half of a candidate's campaign funds go to producing and buying time for television advertising. The candidates compete in an *air war* in which they run ads for themselves and against the competition. There are many battles in the air war with *rapid response* attacks and counterattacks. Of course, ads are not the only way candidates use television. Televised debates provide free airtime, as does news coverage. Whereas the air war is on television, the *ground war* is on the streets, where campaigns try to get out the vote. This is particularly important in close elections. Candidates are experimenting with new technology such as the Internet to mobilize support.

Candidate-centered campaigns are more open, fluid, and responsive to the public than party-centered ones. It is easier for newcomers to compete and for candidates to adapt to a changing political context and to represent local concerns, especially when those concerns are at odds with national party sentiment. The disadvantages of candidate-centered campaigns are that they emphasize personality, or image, over issues, they empower special-interest groups, and they weaken accountability, as elected officials blame others rather than assume responsibility as part of a party. While individual politicians have closer ties to their constituents, political institutions are less responsible to the electorate under the current system.

TAKE NOTE

This is an important chapter to understand for the AP U.S. Government and Politics test. It is not enough to know that the United States has a two-party system that works to link the public to government by organizing voter choices and guiding policymaking. You need to understand how parties have changed over time, how they work, and what effects they have. It is essential to understand how campaign finance works. Patterson addresses this in four separate sections of the book (Chapter 8, pp. 261–63; Chapter 9, pp. 295–300; Chapter 11, pp. 338–40; and Chapter 12, pp. 385, 388–91). It would be useful to reread these sections together when preparing for the test.

Observations from Past Exams

The material here is part of the "Political Parties, Interest Groups, and Media" section of the AP curriculum, which makes up 10 percent to 20 percent of the multiple-choice questions. Questions on parties are identified as "focusing on the functions, organization, development, effect on the political process, and electoral laws and systems." Recent exams reveal a lot of attention to this material. Nine of the multiple-choice questions on the last two released exams reference lessons from this chapter. Since 1999, five free-response questions related to parties or campaigns have appeared.

The 2002 released multiple-choice test asked about the organization of political parties, the education level of convention delegates, the consequences of single-member districts, and the meaning of "critical elections." It also asked questions about a table on party identification. The 1999 multiple-choice test asked questions about types of primaries, when critical elections have occurred, the nature of U.S. parties, and their purposes.

A free-response question on the 1999 exam asked about the role of the mass media in candidate-centered elections. In response to a question on the 2001 exam, students could choose to write about how weak party discipline affected the public policy process. A 2004 question showed a cartoon about a third-party candidate and asked about third parties' contributions and the obstacles to their success. Students were given credit on the 2004 exam for writing about the high cost of campaigns as something that contributed to a decline in trust in government. A free-response question on the 2005 exam asked specifically about campaign finance reforms. Students needed to know terminology such as *soft money* and to explain arguments for and against reform.

What to Do with the Boxes

The visual representation of political party organizations (p. 258) is helpful for understanding the relationship between voters and parties and for seeing the saliency of state parties. The "Debating the Issues" box (p. 263) helps explain the debate over campaign finance laws and clarifies some terminology; both were essential for doing well on a free-response question on the 2005 exam. "Why Should I Care?" box (p. 253) is worth your attention because its lesson is counterintuitive.

A useful preparation for the stimuli-based questions on the test is to try to write a summary for Figure 8-2 (p. 247), Figure 8-3 (p. 248), Figure 8-4 (p. 252), and Figure 8-6 (p. 261) before you read or review the one provided under the title. Try to come up with arguments for why the information looks the way it does. These figures also use terms that you need to be familiar with. These are: party identification, split-ticket voting, and demographic groups. It is important to know the differences between presidential elections and congressional elections (sometimes referred to as *off-year elections*) and the difference between soft money and hard money.

"How the United States Compares" box (p. 249) includes some information that you do not need to remember (the number of competitive parties in other countries) and some that you do (the difference between the U.S. single-member, plurality district system and other electoral systems). Although the state variations revealed in the "States in the Nation" box (p. 264) are not part of the AP curriculum, the lesson that some states do not offer public campaign funding for state-level races is worth remembering. Although the discussion of political strategy found in the "Citizenship" box (p. 269) might seem obvious, the box provides a nice review of material from Chapter 2. The "Liberty, Equality & Self-Government" box (p. 272) reiterates the "class bias" lesson from Chapter 7.

Because of the focus of the AP test, you do not need to concentrate on the biographical sketch of Andrew Jackson (p. 244) or Abraham Lincoln (p. 245), the graphic history of American parties (p. 243), or the television campaign processes in other democracies (p. 268).

Key Terms

Don't just memorize these terms. Understand what they mean and how they compare to other concepts. Be able to give examples of each.

Political party (p. 241, 242)
Party-centered politics (p. 241, 242)
Candidate-centered politics (p. 241, 242)
Party competition (p. 242)
Grassroots parties (p. 244)
Party realignment (p. 245) Note that this occurs during a "critical election"
Party alignment (p. 246)
GOP (p. 246)
Dealignment (p. 247)
Split ticket (p. 247)
Two-party system (p. 248)
Multiparty system (p. 248)
Single-member districts (p. 248)
Plurality system (p. 248, 249)
Proportional representation (p. 249)
Party coalition (p. 251)
Minor parties (pp. 253–56)
Single-issue parties (p. 254)
Factional parties (p. 254)
Ideological parties (p. 255)
Party organizations (p. 256)
Nomination (p. 256)
Primary election/direct primary (p. 256)
Closed primary (p. 256)
Open primary (p. 256)
Blanket primary (p. 256)
Runoff primary (p. 257)
Patronage (p. 257)
Merit system (p. 257)
Party machine (p. 259)
National party organizations (p. 260)
Service relationship (p. 261)
Hard money (p. 262)
Soft money (p. 262)
527 groups (p. 262)

Issue advocacy (p. 263)
Money chase (p. 265)
Hired guns (p. 265)
Direct-mail operations (p. 266)
Focus groups (p. 266)
Packaging (p. 267)
Air wars (p. 267)
Rapid response (p. 267)
Ground wars (p. 268)
Strategy (p. 269)

Making Connections to Previous Chapters

You can apply Chapter 1's theories of power to political parties and campaigns. Ideally, parties would support the majoritarian model, but low turnout and candidate-centered campaigns undermine this. Think about the impact that the money chase, party realignments, single-member plurality districts, and the weakening of party organizations each have on what model of power is at work in modern elections. You can also apply the core American values to political parties. What value does each of the parties prioritize? Do candidate-centered campaigns enhance or diminish self-government?

Think of the first party system as an extension of the debate between Federalists and Anti-Federalists discussed in Chapters 2 and 3. It might be a good idea to review Chapter 2's discussion of how the Constitution was altered to provide more power to the public (pp. 61–66) after reading this chapter. Now that you know more about primary elections, do you think that this reform ultimately helped or hurt the public? What would the progressives say about the current state of campaigning?

Recall that voting is a state power (p. 74). What impact does this seem to have on campaigns? How are the loose associations between national, state, and local party organizations reflective of federalism (Chapter 3)? How are they different?

Freedom of expression is a civil liberty (Chapter 4) and core American value (Chapter 1). It is important to understand the central role it plays in the debate over campaign finance reform.

The nature of public opinion (Chapter 6) should help you understand why third parties are weak. Without an ideological, issue-driven electorate, it is hard for minor parties to thrive. Since party identifications are acquired during childhood and rarely changed, it is difficult for new parties to thrive. Given the moderate attitudes of the public, it makes sense that candidates "seek the center" (p. 250) and run "candidate-centered" campaigns. Take some time to review the sections in Chapter 6 on "Group Thinking" and "Partisan Thinking" (pp. 200–205) after you read Chapter 8's section on "Politics and Coalitions in the Two-Party System" (pp. 250–53) as they reinforce each other well.

Relate Chapter 7's discussion of class bias in participation to the information in the "Liberty, Equality & Self-Government" box. Compare the figure on page 216 with the one on page 247. You can see an increase in nonpartisanship in the figure on page 247. This dealignment—when larger numbers of people called themselves Independents rather than partisans) coincides with a drop in voter turnout (illustrated on p. 216). This is because partisanship is related to political interest and is considered by some political scientists to be another civic attitude. Recall from Chapter 7 that civic attitudes influence voter turnout. People who lack a sense of civic duty and feel apathy and alienation are less likely to vote than those who feel engaged. People who identify with one of the two major parties are also more likely to vote than those who do not.

SAMPLE QUESTIONS

Multiple-Choice Questions

1. All political parties in the United States:
   a. attempt to bring like-minded people together to support their candidates
   b. represent diverse coalitions of people
   c. take moderate positions in order to win elections
   d. were originally part of another party
   e. are "candidate-centered"

2. Split-ticket voting:
   a. is most common immediately after a realignment
   b. is more common today than it was in the 1970s
   c. may result in divided government but doesn't have to
   d. is more common among partisans than independents
   e. is more common in closed primaries than in open primaries

3. The figure below shows that there has been:

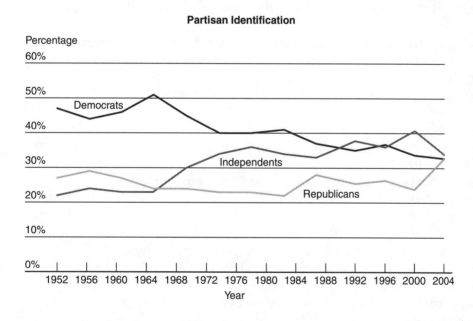

Partisan Identification

   I.   an increase in Republican identification during the 2000s, largely at the expense of Independents
   II. an increase in Independents from the mid-1960s to the early 1980s at the expense of Democrats
   III. a realignment

   a. I
   b. II
   c. I and II
   d. I and III
   e. I, II, and III

4. The figure below demonstrates that:

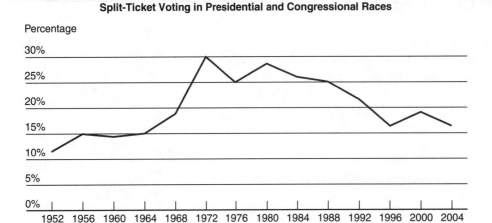

Split-Ticket Voting in Presidential and Congressional Races

a.   the percentage of people who voted for president but did not vote in congressional races
     was greatest in 1972
b.   15 percent of the voters in 1964 voted for a Democratic president and a Republican
     congressperson
c.   split-ticket voting is greater in presidential election years than midterm years
d.   voters are more likely to vote for a president and congressperson from the same party in
     1996 than they were to do so in 1972
e.   in 1980 more people voted a split ticket than did not vote that way

5. Single-member districts
    a.   prohibit Democrats from voting in Republican primaries
    b.   allocate votes proportionately
    c.   make it harder for third parties to gain representation in government
    d.   were found unconstitutional in *Baker v. Carr*
    e.   promote candidates from racial minorities

6. Which of the following is true about the United States' two-party system?
    a.   Candidates with extreme ideologies have a good chance of winning.
    b.   Party coalitions are diverse and overlapping.
    c.   People without party identifications have little influence.
    d.   Third parties are not permitted to have their names on ballots.
    e.   Realignments are necessary for there to be major policy changes.

7. Which of the following characteristics describe the Democratic and Republican party
   organizations?
    a.   They play the dominant role in selecting who will be the presidential candidates.
    b.   They are equally good at offering a range of services such as campaign management
         training to their followers.
    c.   They have more of a service relationship than a power relationship with their candidates.
    d.   Their national committees (the Democratic National Committee and the Republican
         National Committee) direct day-to-day party operations.
    e.   The state party organizations take orders from the national party organization.

8. What does the term "soft money" refer to?
   a. campaign funds given to candidates by private individuals
   b. campaign funds given to candidates by political parties
   c. a term introduced by the campaign finance reform passed in 2002 to replace "hard money"
   d. campaign funds given to candidates by not-for-profit political groups known as "527"s
   e. campaign funds given to political parties prior to the 2002 campaign finance reform law

Multiple-Choice Questions That Link Chapter 8 to Lessons in Earlier Chapters

9. People who oppose limiting campaign finance contributions and spending are placing a priority in which core American value?
   a. due process
   b. unity
   c. freedom
   d. equality
   e. patriotism

10. Which of these political parties is most likely to advocate a limited government in both economic area and personal-value choices?
    a. Populist Party
    b. Communist Party
    c. Green Party
    d. Libertarian Party
    e. Republican Party

Multiple-Choice Answers

1. A; 2. C; 3. C; 4. D; 5. C; 6. B; 7. C; 8. E; 9. C; and 10. D

Free-Response Questions

1. Patterson writes, "Although the influence of party organizations has declined, parties are not about to die out."

   a. Identify a factor having to do with party organizations that has contributed to the parties' decline. Explain how or why it has contributed to a decline in parties. (2 points)

   b. Identify a factor having to do with the public that has contributed to the parties' decline. Explain how or why it has contributed to a decline in parties. (2 points)

   c. Explain why parties are "not about to die." Be sure to describe something about political parties today rather than talk about their past longevity. (1 point)

   This question is worth five points.

   Part "a" is worth two points. One point is earned for correctly identifying a factor about party organizations that has contributed to their decline. Possible answers include: no longer in control of candidate recruitment, increased use of primary elections, use of open primaries and blanket primaries, loss of patronage with merit system, competing sources for campaign funding, competing sources for campaign management expertise, competing sources for information dissemination (particularly the rise of mass media). No points are given for something about parties that has not changed over time, such as "loose associations" or two-party system. A second point is earned for explaining how or why it contributes to decline.

Part "b" is worth two points. One point is earned for correctly identifying something about the public that contributes to party decline. Possible answers include: dealignment, a long time from the last realignment, rise in independent voters, decline in strength of association with parties, image-based voting, single-issue voting. No points are given for something about voters that might be true but is not relevant to party decline, such as lack of trust in government or a lack of voter turnout. A second point is earned for explaining how or why it contributes to decline.

Part "c" is worth one point for adequately explaining why parties are not about to die. Possible answers include: the need for service organizations, the need for ongoing organizations to link politicians to activists, the abilities of parties to adapt (the Republican and Democratic national committee changes noted on p. 261). No points are given for saying that parties have been around a long time so they should continue, for describing parties, or for talking about factors that contribute to a two-party system.

2. Campaigns may be either "candidate-centered" or "party-centered."

   a. Which of these two terms best describes contemporary campaigns in the United States? Describe how it is different from the other type of campaign. (2 points)

   b. Identify a weakness of having this type of campaign. Explain why it is a weakness. (2 points)

   c. Choose one of the following: election procedures or laws, political culture, or mass media. Describe a current feature of the selected idea that encourages either a "candidate-centered" or a "party-centered" campaign. Explain how it encourages one or the other. (2 points)

   This question is worth six points.

   Part "a" is worth two points. One point is earned for correctly identifying candidate-centered. One point is earned for describing how they are different.

   Part "b" is worth two points. One point is earned for identifying a weakness in candidate-centered campaigns. Possible answers include: high cost, image/personality focus rather than issue or ideology, increased power for powerful special interest groups, weakened accountability, further weakens party. No points for answers that describe a weakness of party-centered campaigns. One point is earned for explaining why it is a weakness. To get the second point, it has to be clear why this is a problem.

   Part "c" is worth two points. One point is earned for describing a feature that encourages one type of campaign. Possible answers: candidate-centered campaigns are encouraged by primaries, individualism, and strategy orientation of the mass media. One point is earned for correctly explaining how the feature encourages one type of campaign.

CHAPTER NINE

Interest Groups: Organizing for Influence

SUMMARY

A common belief is that special interests play too large a role in politics. This chapter provides more information about interest groups to better evaluate that assertion. Interest groups are organizations that push for their members' concerns. They differ from parties in that they represent narrower interests and smaller groups of people and are focused on influencing policy as well as the outcome of elections. The various types of interest groups, the goals they pursue, and the methods they use to achieve these goals are the major topics of this chapter. The most important lesson is that the interest-group system has an upper-class bias.

The Interest-Group System

America is a country of "joiners," but not everyone has the money, time, and knowledge to join together. As a result, some people's interests are better represented in government. Three types of groups are discussed in this section: economic, citizen, and governments.

Economic interest groups are the best organized, and their lobbyists outnumber those of other groups. They have more financial resources, from corporate coffers or membership dues. People have a *material incentive* to join these groups because their success leads to additional *private goods.* There are four types of economic groups: businesses, such as the U.S. Chamber of Commerce; labor, such as the AFL-CIO; agriculture, such as the American Farm Bureau Federation or groups for specific commodities; and professional, such as the American Medical Association. Groups vary in size. Although there can sometimes be "power in numbers" that encourages groups to grow and work with other groups, smaller groups are sometimes more effective because they are more cohesive. Overall, labor-group membership has dropped. This is especially true among skilled and unskilled laborers such as auto workers. The largest labor groups now are those representing service and public employees, such as teachers.

Citizen groups fight for causes rather than for economic gain or security. *Purposive incentives,* such as the desire to help the environment, attract their members. They have fewer resources than economic groups. One reason for this is that they fight for *collective goods* that can be enjoyed by people outside of the group. In other words, if an environmental group succeeds, its members will not be the only people enjoying cleaner air. Because of this, such groups have a *free-rider problem.* Free riders are people who enjoy the benefits of a group's success without contributing to the group's efforts. Citizens' groups try to overcome this problem by offering individual benefits to group members and by better identifying people with the resources and interest in the group's goals. Direct mail and the Internet have helped them do this. There are three types of *public-interest groups:* public-interest groups that fight for society such as Common Cause, which tries to clean up politics; single-issue groups such as the National Rifle Association; and *ideological groups* such as the Christian Coalition of America, which advocates traditional values).

Another category of interest groups is foreign and subnational, or state and local, governments. Although foreign governments cannot contribute to U.S. election campaigns, they can lobby for policies that help them. American cities and states, on their own or in groups, also have lobbyists.

Inside Lobbying: Seeking Influence through Official Contacts

To lobby means to contact politicians to influence policy. Because government today is active in so many issues, interest groups have lots of opportunities to lobby. They do this directly through inside lobbying and indirectly by mobilizing the public to contact government officials. Inside lobbying seeks access to politicians because access can lead to influence. Lobbyists sometimes provide tangible benefits to politicians, such as trips or dinners, but usually they have something more useful to offer. This is information. Lobbying is usually targeted at officials who are supportive or at least open to the goals of the group. *Inside lobbying* is expensive and targets all three branches of government.

Inside lobbying of Congress helps both the interest group and legislators. Lobbyists provide Congress with honest and useful information and help them write bills. Bureaucrats in the executive branch, especially those in regulatory agencies, are increasingly lobbied because they make important decisions about policy development and implementation. Regulatory agencies use information from the industries they regulate. When an agency's regulation helps the industry they are supposed to control more than it helps the public interest, it is called *agency capture*. Interest groups increasingly try to influence the courts by advocating or opposing nominations and by filing lawsuits. Sometimes interest groups are on opposite sides of legal court cases.

Groups play an important part in policy processes through their inclusion in *iron triangles* and *issue networks.* The term iron triangle describes the long-standing cooperative relationship among interest groups, government agencies in the executive branch, and congressional committees and subcommittees in particular issue areas. These groups share a self-interest and help each other promote and protect particular policies. For example, agricultural groups contribute to the campaigns of legislators on the Agriculture Committee who pass legislation that helps farmers and provides funding for the Department of Agriculture. This department assists farmers and helps members of the Agriculture Committee with services to their constituents.

Policymaking is not always the result of such cooperative relationships. Sometimes interest groups, legislators, and administrators disagree with each other and among themselves over the best policy to pursue in an issue area. They might agree on some policies but not on others. Issue networks describe a more fluid relationship among politicians, experts, and interest groups who come together temporarily to resolve issues. A specific issue group might be instrumental in one issue network and left out of the next one because once an issue is resolved the issue network disappears. Actors in issue networks have self-interests that do not necessarily coincide permanently. Scholars believe that issue networks are now more common than iron triangles.

Outside Lobbying: Seeking Influence through Public Pressure

Lobbying is most effective when policy makers believe that the interests of a group reflect concerns of a popular constituency. One way to do this is to combine inside lobbying with *grassroots lobbying* that conveys this impression. Getting people to call or write to politicians and having the mass media convey public concern over an issue are tactics of grassroots lobbying. Success of grassroots lobbying can be seen when the American Association of Retired Persons encourages its large membership to pressure Congress.

In addition to grassroots efforts, *outside lobbying* entails electoral action. Interest groups can influence the voting decisions of their members and mobilize them to participate. They can also contribute money to campaigns through *Political Action Groups (PACs)*. PACs can legally raise money from organizations or individuals and give a $10,000 contribution to as many federal candidates as they want. State laws regulate the limits on contributions to candidates for state and local positions. PACs often decide to give some money to both competitors and both parties to hedge their bets, although much more money is contributed to incumbents than to challengers. More than 40 percent of PACs are corporate. While these business PACs give more money to Republicans than to Democrats, Democratic incumbents still receive support. Citizens' groups are the second-largest groups of PACs. The growing influence of special interests through the proliferation of PACs has many critics.

The Group System: Indispensable but Biased

The pluralist theory of power can be evaluated by looking at how well the interest-group system facilitates self-government and equality. While interest groups do help express public concerns to government, not all interests are equally represented.

Some advocates of pluralism argue that through the multitude of special interests promoted through interest groups, the collective interest of the mass public is represented. Critics disagree, arguing that interest groups represent better-organized and better-financed minority interests that are often counter to what is preferred by or good for the public at large. Despite the growing number of public interest groups since the 1960s, two-thirds of the groups that lobby are business groups. Interest-group politics is another place where people high in socioeconomic status are more active than those with fewer resources. This amplifies the political power of the higher-status groups.

The tendency of government officials to support positions of self-interested groups rather than the public interest is called *interest-group liberalism*. Critics claim that this is wasteful as well as unfair. Advocates of interest groups argue that they serve the important function of forcing politicians and parties to address issues that might seem too controversial to tackle.

Liberty invites individuals and groups to advocate for their self-interest. James Madison wrote about this in *Federalist* No. 10. He believed a system of checks and balances would help prevent some of the problems that could stem from self-interest because it would keep majority factions from gaining too much power. Yet decentralization provides multiple points of access for minority factions to influence public policy, making it easier for these factions to get and hold on to benefits. Patterson calls this the Madisonian Dilemma.

TAKE NOTE

This is a very important chapter for the AP U.S. Government and Politics test. Not only will you be asked questions about what interest groups are and what they do, but you also need to understand how they affect the policy process. You need to know why both parties and interest groups are considered "linkage institutions" and what are the advantages and disadvantages of each for fulfilling that function. It is particularly important for free-response questions to be familiar with the agendas, techniques, and impact of some specific interest groups.

Missing from this chapter is the term *amicus curiae* (meaning "friend of the court") briefs. Filing *amicus curiae* briefs is another technique interest groups use to lobby the court. It is described in Chapter 14 (p. 465). It is also important to understand that litigation strategy can involve *class-action suits*. These are cases brought to the court that include many people who claim to have been harmed. For example, rather than sue the tobacco companies for selling a product that hurt a particular plaintiff (who might die before the case comes to trial thereby making it a moot case), a class-action suit claims that a class of people such as smokers was harmed. It is also important to realize that the unconventional forms of participation discussed in Chapter 7 are forms of outside lobbying.

Observations from Past Exams

The material in this chapter falls under the "Political Parties, Interest Groups, and Media" section that is supposed to make up 10 percent to 20 percent of the multiple-choice questions. Questions on interest groups are identified as focusing on the range of interests represented, activities of groups, effects on the political process, and the role of PACs.

There were four multiple-choice questions about interest groups on the released 1999 exam. They asked about the function of PACs, whom lobbyists interact with, the purpose of interest groups, and participants in iron triangles. Lobbying and PACs also appeared as answers to questions about campaigns and Congress. The 2002 exam had two multiple-choice questions about interest groups. One asked about the dominant techniques used by lobbyists and the other asked which types of PACs had increased since the 1970s.

Tests for four years out of the last seven have included free-response questions about interest groups. In 2002, one question asked why government benefits go toward the elderly. A discussion of interest groups was an acceptable answer. The 1999 free-response question asked students to select an interest group from a list (American Association of Retired People, American Medical Association, National Association for the Advancement of Colored People, or National Association of Manufacturers) and discuss how its resources or characteristics influenced what policymaking institution it would target. The 2000 free-response question asked students to describe two methods interest groups use to influence the Supreme Court appointment process. The 2001 question asked students to explain how the growth in the number of interest groups and PACs made it harder for federal government to enact public policy. In 2004, a question required students to select one interest group from a list (American Medical Association, Sierra Club, National Rifle Association, or National Association for the Advancement of Colored People) and identify which technique (litigation, campaign contributions, or grass root lobbying) it was most likely to use and explain why. The question also required that the three techniques be defined.

What to Do with the Boxes

Table 9-2 (p. 286) and Table 9-3 (p. 295) are helpful summaries of important information about interest groups. Figure 9-1 (p. 293) is extremely useful for understanding how iron triangles work.

A useful preparation for the illustration-based questions on the test is to try to write a summary for Figures 9-2 and 9-3 on page 298 before you read or review the one provided under the title. Try to come up with arguments for why the information looks the way it does.

The "Citizenship" box (p. 288) reinforces the lessons about social capital already discussed in Chapter 7 (p. 228). The "Why Should I Care?" box (p. 290) describes an important concept— the *revolving door*. The "Debating the Issue" box (p. 296) debates the influence of interest groups on the *initiative process*—another term to know. The "Liberty, Equality & Self-Government" box (p. 302) provides an excellent example of the tension between liberty and equality that was first introduced in Chapter 1.

Because of the focus of the AP test, you do not need to concentrate on international comparisons ("How the United States Compares" box, p. 280). You also do not need to know the state differences limiting PAC contributions or the reasons for these differences ("States in the Nation" box, p. 299); however, you need to remember that federal candidates face the same PAC contributions limits. This means that someone running for the U.S. Senate in Texas is limited to the same donation from a particular PAC as one running in Florida, even though a candidate for the governorship of Texas can receive unlimited contributions and someone running for governor in Florida is limited to $2,000 contribution from any specific PAC. The specificity in Table 9-1 (p. 283) is unlikely to be required on the AP test.

Key Terms

Don't just memorize these terms. Understand what they mean and how they compare to other concepts. Be able to give examples of each.

Single-issue politics (pp. 277, 278) and single-issue groups (p. 286)
Interest group (p. 278)
Economic groups (p. 280)
Private (individual) goods (p. 281)
Material incentive (p. 281)
Citizens' (noneconomic) groups (p. 283)
Purposive incentives (p. 283)
Collective (public) goods (p. 283)
Free-rider problem (p. 284)
Public-interest groups (p. 285)
Ideological groups (p. 286)
Lobbying (p. 289)
Inside lobbying (p. 289)
Revolving door (p. 290)
Agency capture (p. 291)
Iron triangles (p. 292); these are sometimes called "cozy triangles"
Issue network (p. 292)
Outside lobbying (p. 294)
Grassroots lobbying (p. 294)
Political Action Committees or PACs (p. 296)
Initiatives (p. 296)
Interest-group liberalism (p. 301)
Federalist No. 10 (p. 302)
Madisonian dilemma (p. 303)

Making Connections to Previous Chapters

You can apply Chapter 1's theories of power to interest groups and gain a better understanding of the pluralism model. Think about how the power of interest groups puts the core American values of liberty and equality in conflict. Be prepared to argue both sides of the question, "Do interest groups promote self-government?"

It would be a good idea to review the section on "Using Power to Offset Power" and "Separate Institutions Sharing Power" in Chapter 2 so that you can better understand the

Madisonian dilemma (p. 303). A review of Chapter 3 can help you think about what kind of issues subnational governments lobby for. The limitations on PAC contributions for federal and state offices and the diversity of state limits (discussed under "boxes") are nice illustrations of how federalism works (Chapter 3).

The freedom of expression is a civil liberty (Chapter 4) and core American value (Chapter 1). It is important to understand the central role it plays in the debate over limitations on PAC contributions. It is essential to understand how campaign finance works. Patterson addresses this in four separate sections of the book: Chapter 8, pp. 261–63; Chapter 9, pp. 295–300; Chapter 11, pp. 338–40; and Chapter 12, pp. 385, 388–91. It would be useful to reread these sections together when preparing for the test.

Chapter 5's discussion of how various groups fought for equality (pp. 144–61) is a vivid illustration of how social movements (discussed in Chapter 7) and interest group lobbying can be effective. These examples are exceptions to the upper-class bias of interest-group advocacy. The upper-class bias of interest groups is consistent with lessons from Chapter 7 regarding political participation, including voter turnout.

It is important to avoid confusing the term interest-group liberalism with liberalism. A review of the section on ideological thinking in Chapter 6 (pp. 197–200) will help you distinguish between the two.

Political parties (Chapter 8) and interest groups are both linkage institutions connecting the public to government. Whereas parties are getting weaker, interest groups are growing in strength. It is important to understand how they are similar and how they are different. One difference is that parties run candidates whereas interest groups do not. Another is that parties represent a greater range of issues and people than interest groups do. An exception to both of these statements is single-issue minor parties (p. 254). You can think of these as either issue groups running candidates, as parties do, or parties representing more narrow interests, as interest groups do. Campaign finance laws treat political parties and PACs the same in terms of restricting the contributions they can make directly to federal candidates. Even though 527s are discussed in the chapter on parties (specifically pages 262–63) remember that they are interest groups with a growing influence on electoral politics.

SAMPLE QUESTIONS

Multiple-Choice Questions

1. The greatest number of lobbyists in Washington represents which type of interest group?
   a. those advocating economic groups such as corporations and professional associations
   b. those advocating public interests, such as Common Cause
   c. those advocating the interests of unskilled laborers
   d. those advocating single issues, such as the National Rifle Association
   e. those advocating the interests of foreign governments

2. What is meant by the "free-rider problem"?
   a. Legislators can add an amendment to a bill, thereby hurting its chances of passing.
   b. Legislators can add an amendment to a bill, thereby getting special benefits for their districts.
   c. Interest groups get financial benefits at the expense of taxpayers.
   d. Benefits won by an interest group are also available to people outside of the group.
   e. Benefits won by an interest group are at the expense of people outside of the group.

3. Which of the following is the most valuable resource of lobbyists?
   a. campaign funds
   b. information about technical issues
   c. information about opponents' weaknesses
   d. advertising skills
   e. persuasive skills

4. Which of the following is true of iron triangles?
   a. They were done away with when Republicans became the Congressional majority.
   b. They exist in all policy areas.
   c. Their members are cooperative because of mutual self-interest.
   d. Their members are combative because of competition among them.
   e. They are strong proponents of presidential power.

5. In what way do issue networks differ from iron triangles?
   a. Iron triangles no longer exist because issue networks replaced them.
   b. Issue networks work on the state level and iron triangles work on the national level.
   c. Iron triangles are stable and long-lasting while issue networks are temporary.
   d. Iron triangles are temporary, and issue networks are stable and long-lasting.
   e. Iron triangles include bureaucrats and legislators, and issue networks do not.

6. Which of the following is true of interest groups' financial contributions to campaigns?
   a. Most interest groups give money to Democrats or Republicans but not to both.
   b. Most of the money is directed to presidential candidates.
   c. Most of the money comes from corporate accounts and union dues rather than individual donations.
   d. Most of the money is given to incumbents.
   e. Most of the money is given to Republicans.

7. Which interest group is most likely to participate in grassroots lobbying?
   a. American Bar Association
   b. U.S. Chamber of Commerce
   c. American Farm Bureau Federation
   d. U.S. Conference of Mayors
   e. American Association of Retired Persons

8. Political action committees are most closely associated with:
   a. interest groups
   b. campaign organizations
   c. political parties
   d. foreign-policy issues
   e. social movements

Multiple-Choice Questions That Link Chapter 8 to Lessons in Earlier Chapters

9. What did James Madison think about interest groups?
   a. They needed to be eliminated.
   b. They were dangerous because they never represented majorities.
   c. Nothing; they were not around in the 1700s.
   d. Their power could be limited by separation of power.
   e. They needed to be nurtured through democratic institutions.

10. Which of the following theories of how power in America is held and exercised gives the most weight to the power of interest groups?
    a. majoritarianism
    b. pluralism
    c. elitism
    d. bureaucratic rule
    e. autocracy

Multiple-Choice Answers

1. A; 2. D; 3. B; 4. C; 5. C; 6. D; 7. E; 8. A; 9. D; and 10. B

Free-Response Questions

1. Examine the figure below.

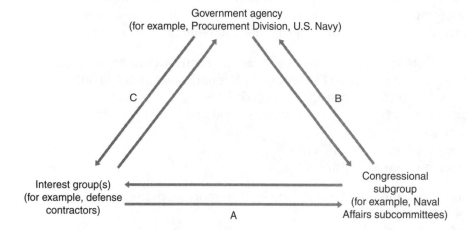

a. Identify the concept illustrated in the figure and describe the type of relationship the three political actors have with each other. (1 point)

b. Describe two ways that interest groups influence congressional subcommittees (Arrow A). (2 points)

c. Describe one way that congressional subcommittees influence government agencies (Arrow B). (1 point)

d. Provide an example of how this phenomenon works. Be sure to describe an outcome from this process. (2 points)

This question is worth six points.

Part "a" is worth one point. Answers must correctly name the triangle and briefly describe it. Acceptable answers are iron triangle or cozy triangle. Descriptions need to include a sense that the relationships among the parties are cooperative.

Part "b" is worth two points. Each way that interest groups influence subcommittees is worth one point. Acceptable answers include: donate money to members' campaigns through PACs, indirectly advocate candidates through issue advocacy ads, provide information about issues, provide information about constituency attitudes, write legislation, identify bills that need attention, provide questions to ask at hearings, and provide information to assist in oversight.

Part "c" is worth one point. Acceptable answers include: limited oversight, failing to audit the agency's programs, expanding the agency's budget, maintaining the agency's budget in the face of congressional or presidential threats to cut it, passing bills that expand programs or develop new programs.

Part "d" is worth two points. An example that includes correct information is worth one point. An example that is thorough (including all three players and the outcome) earns the second point.

2. E. E. Schattschneider wrote, "The flaw in the pluralist heaven is that the heavenly chorus sings with a strong upper-class bias."

   a. Explain what he meant by "the pluralist heaven" and explain what he meant by "sings with a strong upper-class bias." (2 points)

   b. Describe a feature of the political system that encourages this bias and explain how it encourages it. (2 points)

   c. Identify and describe a technique used by interest groups. Explain how it benefits particular types of interest group over others. (2 points)

   This question is worth six points.

   Part "a" is worth two points. One point is earned for correctly explaining what is meant by "pluralist heaven" (interest groups). One point is earned for correctly explaining what is meant by "sings with a strong upper-class bias" (groups that represent upper-class or business interests are more powerful and /or plentiful).

   Part "b" is worth two points. One point is earned for correctly describing a feature that encourages this bias. Answers may include: expensive campaigns; lack of limits on 527s; lack of limits on the number of candidates to which PACs can contribute; expense of hired guns for advertising; expense of professional lobbyists; expense of lobbying—that is, of providing benefits to politicians and the cost of acquiring information through research and polling, litigating, direct-mail campaigns, and advertising; expense of an interest groups' staff, headquarters, and communications; resources of upper class make it easier to pay dues, attend functions, contribute money; easier to attract members because there are economic benefits, more access for people of similar class as politicians (includes the revolving door). The second point is earned for correctly explaining how the feature encourages upper-class bias.

   Part "c" is worth two points. One point is earned for correctly identifying and describing a technique used by interest groups. Answers may include: inside lobbying (contacting politicians, providing information to politicians, providing assistance to politicians), outside lobbying (encouraging members to contact officials, getting media coverage, contributing to campaigns, running issue advocacy ads, encouraging members to vote for certain candidates, filing friend of the court briefs, litigation, protest). The second point is earned for explaining how the technique benefits particular types of interest groups over others.

CHAPTER TEN

The News Media:
Communicating Political Images

SUMMARY

Television and radio networks, newspapers, magazines, and, in recent years, websites—collectively known as the media—choose news that will gain and hold large audiences because their primary objective is making a profit. Therefore, the media emphasize new, exciting events rather than information that would better serve Americans in their political roles. This chapter looks at how the *news media* (also called the *press*) changed from an explicitly political entity to one in which their political role is less intentional but nevertheless important. The functions the press serves and its limitations are the focus of the chapter.

The Development of the News Media: From Partisanship to Objective Journalism

Freedom of the press is essential to a democracy because people need information for the choices they make to self-govern. Although freedom of the press belongs to everyone, most people cannot afford to run a newspaper or own a television or radio station. The Internet is a place where ordinary people, and politicians, can exercise this right.

The approach the press has taken to news reporting has changed over time. In the nation's early years, there was a *partisan press*. Newspapers took sides on political issues in keeping with the party that funded them. Later, newspapers had technology that helped them make more papers quickly and cheaply. These were the days when papers were a penny, their circulation increased dramatically, and financial backing for the industry shifted to advertising. Circulation was further enhanced by *yellow journalism,* which sensationalized events. The excesses of this period were corrected in a new phase of *objective journalism* in which opinion is separated from facts and reports cover both parties' sides in debates. Although objective journalism is the dominant approach today, the media is increasingly doing *interpretive reporting.* This approach tries to explain why things happen, rather than just explaining what happened (the *descriptive reporting* common to objective journalism). Interpretive reporting is more common in television news stories than in newspaper reports.

Radio was the first national mass medium, followed by television. Through the Federal Communications Commission, government regulates both. The justification for regulation—to prevent transmission interference and because airwaves were a scarce resource and public good—was established in the 1934 Communications Act. One regulation is the *equal-time restriction* requiring broadcasters who sell or give time to one candidate to offer the same to other candidates running in the same race. The reason that third-party candidates are often excluded from debates is because debates are exempted from this rule.

Freedom and Conformity in the U.S. News Media

Despite some regulations on radio and television, the news media in the United States have more freedom from government restrictions than the media do in most Western democracies. Even in the case of libel, the laws favor news organizations by making the barriers to winning libel suits high. The government also supports the media by keeping the costs of mailing newspapers and broadcast licenses cheap. This has allowed the media to flourish.

Despite the large number of media outlets, there is limited diversity in news content. The media tend to cover the same events, mostly without a partisan slant. Many rely on wire services, such as the Associated Press (AP), for newsgathering outside their immediate area. Similarly, local television stations often get their video from the six major networks. News organizations send reporters to the same *beats,* places like the White House, where they see the same things and sometimes consult about what it means. Reporters have been trained similarly and do not want to miss something that other reporters covered. Often, they have little time to come up with a novel interpretation. These things make news content homogeneous; though the reporting styles vary. Newspapers tend to do more in-depth coverage and television provides a narrative description. Some outlets are more prone to sensationalism than others. The increased concentration of media ownership not only contributes to the sameness of news reporting, but also has resulted in corporations putting profit ahead of news quality. Infotainment (a mix of entertainment and news that focuses on human-interest stories) gets larger audiences and advertising revenue than in-depth political news reporting.

The News Media as Link: Roles the Press Can and Cannot Perform

Unlike the partisan press, the modern press separates political opinion from news coverage. It can fulfill only the responsibilities that are consistent with the journalistic values of choosing news that seem interesting or important. It cannot live up to the responsibility of advising the public on how to make political decisions, as parties and interest groups do. This is why the media are more successful at acting as signalers, common carriers, and watchdogs than as public representatives.

The *signaler role* entails quickly alerting the public to important events. The media does this reasonably well by sending reporters to hot spots such as war or disaster sites or covering political developments in Washington. The public's interest and priorities follow the attention something or someone gets in the press. This is called *agenda setting.*

Another role of the press is that of *common carrier.* In this capacity, the media act as a channel carrying the messages of politicians to the people. Most national news is about politics and politicians who compete to place their spin, or interpretation, on events. While they are often successful, reporters also get their say. This is evident from the fact that viewers hear television journalists talk for much longer than sources or subjects do. In fact, *sound bites* (direct quotes from subjects and sources on television news) have been getting shorter over time. For example, candidates in the 1960s could be heard uninterrupted for 40-second intervals on average, while candidates today are heard in 10-second bursts.

The *watchdog role* of the press is intended to protect the public from official wrongdoing by alerting readers, listeners, and viewers to problems. Watergate is a good example of the press fulfilling this responsibility. Whereas the common-carrier role assumes that what government officials say is truthful, the watchdog role does not. The distrust of government that underlies the watchdog role has resulted in a negativity bias that some critics think has gone too far. This attention to bad news targets both Democrats and Republicans.

The *role of public representative* assumes that the media can be the public's advocate. There are two reasons that the media are not well suited for this role and fail to perform it well. First, the media are not elected by voters and therefore are not accountable to them in the same way as elected officials. Second, being an advocate is at odds with neutrality, something the press tries hard to maintain. The motivation of most news organizations is to cover a "good story." To journalists this means something dramatic and compelling to the audience, not to promoting points of view. There are exceptions to this rule, such as Fox News, which combines an attention-getting goal with a conservative agenda.

The roles of signaler, common carrier, and watchdog are important for a democracy. But for effective self-government, the job of organizing and mobilizing the public cannot rest with the mass media because it is an institution ill-suited for that purpose.

TAKE NOTE

Despite the fact that the mass media is identified as part of the AP U.S. Government and Politics curriculum, most of the material in this chapter is unlikely to be on the test. Many of the accepted media-related answers to past free-response test questions are not learned from Chapter 10 but are instead drawn from material about the media that is integrated into other chapters.

Overall, the most relevant material in Chapter 10 is about the more explicitly political aspects of the news media rather than their history or production aspects. Throughout the chapter, ask yourself the questions: "How is this politically relevant?" or "What impact is this likely to have on the public and politicians?" It is useful to think of the mass media as another linkage institution, like parties and interest groups, but one that is inherently flawed because it was not designed for the task.

Observations from Previous Exams

Material on the media is part of the "Political Parties, Interest Groups, and Media" section that is supposed to make up 10 percent to 20 percent of the multiple-choice questions. Questions on media focus "on the functions and structures of the media and the media's influence on politics." An examination of the recently released exams indicates that most of the questions from this section have been about parties and interest groups.

The one question on the released 1999 multiple-choice test about the media asked about how the press covered campaigns. Similarly, the 2002 multiple-choice test's question on the media was about the term "horse-race journalism." This term does not appear in this textbook. It refers to how news coverage focuses on who is ahead and who is behind and what strategies the candidates are doing to influence that. Polls are used extensively to report the horse race.

One free-response question in the last six years has focused on the media. In 1999, a question asked about ways the media contribute to candidate-centered campaigns and how presidential candidates use the media. In addition, answers to free-response questions appearing on the other five tests accepted media explanations in their answers.

On the 2000 exam, media could be identified as one of the methods used by interest groups to influence the court appointment process. On the 2001 exam, media could be used in responses to two free-response questions. The first was to explain the incumbency advantage in elections and the second was to explain how interest groups make it harder for the government to enact public policy. On the 2002 exam, media could be used as one of the explanations for how the president overcomes the problem of divided government. It could also be used on that year's test to explain why voter turnout has gone down over time and why presidential elections get higher turnout than midterm elections.

The 2003 exam accepted media explanations for three of the four free-response questions: why presidential approval ratings fluctuate; how people participate politically outside of voting; and what strategies Congressional leaders use. On the 2004 test, media attention could be used as an informal advantage the president has over Congress in conducting foreign policy. An understanding of media could also contribute to an answer about how divided government leads to lower trust in government. Finally, on the 2005 exam the lack of media access to the Court was accepted as one of the reasons for that institution's insulation from public opinion.

What to Do with the Boxes

A useful preparation for the illustration-based questions on the test is to try to write a summary for Figure 10-1 (p. 314), Figure 10-2 (p. 323), and Figure 10-3 (p. 325) before you read or review the one provided under the title. Try to come up with arguments for why the information looks the way it does.

The "Liberty, Equality & Self-Government" box (p. 315) describes *prior restraint*—a concept that might appear on the test. Although media mergers ("Debating the Issues" box, p. 319) are unlikely to be the topic of multiple-choice questions, understanding how they work and what impact they have on news homogeneity is useful. The discussion in "Global Perspectives" box (p. 324) would be appropriate for explaining how the mass media influence foreign policy. The "Why Should I Care?" box (p. 329) reiterates points made in the text about how the media put a higher priority on entertaining news and the disadvantages of this approach for the public.

Because of the focus of the AP test, you do not need to concentrate on the "States in the Nation" box (p. 316) or the degree of neutrality in other countries' news ("How the United States Compares, p. 320).

Key Terms

Don't just memorize these terms. Understand what they mean and how they compare to other concepts. Be able to give examples of each.

News (p. 308)
News media or press (p. 308)
Partisan press (p. 309)
Yellow journalism (p. 310)
Objective journalism (p. 310)
Interpretive reporting (p. 311)
Descriptive reporting (p. 311)
Equal-time restriction (p. 312)
Prior restraint (p. 315)
Beats (p. 318)
Mergers (pp. 318–19)
Infotainment (p. 320)
Signaler role (p. 321)
Agenda setting (p. 322)
Common-carrier role (p. 322)

Spin (p. 322)
Watchdog role (p. 323)
Negativity bias (p. 325)
Public-representative role (p. 326)

Making Connections to Previous Chapters

Think about the equal-time restriction in terms of the core American values of liberty, equality, and self-government discussed in Chapter 1. To which core value does the restriction give the highest priority? How?

The sections on freedom of expression in Chapter 4 are relevant to this chapter's discussion of libel, prior restraint, and government regulation of television and radio. A review of the important court cases on libel will better explain how limited government's restrictions on a free press are. Think about whether this is what you would expect from the Federalists prevailing over the Anti-Federalists (Chapter 2). You also want to remember that the Federalists used a New York newspaper to promote ratification of the Constitution by having their essays, known today as the *Federalist Papers,* published there.

Recall the limits to the public's knowledge of politics and the public's ideological thinking (Chapter 6). How do the mass media affect these limits? The mass media were one of the agents of socialization (Chapter 6). What perceptions are most likely to be acquired from the media given what this chapter reveals about their roles and limitations?

It would be useful to reread the section called "Following Politics in the Media" (Chapter 7) now that you know more about the different approaches that television and newspapers have to covering news. Do these differences make the information in this section more troubling or less? Chapter 7 described social-movement events as designed to bring attention to an issue. Reconsider the likelihood of this strategy working and what conditions would influence its working now that you know more about how reporters choose and cover stories.

Chapter 8 described the declining strength of party organizations. Consider how changes in the media may have contributed to this decline. How have changes in the media contributed to the change from party-centered to candidate-centered campaigns? Review the section on media consultants (p. 266) and air wars (p. 267) now that you have a more comprehensive understanding of the mass media.

How might the news media be used for outside lobbying (Chapter 9)? Do you think that outside lobbying through the media is enhanced or diminished by the rise in interpretive reporting or by the consolidation of the media?

SAMPLE QUESTIONS

Multiple-Choice Questions

1. Which of the following is the most common problem in today's news coverage?
   a. a lack of diversity of topics and interpretations
   b. a lack of ideological balance
   c. too much yellow journalism
   d. too much descriptive reporting
   e. too little coverage of the president

2. Interpretive reporting is least appropriate for which of the following roles of the mass media?
   a. watchdog role
   b. signaler role
   c. public-representative role
   d. common-carrier role
   e. agenda-setting role

3. This figure demonstrates that:

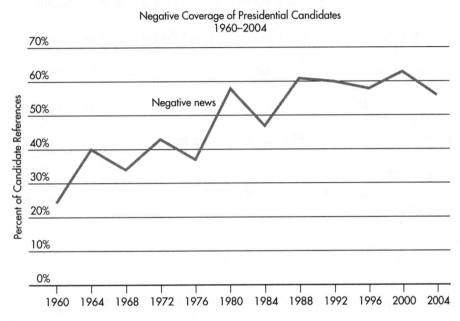

Negative Coverage of Presidential Candidates
1960–2004

From Thomas E. Patterson, *Out of Order*, Alfred A. Knopf, 1993, p. 20. Copyright
© 1993 Thomas E. Patterson.

   a. the media have a liberal bias
   b. the media have generally increased their coverage of presidential candidates over time
   c. press coverage of presidential candidates has been more negative than positive
   d. the greatest increase in negative news about presidential candidates was between 1976 and 1980
   e. the race between George W. Bush and John Kerry got more negative coverage than the race between George W. Bush and Al Gore

4. Which of the following accurately describes the history of American journalism?
   a. The press has always practiced objective journalism.
   b. The press has never practiced objective journalism.
   c. Throughout American history, there have always been some newspapers that practiced objective journalism and some that did not.
   d. Over time, the practice of objective journalism has fluctuated.
   e. In the nation's early years, the press did not practice objective journalism, but over time, it became the dominant approach in the press.

5. Which of the following violates the equal-time restriction?
   a. one candidate buying airtime and another not getting the opportunity to buy comparable airtime
   b. a televised debate in which third-party candidates are excluded
   c. one candidate getting more news coverage than the other candidate
   d. one candidate buying more advertising time than the other candidate
   e. no candidate getting free airtime

6. Which of the following is true about restrictions on freedom of the press?
   a. Government can stop publication or broadcast of material that is not in the public's interest.
   b. Government can stop publication or broadcast of material that is not in the interest of the government as a whole.
   c. Government can stop publication or broadcast of material that is not in the interest of the president.
   d. Government can stop publication or broadcast of material if a court deems it harmful to the nation to reveal that information.
   e. Government cannot stop publication or broadcast of any material.

7. Which of the following is a trend in news coverage?
   a. more descriptive reporting and less interpretive reporting
   b. longer sound bites for politicians
   c. less reliance on the beat system
   d. less negativity
   e. less political coverage relative to other types of stories

Multiple-Choice Questions That Link Chapter 8 to Lessons in Earlier Chapters

8. Which of the following is part of an outside strategy that uses the mass media?
   a. the March on Washington during the civil rights movement
   b. contributing money to a candidate's campaign that the candidate uses to pay for advertising
   c. suing the tobacco industry for causing lung-cancer deaths
   d. providing technical information to a senator so that the senator can ask an important question during a televised debate
   e. developing contacts with legislators and members of the executive agencies who are most likely to appear in the news

9. Which of the following statements is true about the American public and the national evening news regarding political ideology?
   a. The American public is ideological, but the major evening news shows are not.
   b. The major evening news shows are ideological, but the American public is not.
   c. Neither the American public nor the major evening news shows are ideological.
   d. Both the American public and the major evening news shows are ideological.
   e. No generalization can be made about the ideological nature of either the American public or the major evening news shows.

10. The *New York Times v. Sullivan* case illustrates:
    a. that the freedom of the press is limited
    b. that the freedom of speech is limited
    c. the press needs to be very careful when criticizing public officials
    d. the press is virtually immune to being convicted of libel against public officials
    e. that the press can knowingly exhibit reckless disregard for the truth

Multiple-Choice Answers

1. A; 2. D; 3. D; 4. E; 5. A; 6. D; 7. E; 8. A; 9. C; and 10. D

Free-Response Questions

1. The mass media serve many roles in the political system.

   a. Identify and describe two roles of the media. (2 points)

   b. Describe how each of these two roles is evident in campaign coverage. (2 points)

   c. Explain how the media can be a tool for interest groups. Explain how the media can be an obstacle. (2 points)

   This answer is worth six points.

   Part "a" is worth two points. One point is earned for correctly identifying and describing one role. The second point is earned for correctly identifying and describing the second role. Acceptable answers include: signaler role, common-carrier role, watchdog role, and public-representative role. Simply naming one of these roles without correctly describing it earns no points. It is acceptable to call the role something else if it is clear from the description that it is one of these four.

   Part "b" is worth two points. One point is earned for describing how campaign coverage illustrates one role. The second point is earned for describing how campaign coverage illustrates a second role. Acceptable answers include: campaign events and candidate positions are revealed to the public through the signaler role; candidates, parties, and government officials talk about issues and candidates, and this communication is carried by the media in the "common carrier role" as coverage of debates and of speeches at party conventions; the inadequacies of candidates, their issue positions, and campaigning are revealed through the media as part of its watchdog role; and reporting of public-opinion polls about the candidates, televised or public forums organized by the media, and reporters asking questions of candidates during debates on behalf of the public fit the public-representative role.

   Part "c" is worth two points. One point is earned for describing how the media can be a tool for an interest group. Acceptable answers include: communicating their interests to the public; communicating their interests to politicians, agenda setting, dramatizing a problem of concern to the interest group, ad time and space to raise money for the group or for the group to use to publicize support for an issue or candidate, and by ignoring issues that allow iron triangles to survive. A second point is earned for how the media can be an obstacle for an interest group. Acceptable answers include: ignoring the groups' issues and events, negatively characterizing them or their issues and events, revealing scandals and the unseemly influence they have with politicians (which could result in decreased influence or punishment), giving attention to their opponents or opponents' issues and events, or publicizing congressional oversight that hurts their claims.

2. There are two different models of how the media can serve the public. The first is as a partisan press. The second is as an objective press.

    a. Describe each of these types and provide an example of each. (3 points)

    b. Explain an advantage of each of these types for serving the public. (2 points)

    c. Explain a disadvantage of each of these types for serving the public. Provide an example for each. (3 points)

    This question is worth eight points.

    Part "a" is worth three points. One point is earned for correctly describing the partisan press. One point is earned for correctly describing the objective press. One point is earned for correctly identifying an example of each. One example earns no points. Two examples of the same type of press earn no points. Historical, contemporary, or hypothetical examples are acceptable.

    Part "b" is worth two points. One point is earned for explaining how the partisan press helps the public. Acceptable answers include: explaining issues and rationales, clearly identifying which side stands for different issues, making vote choices clearer, and providing a sense of community or belonging. The second point is earned for explaining how the objective press helps the public. Acceptable answers include: explaining issues, providing more than two sides to issues, providing more than partisan interpretations of issues, information that is trustworthy and accurate, and a forum for ideas and voices outside of the mainstream.

    Part "c" is worth three points. One point is earned for explaining how the partisan press does not serve the public. Acceptable answers include: bad for third parties, bad for alternative ideas, enhances partisan conflict, undermines compromise, and provides incomplete information. One point is earned for explaining how the objective press does not serve the public. Acceptable answers include: does not help people evaluate the facts, undermines development of ideological thinking, less clarity in providing major party positions, gives more weight to the voice of officials, and results in a narrowing of the political debate. One point is earned for providing two examples. One example earns no points. Two examples of the same type of press earn no points. Historical, contemporary, or hypothetical examples are acceptable.

CHAPTER ELEVEN

Congress: Balancing National Goals and Local Interests

SUMMARY

This chapter discusses both the national and local responsibilities of Congress. Congress passes national laws but represents states and districts. These two goals create a tension that is hard to resolve satisfactorily. Congress is structured through committees to be responsive to diverse special interests. Yet Congress is also at the center of national policy debates, and despite the independence of legislators, their decisions sometimes reflect majoritarian opinion advocated by the majority-party leadership. This chapter looks at congressional elections, leadership, organization, and processes.

Congress as a Career: Election to Congress

Congress today is full of career politicians who serve for a long time despite having to be reelected every two years in the House and every six years in the Senate. Almost all of the *incumbents*—those already in office—who run for reelection end up winning. Most of them beat their competitors by large margins. Despite public distrust of Congress, people reelect their own representatives.

Incumbents hold many advantages over their competition. First, they have a record of serving their *constituencies,* the people in their districts or states. They pass legislation that provide constituents with tangible benefits (*pork-barrel projects*) and help them with problems they have with government (*constituency service*). Congressional staffers provide these services and help the members advertise their success back home, often using free mailings (the *franking privilege*). Incumbents also have an easier time raising the large amount of money needed to run a modern campaign than challengers do. They have already developed mailing lists of likely donors, and PACs are more likely to contribute to them. Even more expensive are *open-seat* races, or those without an incumbent.

Threats to an incumbent's winning are troublesome national issues that members might be blamed for, like a bad economy, and their own personal scandals. The *drop-off* turnout in an off-year election—an election held two years after a presidential election—can also hurt some incumbents of the president's party who previously won close elections. This is because the less-partisan voters who gave them their edge seldom vote in midterm elections. A strong challenger, such as someone with House or governor experience, can cause problems for an incumbent senator's reelection. Redistricting also threatens some incumbents. Every ten years *reapportionment* occurs, reallocating House seats based on population shifts measured by the national Census. State governments redistrict by drawing new House district lines to maintain an equal number of people in each district. Redistricting becomes a political act as the party in power creates districts that favor its candidates, a process called *gerrymandering.* One incumbent can be pitted against another in a newly designed district.

The consequence of having so little turnover because of the incumbency advantage is that Congress rarely changes policy direction, even when things are not going well. This weakens the public's control of government. It is also an obstacle to changing the demographic makeup of Congress, which consists overwhelmingly of white, male lawyers.

Congressional Leadership

Because leaders have no real control over who gets into Congress, they have a limited ability to direct members' behavior. Members can be caught in a tension between representing constituents and supporting party leadership.

Congress and its leadership are organized along party lines. Each *party caucus*, which includes all party members in the chamber, selects its *party leaders* at the start of a session, the two-year period between elections. It also decides on its policy program and strategies. House leaders are the *Speaker*, who is elected by the chamber and is thus a member of the majority party, the *majority leader, majority whip, minority leader,* and *minority whip.*

The Speaker's formal powers include: speaking first in debates, recognizing speakers on the floor, choosing the chair and majority members of the *Rules Committee* (the committee that schedules debate), assigning bills to committees, putting time limits on how long bills can be in committee, and choosing who will be on *conference committees.* The Speaker also works with the majority leader and majority whip on the party's issue agenda and the strategy to pass it. As floor manager, the majority leader works to get support for the bills. The whip counts votes and tells members when important bills will come up and what the party's positions on bills are. The minority leader and minority whip do the same with its party's agenda.

Although the Constitution indicates that the vice president is the presiding officer of the Senate, he usually attends sessions only when his vote is needed to break a tie. The *president pro tempore* instead leads Senate deliberations. This is a position of limited power. The Senate also has a minority leader and whips for each party. The most important position in the Senate is that of majority leader. With the exception of recognizing speakers and appointing members of a Rules committee, his job is similar to that of the Speaker. Yet it is a weaker position than Speaker of the House because senators are less likely to defer to leaders, and they have different norms (accepted ways of behaving) and rules. For example, there is unlimited debate in the Senate and strict limits in the House.

For leaders to be effective at building coalitions to pass their agendas, the members of their party must trust them. Because congressional parties are generally cohesive ideologically, leaders' jobs are easier now than they were a few decades ago. The leaders can now manage the self-interested members of the party to be an effective group because their self-interests are less divergent than when the congressional parties had strong party factions (for example, moderate Republicans and conservative Democrats). Still, there are differences of opinion within parties, so leaders need to consider this diversity when choosing a legislative agenda. Leaders no longer can rely on junior members sitting back and deferring to seniority, a norm that was once widely accepted in the House. Now, new members want the publicity that comes from being outspoken so that they can please special interests that support their campaigns and succeed in candidate-centered campaigns.

Committee chairs are also important leaders in Congress because committees are where the work of the institution is done. Chairs are always held by members of the majority and are usually the committee's most senior majority member. *Seniority* is measured by how long a person has served in the chamber, not how old they are. Committee chairs schedule meetings and the order of business in those meetings, lead the discussions, and decide when the bills get to the floor. Committee chairs have additional staff. The seniority system diminishes conflict and gives the most experienced members the most power. It can also undermine leadership control when committee chairs disagree with party leadership. This is why the Republican party placed a limit on how long someone could be chair. Chairs of subcommittees are members of the majority party. In 1994, the new Republican majority in the House reversed decisions made by the Democrats in the 1970s, which had democratized power in the chamber in order to strengthen party leadership. One of these rules gave committee chairs the authority to choose chairs of their subcommittees and to appoint their own staff. This helped strengthen the power of party leadership. This back-and-forth between emphasizing tools for representing national majorities and helping individual members represent district interests is common in the history of an institution that struggles to do both.

The Committee System

Standing committees, those that are permanent and consider policies in particular substantive areas, are where the major work of Congress is done. These committees draft, rewrite, and recommend legislation to their chambers. They also hold hearings. There are nineteen committees in the House and sixteen in the Senate. House committees average between thirty-five and forty members and are larger than Senate committees. Each has its own staff. These committees are essential to managing the large workload of lawmaking, as typically ten thousand bills are introduced in a two-year session.

Select committees are less permanent and do not consider legislation. They are put together for specific tasks. Some investigate political scandals; others oversee agencies. Select committees can be found within each chamber or may be *joint committees* made up of members from both chambers. *Conference committees* are joint committees that work temporarily to resolve differences in the House and Senate versions of the same bill.

Members of the majority party hold more seats on each committee and subcommittee than do members of the minority party. The tradition is that the ratio of Democrats to Republicans in the chamber is reflected, more or less, on each committee. House members serve on two committees and no more than five subcommittees, and Senators sit on between two and four committees, depending on the importance of the committee. As there are a fixed number of seats on each committee, members must wait for vacancies to occur, vacancies caused by other legislators losing an election, retiring, or choosing to relinquish a committee assignment. The decision as to which Republican will get a seat vacated by a Republican is up to a special Republican committee. Democrats have their own committee to make their assignments. The factors that influence most of these decisions are the requests of the members and the type of district the member represents. For example, members from farming districts are more likely to get on the Agriculture committee). Because there is more competition for *prestige committees* such as Foreign Relations or Finance in the Senate and Appropriations or Ways and Means in the House, additional factors are considered for those appointments. These are the personal qualities of the member, such as intelligence, experience, and work ethic, the member's seniority, the member's region, and whether the member's votes tend to be based on ideology or on party loyalty. For subcommittee assignments, the party members on the committee to which the subcommittee reports, make choices using the same considerations.

Regardless of the implication for the likelihood that a bill will pass a committee, by law bills must be referred to committees that have *jurisdiction* over the issue central to that piece of legislation. Complex legislation could fall under more than one committee's jurisdiction. This overlap can lead to "turf wars" that are resolved by the party leadership sending the bill to the committee they prefer consider it. Sometimes bills are divided up so that more than one committee can consider parts of it. Subcommittees also have specific jurisdictions. For issues falling within those jurisdictions, a handful of legislators have the greatest responsibility and authority.

How a Bill Becomes Law

The formal legislative process begins when a *bill,* or proposed legislation, is introduced. Only members of Congress can introduce bills, even though they are often written by people working in the executive branch or for interest groups. Bills are sent to the appropriate committee, which sends it to one of its subcommittees. The subcommittee might choose to conduct a hearing at which interested parties testify to the merits or weaknesses of the bill. If the members of the subcommittee are convinced after this that the bill should be passed, they refer it to the committee. The committee might hold more hearings. The committee—or, in the House, the subcommittee—might choose to revise the bill. This is referred to as *mark up.* If a majority of the committee recommends it, the bill is sent to the full chamber for action. Only 10 percent of the bills that are sent to committees are issued out of them. Since many bills are written to appease constituent interests, this rejection rate is not particularly troubling to most legislators.

In the House, the next hurdle is the *Rules Committee.* It is through this committee that the majority party controls the law-making process because the Rules Committee decides when the bill will be voted on, how much debate will be allowed, and whether it can be amended. A *closed rule* indicates that no amendments can be proposed; an *open rule* allows relevant amendments to any sections of the bill. Some rules indicate that it is permissible to amend some sections, but not others. Closed rules frustrate the minority party. There is typically little debate allowed on a bill; members of the committee reporting the bill voice most of the debate.

The Senate's rules committee does not hold this much power. The majority and minority leaders together schedule bills and allow unlimited debate and any amendment proposals—even *riders,* amendments not relevant to the bill. The exception to unlimited debate is *cloture,* a parliamentary maneuver in which at least three-fifths of the chamber votes for a 30-hour limit on debate. Cloture limits the power of the minority to prevent a bill its members dislike from coming to a vote through a *filibuster.*

After discussion, the bill comes to a vote. On small issues, the vote tends to defer to the committee's recommendation. The rank-and-file members will give more attention to the issue if the committee was split, which usually happens along party lines. On major issues, the party leaders are more involved in shepherding the bill throughout the process. They keep track of voting intentions and push for *party discipline* when the issue comes to a vote.

For a bill to move to the next stage, the same exact version needs to get a simple majority of more "yea" votes than "nay" votes in both chambers. About 10 percent of the time, the Senate passes a different version of the bill than the House does. In these cases, a conference committee is formed to resolve the differences. Typically, a conference committee is composed of members of the standing committees. Once the conference committee drafts a compromise, the new version goes back to each chamber to be voted on again. It cannot be amended by either chamber, but it can be passed, rejected, or sent back to the conference committee for more work. The next stage of the process is for the bill to go to the president. If the president signs the bill, or leaves it unsigned for ten days while Congress is in session, the bill becomes law. If the president rejects the bill by *vetoing* it, Congress still has an opportunity to make it law if two-thirds of each chamber vote for it, rather than 50 percent plus one. This is called *overriding a veto.* Another way that the president can prevent a bill from becoming law is by leaving it unsigned for ten days after Congress has adjourned for the term. This is called a *pocket veto.*

Congress's Policymaking Role

Congress was designed by the Framers of the Constitution to be the branch that led because it was the most representative of the people. Now both the president and Congress share this leadership role. In addition to its role in lawmaking, Congress serves representation and oversight functions. These three functions overlap.

The Lawmaking Function of Congress

The Constitution establishes the power of Congress to make laws that tax, spend, regulate commerce, and declare war. Yet on big issues, fragmentation of power tends to get in the way of Congress taking the lead. Fragmentation is the decentralization of power. It is inherent in such a large institution (535 legislators) that is bicameral (two chambers), in which the members are elected by, and therefore primarily concerned with the desires of, different constituencies. Power is less fragmented in the executive branch, where the president can embrace policy positions he believes are best for the nation. Therefore, the president tends to take the policy initiative and Congress works from his proposals.

Three congressional agencies assist Congress in evaluating policy proposals. The Congressional Budget Office, established by the Budget Impoundment and Control Act of 1974, evaluates the president's budget proposal. The cost and impact of the proposal estimated by the CBO is often different than the projections of the Executive Department's Office of Management and Budget. The second agency, the General Accounting Office, oversees how money appropriated by Congress is being spent by executive agencies. The Congressional Research Service is the third agency. It is a nonpartisan research group that collects and organizes information requested by members of Congress.

Sometimes Congress does lead on broad issues, typically in the areas of labor, environment, education, and urban development. The 1994 Republican Contract with America was an effort to lead on multiple issues. But because its committees are organized around constituent interests, Congress is better equipped to lead on narrow *distributive* issues that deal with what benefits to give to particular groups.

The Representative Function of Congress

Congress is supposed to represent the interests of America. This is often difficult because what is in the interest of particular localities and states might not be in the interest of the nation. There is no consensus on which should be more important to legislators.

The need to get reelected pushes members towards putting the highest priority on the needs and desires of their constituencies. Local representation can be seen in members' vote choices and their committee and subcommittee assignments. It is in these committees that *logrolling* (trading votes so legislators each get what they want in bill) occurs. A limitation on representing the interests of constituents is that there might not be a clear or uniform position in the state or district.

National interests are also important to legislators, especially on major issues. Debates over what is in the interests of the nation tend to be along party lines, with Democrats and Republicans disagreeing over solutions. The influence of party on Congressional decision making can be seen in votes that are individually recorded, or *roll-call votes*. Over the past 20 years there has been more party discipline on these votes than there was for decades before. The parties in Congress are ideologically consistent without the large factions that existed in the past. For example, many southern conservative Democrats vied with liberal Democrats over civil rights legislation in the 1960s. More than half the time, presidential initiatives are supported by the president's party and opposed by legislators of the other party.

The Oversight Function of Congress

It is Congress's job to make sure that the executive branch is following the laws and staying within Congressional appropriations. This *oversight* role is carried out primarily through committees, with each committee checking the parallel agency; for example, the Agriculture committees oversee the Department of Agriculture. This is a big—practically impossible—job and not one that legislators are usually interested in doing unless the problems are scandalous enough to attract media attention.

When there appear to be serious problems within an agency, the oversight committees hold investigative hearings. At these hearings, employees of the executive branch are compelled to answer questions or risk being charged with the crime of contempt. The exception to this is if they claim *executive privilege* because the material is confidential for national-security issues. Congress also has leverage over the executive branch through appropriations. Congress can cut an offending agency's budget or add restrictions to its spending. This punishes an agency.

To prevent problems before they happen, Congress has begun to limit bureaucrat discretion by putting specific instructions in appropriations bills. Congress has also included *sunset laws* that set a date when authorized programs will end. These *legislative vetoes* are a controversial approach to controlling the bureaucracy that may be unconstitutional because it entails agencies asking for Congress's permission before they take specific actions.

TAKE NOTE

This is an extremely important chapter. When it comes to studying Congress, you do not want to "miss the forest for the trees," but you need to see the trees, too. Be prepared for lots of questions about internal aspects of Congress (committees, leadership, processes) and about how this institution works with and against other institutions. Use the systems model on page 32 to help organize the information from this chapter. How do elections, interest groups, public opinion, and media provide input in the form of demands and supports to Congress? What role(s) does Congress play in producing outputs? How and when do other institutions limit Congress's power? How does Congress constrain the president, the bureaucracy, and the courts?

Although the term "divided government" does not appear in this book, it is an important concept relevant to this chapter and to Chapter 12. Divided government is when the president is of one party and another party is in the majority in the House of Representatives and/or the Senate. During periods of divided government, there tends to be more conflict between these two branches of government than when there is "unified government." Although George W. Bush has enjoyed unified government for most of his time in office, divided government has been more common in the postwar era.

Observations from Past Exams

Congress is part of the "Institutions of National Government" section that is supposed to make up 35 percent to 45 percent of the multiple-choice questions. Questions on Congress focus on "formal and informal institutional arrangements of power," relationships between Congress and other institutions, and linkages among Congress and public opinion, voters, interest groups, parties, the media, and subnational governments. Released exams reveal many Congress questions.

Sixteen of the sixty questions on the 1999 multiple-choice test were about Congress. They included questions about which officials are elected directly by the public, the role of conference committees, why the committee system is more important in the House than in the Senate, what standing committees are, the use of the Budget and Impoundment Control Act to regain powers lost to the executive branch, what Congress can do when the Supreme Court finds federal laws unconstitutional, what the War Powers Resolution entailed, what the impact of the 1992 elections was on Congressional membership, what the advantages of incumbency are, which chamber has more formal rules, how congressional districts are determined, what Congress's oversight tools are, what congressional powers have been challenged by the courts, how committees conduct oversight, and one that required students to recognize that the "congressional process is frequently lengthy, decentralized, and characterized by compromise and bargaining." The test also included a illustration-response question using a table that showed how competitive congressional elections were over time.

The 2002 multiple-choice test included seven questions about Congress. These were about the Rules committee, gerrymandering, the franking privilege, which institution redraws congressional districts, the Senate's role in ratifying treaties, the difference between the Senate and the House in terms of unlimited debate, and which congressional committee considers income-tax reform.

Nine free-response questions related to Congress were asked on the last six released exams. A 1999 question asked students to identify a major national-level policy making institution, such as Congress, and describe how interest groups affect it. Another question on that year's test asked about methods and limitations of congressional oversight. The 2000 exam asked about obstacles to congressional reform of campaign finance laws. The 2001 exam included a graph of congressional incumbency reelection rates over time in the Senate and House. The question asked about factors that contribute to incumbency advantage and their consequences. Another question relevant to material in this chapter asked about the impact of divided government and weak party discipline on policy making. The 2002 exam asked about obstacles to presidential appointments caused by divided government. The congressional committee system was the focus of a free-response question on the 2003 exam. It asked about the impact of specialization, logrolling, party representation on committees, and party leadership on the legislative process. A free-response question on the 2004 exam was about Congress's disadvantage, compared to the president, in foreign policy making. The 2005 exam asked about campaign finance reform.

What to Do with the Boxes

Useful summaries of information you should know appear in boxes on page 344 ("Constitutional Qualifications for Serving in Congress") and page 355 (Figure 11-4, "How a Bill Becomes Law").

The "Why Should I Care?" box (p. 337) describes factors that contribute to the incumbency advantage. These are important to remember. The "Debating the Issues" box (p. 343) is worthy of attention because it describes the consequences of gerrymandering, evaluates gerrymandering in light of the Equal Protection Clause, and is a nice illustration of how arguments in amicus curiae briefs look. (You will learn more about these in Chapter 14.) More information on redistricting appears in the "Liberty, Equality & Self-Government" box (p. 362).

A useful preparation for the illustration-based questions on the test is to try to write a summary for Figure 11-1 (p. 338), Figure 11-2 (p. 339), Figure 11-3 (p. 340), Table 11-1 (p. 346), and Figure 11-5 (p. 365); also, for Figure 7-1 (p. 216), the turnout data on the map (p. 219), and Figure 7-2 (p. 221) before you read or review the one provided under the title.

Because of the focus of the AP test, you do not need to know specific data from the "States in the Nation" box (p. 345). Most of the information in the "How the United States Compares" box (p. 348) is also beyond the scope of the AP test; however, the first paragraph of the second column provides a helpful summary of fragmentation in Congress. You do not need to memorize all of the standing committees in Congress found in Table 11-2 (p. 352). Information about standing committees found in the text will suffice. Aside from pointing out that much of the legislative staff's time is spent on constituency service, the "Citizenship" box (p. 367) is not relevant to the test.

Key Terms

Don't just memorize these terms. Understand what they mean and how they compare to other concepts. Be able to give examples of each.

Constituency (p. 337)
Pork-barrel projects (p. 338)
Service strategy (p. 338)
Frank (p. 338)
Open-seat election (p. 339)
Midterm election drop-off (p. 340)
Reapportionment (p. 341)
Redistricting (p. 342)
Gerrymandering (p. 342)
Party caucus (p. 346)
Party leaders (p. 346)
Seniority (p. 350)
Standing committee (p. 351)
Select committee (p. 351)
Joint committee (p. 351)
Conference committee (p. 352)
Prestige committees (pp. 353–54)
Jurisdiction (p. 354)
Bill (p. 355)
Mark up (p. 356)
Rules Committee (p. 356)
Closed rule (p. 356)
Open rule (p. 356)
Cloture (p. 356)
Filibuster (p. 357)
Rider (p. 357)
Party discipline (p. 357)
Law (p. 358)
Veto (p. 358)

Overriding a veto (p. 358)
Pocket veto (p. 358)
Lawmaking function (p. 358)
Distributive benefits (p. 361)
Representation function (p. 362)
Logrolling (p. 363)
Roll-call votes (p. 364)
Oversight function (p. 365)
Executive privilege (p. 366)
Sunset law (p. 366)
Legislative vetoes (p. 366)

Making Connections to Previous Chapters

Perhaps more than any other chapter, this one connects to all the others. This is because Congress was designed to be the most central branch of government. The section on its functions shows why. Congress is included in virtually every chapter of the book, with the first mention of a Congressional act appearing on page 15. Some of these references should be easier to understand after reading Chapter 11. For example, it would be useful to reread the section on "Equal Ballots" in Chapter 5 (pp. 165–66) after reading pages 342–43.

Think about how Congress embodies the ideas about politics on page 18. Think about how the "two Congresses" idea relates to the four models of power (pp. 27–31). Page 368 should help broaden your understanding of pluralism (pp. 29–30).

The workings of contemporary Congress demonstrate well the Founding Fathers' goal of balancing limited government and self-government. Review those concepts from Chapter 2 and take some time to reread the "Debating the Issues" box (p. 65). Has the incumbency advantage compromised the goals of the "Great Compromise" (p. 45); has it further limited popular rule (p. 60)? How do divided government, term limits, increased partisanship in Congress, and gerrymandering relate to the Framers' intentions? Review the chart on checks and balances (p. 54). Then consider whether Congress is living up to its obligation to check and balance presidential power. Evaluate Figure 11-5 (p. 365) with this question in mind.

Patterson explains in Chapter 3 that even though the federal system divides authority between states and national governments, powers overlap. For example, education is an issue for states, but the federal government has a role in it. The discussion on page 354 illustrates this. The section on devolution and the Republican Revolution (pp. 95–97) will probably make more sense after reading Chapter 11.

Chapter 6 explained that most Americans do not pay close attention to politics and that cultural thinking, ideological thinking, group thinking, and partisan thinking influence their attitudes. Chapter 7 demonstrates that voters are disproportionately educated and have high incomes. What implications do these facts have on Congress's fulfilling its representational function?

Chapter 8 is particularly relevant to understand Congress because Congress is organized and led by parties. Think about how realignment, dealignment, decentralized party organizations, candidate-centered elections, single-member district system affect who is elected to Congress and how the members act when they get there.

It is essential to understand how campaign finance works. Patterson addresses this in four separate sections of the book (Chapter 8, pp. 261–63; Chapter 9, pp. 295–300; Chapter 11, pp. 338–40; and Chapter 12, pp. 385, 388–91). It would be useful to reread these sections together when preparing for the test. Lobbying Congress is described briefly in Chapter 9 (pp. 288–91). Now that you understand decentralization of Congress better, you can see why interest groups make this institution a target. What are the obstacles to interest-group influence? The section on iron triangles and subgovernments (pp. 292–93) could just as easily have been put in Chapter 11. How do these relate to Congress's three policymaking functions?

Given what you learned about the media from Chapter 10, what do you think coverage of Congress and legislators looks like? What effect might media coverage have on how Congress works? How does it serve and how does it undermine the power of leaders, the incumbency advantage, and oversight?

SAMPLE QUESTIONS

Multiple-Choice Questions

1. Gerrymandering:
   a. is another word for reapportionment
   b. is legal if it is motivated by a desire for racial equality
   c. is legal if it is motivated by a desire for gender equality
   d. is legal if it is motivated by a desire for partisan inequality
   e. results in more turnover in Congress both in the short and long term

2. The power of leaders in Congress rests primarily on:
   a. the willingness of members to support them
   b. members' fear of censure
   c. members' fear of losing committee assignments
   d. members' desire for career longevity
   e. leaders' formal powers, such as the Speakers' right to recognize members on the floor

3. Which of the following is a reason that the Speaker of the House is more powerful than the president *pro tempore* of the Senate?
   a. The Speaker can vote on all bills, whereas the president *pro tempore* can only vote to break ties.
   b. The House of Representatives has more committees than the Senate, so the leader's power to appoint members to committees is more important there.
   c. The Senate has unlimited debate whereas the House does not.
   d. The Speaker is also the Majority Leader in the House.
   e. The President is more likely to exert pressure on the president *pro tempore* than on the Speaker of the House.

4. Which of the following most directly oversees the executive agencies' spending of money to ensure that they operate in ways prescribed by Congress?
   a. House Appropriations Committee
   b. Congressional Budget Office
   c. General Accounting Office
   d. Office of Management and Budgeting
   e. Senate Budget Committee

5. Which of the following are responsibilities of standing committees?
    I. draft legislation
    II. revise legislation
    III. see that the executive-branch agencies faithfully carry out laws

   a. I
   b. I and II
   c. I, II, and III
   d. I and III
   e. II and III

6. According to this figure:

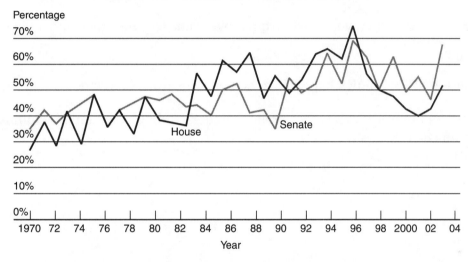

Percentage of Roll-Call Votes in House and Senate in Which a Majority
of Democrats Voted against a Majority of Republicans

   a. in the 1980s, the House had more party discipline than the Senate
   b. bipartisanship in the House was at its highest in 1995
   c. in terms of voting, both the Senate and the House have seen increases in cooperation between the parties over time
   d. for every year in the 1970s, fewer than half of the bills introduced in the House and in the Senate were passed
   e. in the Senate, party discipline has decreased over time

7. In the House of Representatives, where do most bills "die"?
   a. in the hands of the Speaker of the House when he decides not to assign them to committees
   b. in standing committees and standing subcommittees
   c. in the Rules Committee
   d. on the floor of House of Representatives
   e. in conference committees and conference subcommittees

8. Which of the following is the biggest obstacle to congressional oversight?
   a. sunset laws and the legislative veto
   b. the lack of staff
   c. the scope of the task
   d. partisanship
   e. divided government

9. The 1994 Contract with America is an example of:
   a. how the House of Representatives routinely takes the lead in broad national policymaking
   b. how members of the House of Representatives routinely defer to party leaders
   c. how new members of the House of Representatives routinely take the lead with major initiatives
   d. how fragmentation in the House of Representation facilitates bold policymaking in the House
   e. how the House of Representatives can sometimes overcome fragmentation and initiate broad national policies

Multiple-Choice Questions That Link Chapter 11 to Lessons in Earlier Chapters

10. Which of the theories of power is most appropriate to understanding how Congress fulfills its local representational role?
    a. majoritarianism
    b. pluralism
    c. elitism
    d. bureaucratic rule
    e. capitalism

Multiple-Choice Answers

1. D; 2. A; 3. C; 4. C; 5. C; 6. A; 7. B; 8. C; 9. E; and 10. B

Free-Response Questions

1. Congress has a dual nature, being both a lawmaking institution and a representative of localities and states.

   a. Choose one of the three features of Congress listed below that you think enhances Congress's representation of localities and states. Describe the feature and how it results in local and state representation. (2 points)

   b. Choose another one of the three features of Congress listed below that you think enhances Congress as a lawmaking institution. Describe the feature and how it results in Congress fulfilling its lawmaking responsibility. NOTE: This one needs to be different from the one you selected for "a." (2 points)

   c. Describe the remaining feature from the list. Explain how the feature that you have not previously selected reflects both roles of Congress. (2 points)

Features:

1. congressional elections

2. congressional standing committees

3. congressional party leadership

This question is worth six points.

Part "a" is worth two points. One point is earned for accurately describing any of the three features. One point is earned for explaining how it enables Congress to fulfill its representative role. Acceptable explanations for how elections result in representation include: constitutional requirements for residency, short terms of office allowing for replacement of members who do not fulfill expectations, campaign funding from local interests provide access and representation for them, even remote fear of losing office encourages representative voting and constituency service. Acceptable explanations for how standing committees result in representation include: members sit on committees and subcommittees that reflect state/district interests, logrolling, committees as source of pork-barrel legislation, distributive policies that come out of committee reflect constituent interests and allows for effective constituency service through iron triangles. Acceptable explanations for party leadership need to include a connection being made between the party leadership's goals and party interests that are reflective of national interest and of the district's or state's interests. NOTE: It is hardest to make the case for party leadership.

Part "b" is worth two points. One point is earned for correctly describing a feature different from the one in "a." The second point is earned for explaining how it enables Congress to fulfill its lawmaking function. Acceptable answers for elections include: a variety of members who reflect different local interests provide ideas for solving problems, interests expressed through elections push for distributive policies that Congress is effective at passing. Acceptable answers for standing committees include: standing committees allow for division of labor that allows Congress to handle its legislative workload; expertise developed in committees and subcommittees allow problem-solving; expertise developed allows for informed evaluation of executive-branch ideas; distributive policies developed in committees; norm of seniority in the committee system provides experienced leadership; committees draft, rewrite and recommend laws; conference committee membership is usually drawn from standing committees; and standing committees use staff for lawmaking role. Acceptable answers for party leadership include: easier for Congress to function and act when leaders lead, leaders develop agendas and strategies for passing them, leaders promote party discipline that get policies passed, and leaders assign bills they prefer to committees that will more likely act on them. NOTE: It is hardest to make the case for elections.

Part "c" is worth two points. One point is earned for explaining how the remaining feature enables Congress to fulfill the lawmaking function. One point is earned for explaining how this feature enables Congress to fulfill its representative function. See examples above.

2. Consult the figure on page 340.

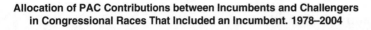

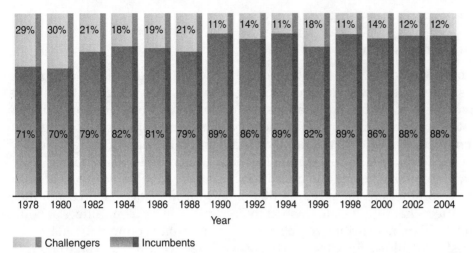

a. Define Political Action Committees (PACs). (1 point)

b. What is the most important finding demonstrated by the figure? (1 point)

c. Explain the implication of this finding for policy making. (2 points)

d. Explain the implications of this finding for campaigning. (2 points)

This question is worth six points.

Part "a" is worth one point for correctly defining PACs.

Part "b" is worth one point for correctly describing the most important finding as incumbents receiving more PAC contributions than challengers.

Part "c" is worth two points. One point is earned for identifying an implication for policymaking. The second point is earned for explaining it clearly. Acceptable answers include: special-interest groups get their way, special interests over majoritarian interests, orientation toward the status quo because little innovation when incumbents get reelected, undermine party discipline because money is coming from interest groups instead of parties, Congress is less responsive to national conditions, and a Congress of white, male lawyers is maintained.

Part "d" is worth two points. One point is earned for identifying an implication for campaigning. The second point is earned for explaining it clearly. Acceptable answers include: candidate-centered rather than party-centered, not issue-driven, not meaningful debate because less competitive, campaigns neglect less-organized and poorer interests.

CHAPTER TWELVE

The Presidency: Leading the Nation

SUMMARY

The Constitution provides the president with few formal powers. Yet there are times in which presidents seem "imperial" in the extent of their influence. At other times, the characteristics of a president and the circumstances that surround him have resulted in limited power. The conditional power of the presidency and presidential elections are the foci of this chapter.

Foundations of the Modern Presidency

Article II of the Constitution enumerates the formal powers of the president. Over time, these powers have been expanded without amending the Constitution. This is because presidents have successfully argued that they were nationally elected and therefore the single authority to lead the nation. Although only Congress has the authority to declare war, presidents have used their power as commander in chief to direct the military to send Americans into military action more than 200 times. Congress must approve ambassador appointments and treaties, yet the president, as chief diplomat, makes *executive agreements* with other nations. These are very much like treaties and have the authority of law. Even though Congress can cancel executive agreements, agreements with other nations take this form more often than as treaties; there are some 10,000 executive agreements as opposed to fewer than 100 treaties. Other constitutional powers of the president are his job as chief executive and legislative leader. As chief executive, he appoints people in the executive branch to execute—that is, to interpret and apply—the laws. As chief legislator, he recommends policies to Congress and vetoes bills.

Despite Andrew Jackson's assertion of presidential power, *Whig theory* prevailed until the presidency of Theodore Roosevelt. This theory saw the presidency as a limited office. Roosevelt replaced this idea with the *stewardship theory*, which envisioned strong presidents limited only by what was prohibited by law. Until his cousin Franklin took office, Teddy Roosevelt's successors, with the exception of Woodrow Wilson, reverted to the more limited view of their power. During and since Franklin D. Roosevelt's presidency, the office of president has been seen as inherently strong. The power of the modern presidency comes largely from the federal government's expanded authority.

While presidents were always the leader of the nation's foreign policy, America's long history of isolationism limited this power. This changed with World War II, when the nation became a global superpower. The need for fast decision-making in international affairs has resulted in presidents typically receiving deference from Congress and the public.

The president's power in domestic policy has also increased as the federal government has taken on more authority in an industrial and post-industrial society. As the federal budget grew, Congress gave the executive branch the authority to initiate the budgetary process. Policy planning during the New Deal came out of the White House and remains there today.

Choosing the President

The process of choosing the president has changed four times since the nation's founding. These changes were justified on the basis of needing to enhance the legitimacy of the office by making the selection process more democratic.

Originally, congressional party caucuses selected presidential party nominees and the president was selected by an Electoral College. The electors were selected by each state although not by the states' voters. The first major change in this system occurred in 1832 when national party conventions made up of delegates chosen by the local and state parties chose the nominees, and electors were tied to the popular votes in their states. The second change came with the Progressive movement in 1904. This is when the *indirect primary* was created so that voters could choose delegates to their party's convention who would then select the nominee. This resulted in little change to the overall system because most states did not institute primaries. The final change began in 1972 when voters were given more control of their nominating process through the use of *open party caucuses,* meetings to determine a party's nominee that are open to party voters. There was also an increase in the number of states that used primaries. Today there are far more primaries than caucuses.

Because voters are the ones who indirectly choose their party's nominee, the nomination process is a campaign. Because the process is staggered geographically and over time, *momentum* from successes in early states is essential for a victory. Press coverage, funding, and public support follow from early victories. As states move their competitions earlier in the process, money becomes even more important. Because of the *Federal Election Campaign Act of 1974,* candidates can receive *federal matching funds* as long as they follow rules on how much they raise and how much they spend. Some candidates, like George Bush and John Kerry in 2004, chose not to take matching funds so they could spend money more strategically, such as outspending their rivals in early primary states to get momentum. The nominating campaigns end with the national party contentions, where the *party delegates* from the states formally choose their nominee. These nominees choose their own vice presidential running mates.

During the general election campaign, the major-party nominees and independent candidates devise strategies that take into consideration the *unit rule:* the rule in 48 states that says that the candidate who wins the most votes in the state gets all of its Electoral College votes. To win the presidency, a candidate needs a majority of the electors' votes (270 or more), not a majority of the popular votes. Each state gets the number of electors equal to its number of representatives in Congress. Recall that each state has two Senators and its number of House seats is based on its population. Candidates spend their time and money in *battleground states*—those in which neither party dominates and in which the race looks like it will be close.

Campaigns are fought in the media, particularly on television through news coverage, debates, and advertising. Since 1976, both of the major parties' candidates have accepted federal funding, which is money predicated on the agreement not to spend additional funds. Third-party candidates receive federal funds if they get 5 percent of the vote or more, unless they spend more than $50,000 of their own money.

The Constitution insists that presidents must be at least 35-years old, be born in the United States, and have lived in the country for 14 years or more. Most of them have previously served in elected office. All of them have been white males. All but one have been Protestant.

Staffing the Presidency

The president appoints the people who will assist in meeting policy goals to positions in the executive branch. They typically are members of the president's party. These appointees provide the president with expertise and influence over the bureaucracy. With the growth of presidential responsibilities has come a growth in the executive bureaucracy. The president appoints a few thousand staff to the Executive Office of the President, the cabinet, and to federal agencies and commissions.

Since its creation in 1939, the *Executive Office of the President* (EOP) has assisted the president most directly. Presidents can select the people and the organizational structure of the office to best help manage the executive branch. Currently the EOP consists of 14 organizations. The *White House Office* includes the people who are closest and most loyal to the president: his chief of staff, counsel, and press secretary. The *Office of Management and Budget* (OMB) is in charge of formulating and carrying out the budget—according to the president's goals, of course. Policy experts who provide the president with advice and information make up many of the executive offices such as the National Economic Council, National Security Council, and the Council of Economic Advisors. The *Office of the Vice President* is part of the EOP. The role of the vice president has evolved over time into an important one despite its authority remaining undefined in the Constitution.

The *cabinet* consists of the heads, called secretaries, of the executive departments, of which there are currently 15. Of these, the most important is the secretary of state. Unlike the EOP appointments, these need to be confirmed by the Senate. Although they were once the primary advisory group with whom the president frequently met, they now infrequently operate as a group working collectively only on general issues.

Although presidential appointees are supposed to be tools for presidents, they sometimes create problems for the chief executive. There are too many to control. Sometimes the policy experts are unaware of the political context or consequences of programs they recommend. Sometimes the political experts are too independent. It is particularly difficult for the president to control department and agency appointees because they can grow to identify more with the groups for which they work, or with their own self-interest, than with the president.

Factors in Presidential Leadership

Because the president works within a large branch and must depend on the other two branches to lead effectively, the president cannot act alone and is particularly dependent upon a cooperative Congress for power. The degree to which a president succeeds depends a lot on five factors: circumstances, the stage in the presidential term, the nature of the issue, the president's relations with Congress, and public support.

Circumstances most conducive to strong presidential leadership are rare; therefore, presidents have to do what they can with the conditions they face. Presidents have been most successful when they were elected decisively, face a problem that Congress and the public believe the president should act on, and when the president is vigorous and responsive to these expectations. Presidents can be most effective during the first few months of the presidencies, a time called the *honeymoon period*. Therefore, it is important for them to act on their priorities quickly; this is referred to as the *strategic presidency*. Unfortunately, this means that presidents are most effective when they are rookies and know the least.

Although the difference is not as stark as it once was, presidents tend to be more effective on foreign issues than they are on domestic issues. This is because the executive has more authority to act on foreign issues; legislators, even those of the opposing party, are more likely to defer to the president in this realm; fewer interest groups are involved in foreign affairs problems; other nations view the president as the embodiment of the United States; and the federal agencies dealing with foreign policies—the Department of Defense, the Department of State, and the Central Intelligence Agency—are more deferential to the president than other agencies are.

The president can bring Congressional attention to a problem, but this does not guarantee that the president's interests are followed in their deliberation; nor should it, by Constitutional design or intent. In our system of separate powers, both chambers need to consider each other's positions. The presidential veto can stop Congress from doing something as long as the veto is not overridden by a two-thirds majority, but it cannot make Congress do something. Although presidential vetoes, or the threat of them, are usually successful, having to use a veto is a sign of presidential weakness. More effective is a president who can persuade Congress to over-come the various divisions within that institution. A president's ability to do this is enhanced if the president's party is in the majority because partisanship is the greatest source of unity.

When presidents ignore congressional authority, Congress can fight back with two weapons—*impeachment* and legislation. As one of the checks and balances, Congress has the constitutional authority to remove presidents from office. This is done by first impeaching him in the House of Representatives and then trying him in the Senate. A vote by two-thirds of the Senate is necessary to take a president out of office. Andrew Johnson and Bill Clinton were both impeached by the House and acquitted in the Senate. Richard Nixon resigned while the House was considering impeachment.

Passing legislation to reign in presidential power is more common than impeachment. One example was the *Budget Impoundment and Control Act of 1974;* it forces presidents to spend the money that Congress appropriates rather than obstruct Congress's intentions by withholding that money. Another was the *War Powers Act*. It was passed over a presidential veto in 1973 as a response to the unleashed authority of presidents during the war in Vietnam, which was never declared by Congress. The act said that within 48 hours of sending troops into combat, the president had to tell Congress the reason for the deployment. Then it was up to Congress whether the troops could stay there after a 60-day period. This was a controversial act, which many people, including presidents, think is unconstitutional.

Public support also affects presidential power. Throughout presidents' terms, their *approval ratings* are measured by polls. While the ratings start out high, they invariably drop, in part because the public has unrealistically high expectations. When presidential approval falls, it is easier for other politicians to mount challenges. Approval ratings tend to go up after an international threat (this is called the *rally 'round the flag* reaction) and go down after a sustained conflict. The economy can also hurt a president's popularity. Presidents try to manage public opinion by *going public*—using the media to appeal directly to the people. Of course, there is no guarantee that the press will cover the president's version of events and issues positively. The media's bias toward negativity can create problems for presidents, especially when a scandal results in a media *feeding frenzy*. Presidents try to go around an adversarial national press by giving interviews to local and regional press. Inevitably, real events, and not the spin given to them by politicians or reporters, are what have the largest impact on public opinion. A president mired in problems has less power to solve them because power is tied to political legitimacy.

TAKE NOTE

This chapter is very important for the AP test. It is essential to distinguish between "formal powers" (those specified in the Constitution) and "informal power" (what presidents do with their prestige and popularity to persuade others). Although these terms are not used in this chapter, the ideas are. In addition to differentiating executive agreements from treaties (pp. 375–76), you should be aware that executive orders also carry the authority of law although they do not go through Congress. Another source of increased presidential power missing from this chapter is executive privilege. It is discussed on page 366. Since George W. Bush's presidency has given more support to the idea of a new "imperial president" (p. 373), it is likely that questions about tools and abuses of presidential power will continue to be on the test.

Observations from Past Exams

The presidency is part of the "Institutions of National Government" section that is supposed to make up 35 percent to 45 percent of the multiple-choice questions. Questions on the president focus on "formal and informal institutional arrangements of power," relationships between Congress and other institutions, and linkages between the president and public opinion, voters, interest groups, parties, the media, and subnational governments. There are many questions about the president on the released exams.

The last two multiple-choice tests released included 25 questions related to this chapter. The 13 questions on the 1999 exam asked about presidential appointment power, methods of selecting party convention delegates, how vice presidents are chosen, method of electing the president, strategies presidents use to influence Congress, how the president influences the federal judiciary, acts that limit presidential power, the presidential nominating process, the impact of the War Powers Resolution on the president, how presidents are removed from office, what contributed to the increase in presidential power, the line-item veto, and why the cabinet has a limited influence on the president's decisions.

The twelve questions on the 2002 multiple-choice exam focused on when presidential vetoes are upheld, the Electoral College (two questions), the office in which the president's principal staff reside, the education level of delegates to party conventions, the constitutional roles of the executive, the constitutional checks that Congress has over presidential power, when presidents need to seek consent of Congress, line-item vetoes, the location of the president's closest staff (in the White House Office), and why use of executive orders has increased. One question asked students to interpret a figure on presidential approval ratings.

Six free-response questions on tests since 1999 were based on information from this chapter. In 1999 there was a question about the media and presidential election campaigns. Another question from that year's exam asked students to identify a major national-level policymaking institution (such as the presidency) and describe how interest groups affect it. A question on the 2001 exam asked about the impact of divided government and weak party discipline on policy making. The 2002 exam asked what problems divided government gives presidents when they try to make appointments to federal offices and to explain how the president can overcome these. The 2003 exam asked what factors influence presidential approval ratings. A question about the president's formal and informal powers in foreign policy and how they contribute to the president's advantage over Congress appeared on the 2004 exam.

What to Do with the Boxes

A number of boxes in this chapter provide helpful summaries of important information. The first (p. 376) describes the president's constitutional authority. Systems of presidential selection are nicely summarized on page 382, but because of the contemporary focus of the exam, the first two systems are unlikely to be asked about. The "Formal and Informal Requirements for Becoming President" are described clearly on page 391. Figure 12-1 (p. 393) provides a comprehensive list of the councils and offices that make up the Executive Office of the President. The box on page 405 describes the impeachment process.

A useful preparation for the illustration-based questions on the test is to try to write a summary for Figure 12-2 (p. 403) and Table 12-3 (p. 407) before you read or review the one provided under the title.

It is essential to understand how the Electoral College works and what the advantages and disadvantages of it are; therefore, the "Debating the Issues" box (p. 383) and the text in "States in the Nation" (p. 389) are worthy of your attention. Use the "Why Should I Care?" box (p. 386) to learn about frontloading and its consequences for voter turnout. While the AP test is unlikely to ask specifically about fast-tracking trade authority ("Global Perspectives," p. 401), this is a useful example of the struggle between Congress and the presidency for policymaking authority.

Because of the focus of the AP test, you do not need to know specific data in the "Liberty, Equality & Self-Government" box (p. 378), Table 12-2 (p. 387), "States in the Nation" box (p. 395), "How the United States Compares" box (p. 397), "America's Greatest Presidents?" box (p. 400), or the description of Richard Nixon's presidency (p. 406).

Key Terms

Don't just memorize these terms. Understand what they mean and how they compare to other concepts. Be able to give examples of each.

Imperial presidency (p. 373)
Lame duck (p. 373)
Executive agreements (p. 375)
Commander in chief (p. 376)
Chief executive (p. 376)
Chief diplomat (p. 376)
Legislative leader (p. 376)
Whig theory (p. 377)
Stewardship theory (p. 377)
Legitimacy (of election) (p. 381)
Electoral College (pp. 381, 383, and 388)
National convention (p. 382)
Party delegates (p. 383)
Indirect primary (p. 383)
Open party caucuses (p. 384)
Momentum (p. 385)
Federal Election Campaign Act of 1974 (p. 385)
Federal matching funds (p. 385)
Front-loading (p. 386)
Unit rule (p. 388)

Battleground states (p. 388)
Executive Office of the President (pp. 392–94)
White House Office (p. 392)
Office of Management and Budget (p. 392)
Office of the Vice President (p. 393)
Cabinet (p. 394)
Honeymoon period (p. 399)
Strategic presidency (p. 399)
Veto (p. 402)
Impeachment (pp. 404, 405)
Budget Impoundment and Control Act of 1974 (p. 405)
War Powers Act (pp. 405–6)
Presidential approval ratings (p. 406)
Rally 'round the flag effect (p. 406)
Going public or bully pulpit (p. 407)
Feeding frenzy (p. 408)

Making Connections to Previous Chapters

Consider what model of power (pp. 27–31) does the singular authority (p. 377) of the president support? When? Why? Evaluate the president's power in terms of the fears of the Anti-Federalists (p. 48). Review the president's role in checks and balances (p. 53–55). Can strong presidents sidestep these constraints? How? What obstacles to presidential leadership does Congress present? A review of pages 358–68 helps answer these questions.

Although this chapter includes a section on presidential elections (in "Choosing the President," pp. 381–91), it is useful to study it in conjunction with material on the same topic from other chapters. Chapter 2 describes the logic behind the Electoral College for limiting popular rule and how and why it was reformed (p. 63). Chapter 6 describes the expansion of suffrage over time (p. 214) and two approaches to voting that help predict which presidential candidate will win (pp. 226–27). Although realignments (pp. 244–48) involve more than presidential elections, the shift in party control is reflected in presidential races and has a profound effect on what leaders can accomplish in office. The centrist nature of the two-party system and the differences in party coalitions (pp. 250–53) also help explain challenges presidents face in leading Congress. Chapter 8's extensive discussion on national party organizations, money, and candidate-centered campaigns are important for understanding how Americans choose their presidents. PAC money (from Chapter 9, pp. 295–300) and its influence on elections is also relevant to presidential campaigns. It is essential to understand how campaign finance works. Patterson addresses this in four separate sections of the book (Chapter 8, pp. 261–63; Chapter 9, pp. 295–300; Chapter 11, pp. 338–40; and Chapter 12, pp. 385, 388–91). It would be useful to reread these sections together when preparing for the test.

Since public support has an impact on a president's effectiveness (pp. 406–9), it is important to review factors that influence public opinion (Chapter 6) and realize that people interpret the events that presidents confront in partisan ways (pp. 204–5). The role of the media in helping to shape public perceptions about the president is easier to understand after a review of Chapter 10, pages 322–26.

SAMPLE QUESTIONS

Multiple-Choice Questions

1. When do presidents have the greatest success, according to the figure?

Percentage of bills on which Congress
supported president's position

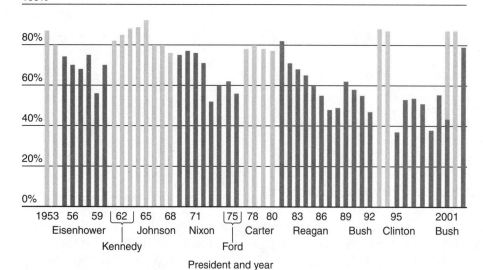

Control of Congress

President's party

Other party (one or both houses)

From *Congressional Quarterly Weekly Report,* December 11, 1999. Copyright © 1999 by
Congressional Quarterly Inc. Reproduced with permission of Congressional Quarterly
Inc. in the format textbook via Copyright Clearance Center.

a.   during the 1950s
b.   when they are Democrats
c.   when they are in their second term of office
d.   when the president's party controls both chambers
e.   during presidential election years

2. Which of the following powers of the president is explicitly listed in the Constitution?
a.   the power to declare war
b.   the power to appoint ambassadors
c.   the power to make executive agreements
d.   the power to propose legislation
e.   the power to withhold money from executive agencies

3. How does the president's power today compare to the intentions of the Founding Fathers?
a.   It is more limited overall.
b.   It is greater overall.
c.   It is greater in domestic policy and more limited in foreign policy.
d.   It is greater in foreign policy and more limited in domestic policy.
e.   It is the same as they intended.

4. Which of the following can a president hire and fire at will?
   a. senators
   b. ambassadors
   c. civil servants
   d. White House Office staff
   e. commissioners on the Federal Election Commission

5. Based on evidence from the last 40 years, which is most likely to be elected president?
   a. a governor
   b. a senator
   c. a member of the House of Representatives
   d. a military leader
   e. a religious leader

6. All of the following are true about "front-loading," except:
   a. it results in some states getting much more media attention than others
   b. it tends to help unknown and poorly funded candidates establish themselves
   c. it results in some states having more influence on who is nominated than others
   d. it disenfranchises millions of voters
   e. it results in candidates spending a lot of time in Iowa and New Hampshire

7. In which of the following scenarios would a presidential candidate win the popular vote but lose the election?
   I. if the candidate got 49 percent of the votes in less-populated states and 51 percent of the votes in highly populated states
   II. if the candidate won in the caucuses and conventions but lost in the primaries
   III. if the candidate won in some states by large margins and barely lost in other states

   a. I
   b. II
   c. III
   d. I and III
   e. I, II, and III

8. Which of the following is typically true about the president's public approval ratings?
   a. They improve over the term in office because he gains experience in office.
   b. They improve over the term in office because he is constantly campaigning for reelection.
   c. They go down over the term in office because international events undermine national security.
   d. They go down over the term in office because opposition mounts and mistakes are made.
   e. Approval ratings have no consistent pattern.

9. In which of the following areas is Congress most likely to challenge a president?
   a. executive agreements
   b. executive orders
   c. appointments to the Executive Office of the President
   d. Foreign policy
   e. funding public-works projects

10. How can a president be removed from office?
    a. The Senate impeaches him.
    b. The House impeaches him.
    c. The Senate impeaches him and the Supreme Court convicts him.
    d. The House impeaches him and the Supreme Court convicts him.
    e. The House impeaches him and the Senate convicts him.

Multiple-Choice Answers

1. D; 2. B; 3. B; 4. D; 5. A; 6. B; 7. C; 8. D; 9. E; and 10. E

Free-Response Questions

1. Despite having the same formal powers, presidential power varies between presidents and within their terms of office.

    a. Identify a factor beyond a president's control that influences his effectiveness. Describe this factor and explain how or why it influences his effectiveness. (2 points)

    b. Identify another factor that is primarily in the president's control that influences his effectiveness. Describe the factor and explain how or why it influences his effectiveness. (2 points)

    c. Identify another factor that is not primarily in his control but is not entirely beyond his influence. Describe this factor and how the president can influence it. Explain how or why the factor influences his effectiveness. (2 points)

    This question is worth six points.

    Part "a" is worth two points. One point is earned for correctly identifying and describing a factor that is beyond the president's control. Acceptable factors include: domestic and international circumstances that the president faces, the stage in the term, and party control of Congress. The second point is earned for explaining how or why the factor influences his effectiveness. NOTE: The factor needs to be beyond his control to receive the first point. The second point can be earned for explaining how or why a factor influences his popularity even if the first point is not earned.

    Part "b" is worth two points. One point is earned for correctly identifying and describing a factor that is primarily in his control. Acceptable factors include: personal qualities of leadership (for example, adapting to changing situations, political strategies, agenda, effective use of the media), decisive victory, or popularity. The second point is earned for explaining how or why the factor influences his effectiveness. NOTE: The factor needs to be primarily within his control to receive the first point. The second point can be earned for explaining how or why a factor influences his popularity even if the first point is not earned. If the factor in "a" is the same as the one in "b," it receives no points.

    Part "c" is worth two points. One point is earned for correctly identifying and describing a factor that is not primarily in his control but is not entirely beyond his influence. The second point is earned for describing how the president can influence that factor. The third point is awarded for explaining how or why it influences his effectiveness. Acceptable factors include: stage in presidential term (the president could utilize a "hitting the ground running" strategy early in the term), party control of Congress (the president could campaign for members of his party and try to maximize their number in Congress; he could offer a bipartisan agenda during divided government), or popularity.

NOTE: Some of the same factors, such as popularity, are on more than one list. They need to be described in such a way that is true to the category they are being used for.

2. The power of the president has increased over time.

   a. Describe two factors that have contributed to this change. (2 points)

   b. Explain how or why each has contributed to this change. (2 points)

   c. Describe a formal power that Congress has to constrain presidential power. Identify a factor that influences the likelihood that Congress will use this power. (2 points)

   This question is worth six points.

   Part "a" is worth two points. One point is awarded for each factor correctly described. Acceptable factors include: increase in national power relative to states', increase in government involvement in economy, increased role of the United States in world affairs, industrialization increased regulatory and policy leadership of government, growth in the size of bureaucracy, executive agreements determined to be constitutional, increased size of budget (discretionary funds), public expectations for activist presidents, television focuses attention on president. NOTE: No points are awarded for factors that have not changed over time (for example, power to veto bills).

   Part "b" is worth two points. One point is awarded for explaining how or why the first factor contributed to the change. Second point is awarded for explaining how or why the second factor contributed to the change.

   Part "c" is worth two points. One point is awarded for identifying and describing a check on the presidential power. Acceptable answers include: impeachment, override veto, approve treaties, approve appointments, enact laws within which the president can act, approve budget, investigate presidential action, and oversee implementation of policy. A second point is awarded for explaining how a factor that influences whether Congress will exercise constraint on the president affects Congress's decision. Acceptable answers include: public opinion regarding issues, presidential popularity, partisan makeup of Congress (divided government, size of majority), and nature of the issue.

CHAPTER THIRTEEN

The Federal Bureaucracy: Administering the Government

SUMMARY

This chapter tries to answer these questions: How can a government bureaucracy be efficient, responsive, and accountable? What encourages and discourages these characteristics in the large bureaucracy needed to administer the plethora of federal programs? This chapter describes the structure, practices, and responsibilities of the bureaucracy, why it is difficult to manage, and what methods are used to try to manage it.

Federal Administration: Form, Personnel, and Activities

Bureaucracies are organizations with structures designed to promote efficiency. These are: *hierarchical authority* (a chain of command that speeds decision making), *job specialization* (which divides labor according to skill and knowledge), and *formalized rules* (standard procedures that encourage quick and consistent decisions). Bureaucracies are found within and outside of government. Despite their reputation for lacking a "human touch," they are essential for large organizations to function. Federal government bureaucrats are numerous, at about 2.5 million, and powerful.

The federal bureaucracy is organized around policy areas, with different departments, agencies, corporations, and commissions having specific expertise and responsibilities. There are currently 15 *executive departments*, the top appointed officials of which make up the *cabinet.* Each works on a general policy area and is made up of bureaus, agencies, divisions, and/or services. For example, the Federal Bureau of Investigations (FBI) is a part of the Department of Justice. *Independent agencies,* such as the Central Intelligence Agency (CIA), are like departments in that they specialize and are divided into smaller units. However, their responsibilities are not as broad as departments' are. *Regulatory agencies,* such as the Environmental Protection Agency (EPA), have three functions: executive, in which they oversee programs; legislative, in which they issue regulations; and judicial, in which they penalize those who don't comply with their regulations. As with the independent agencies, the president appoints the leaders of these regulatory agencies, with Congressional approval. Some he can remove, others he cannot. Government corporations, like the U.S. Postal Service, receive federal funds and are operated by directors appointed by the president with Senate approval. *Presidential commissions* provide the president with recommendations in particular areas of interest, such as the Commission on Civil Rights. Some are permanent and others are temporary. The president appoints their members.

Only bureaucrats at the top level of bureaucrats are appointed. The other 90 percent are hired on their merit; that is, for the expertise in a particular area or for their ability to serve in staff positions). The merit system encourages nonpartisanship because the civil servants cannot be fired for political reasons. Because of the *Taft-Hartley Act of 1947,* they cannot strike, even if they are part of a union. In addition, the *Hatch Act of 1939* prevented them from working on campaigns, a restriction that has since been relaxed for all but the highest-ranking bureaucrats.

The federal bureaucracy's primary function is to implement policies made by the three branches of government. This does not mean that bureaucracy is simply a tool or extension of these institutions. Because congressional acts are general, there is immense discretion left in the implementation process; therefore, bureaucrats are making public policy through their *rulemaking* (deciding precisely how the law will work) and "street-level bureaucracy" (using discretion in the delivery of services or execution of their responsibilities).

Development of the Federal Bureaucracy: Politics and Administration

Patterson argues (p. 421) that bureaucracy has "two simultaneous but incompatible demands: that it administer programs fairly and competently and that it respond to partisan claims." In essence, the federal bureaucracy is expected to be both political and not political. It tries to do this by blending these two goals. Approaches to this blending have changed over time. The system today has features that promote each of the three expectations for bureaucracy: to be fair and competent, to respond to politics, and to be efficient.

The modern large bureaucracy tilts less toward the political than did the original *patronage system;* a patronage system is a bureaucracy with a large number of appointees. Initially, the patronage system resulted in a small, educated, wealthy elite serving for a long time. Andrew Jackson changed this by awarding jobs for shorter periods to partisans whom he wanted to reward and who he thought were more representative of common people. This was called a *spoils system* by some of his critics.

After the Industrial Revolution the economy expanded, and groups looked to the government for help. This facilitated an expansion of the federal government and its employees. The *Pendleton Act* of 1883 established the *civil service,* a *merit system* for acquiring government jobs. The act created the Civil Service Commission, which uses exams and qualifications for hiring bureaucrats. The number of positions that were filled through this system was small at first but grew during the Progressive Era, reaching 70 of federal employees in 1920. The number of federal jobs increased dramatically with the New Deal in the 1930s. Since 1978, two independent agencies have administered the civil service system, the Civil Service Commission and the Office of Personnel Management. The goal of a merit system is to have *neutral competence,* meaning that objective and not political standards dominate.

The system today retains many of the features of a merit system and some of the patronage system. It tries to deal with fragmentation by positioning the president to coordinate the institution's overall goals and processes. The development and expansion of the White House Office and the role of the president and the Office of Management and Budget are at the heart of this *executive leadership system.* The benefit of this system is that it is more efficient and responsive to an elected official and therefore theoretically more responsive to the public. The problem is that it has given more power to the president and hurt Congress's ability to check this power. It can also lead to agencies telling the president what he wants to hear rather than challenging him with other information and opinions.

The Bureaucracy's Power Imperative

Bureaucratic agencies seek political support to see that their priorities are carried out. This support may come from the president, who is the head of the branch they are in, but it can also come from Congress, the institution that authorizes their programs and appropriates the funds needed to carry these out. Regardless of what the president and Congress believe, bureaucrats see their agency's interests as being more important than others'. This is called the *agency point of view.* Loyalty comes from time spent in an agency and the training and experience that it took to get there. Bureaucrats' expertise, interest groups, and political support help them promote the agency point of view.

Having spent careers working in particular subject areas give bureaucrats the advantage of being specialists. Compared with other government officials who are generalists, they can understand the complexity of the issues and are deferred to by others who don't. Agencies also get support from their clientele groups, the special interests that get something from the programs. These groups can help the agencies pressure Congress for additional funds or to authorize new programs. Congressional committees and subcommittees can also be allies because their members often agree with the agency's priorities, and they benefit from a mutually supportive relationship. The president also needs agencies to accomplish the administration's goals; therefore, the president and the agencies can have reciprocal relationships.

Bureaucratic Accountability

Government bureaucracy tends to be a scapegoat for politicians and the public. One common perception is that the federal bureaucracy is inefficient. Not only does evidence fail to confirm this, but also efficiency is not the primary goal of government. Government tries to promote fairness; therefore, bureaucracy needs to be judged by that criterion. Efficiency and fairness do not always go hand in hand. Another criticism of bureaucracy is that it is undemocratic. To encourage *bureaucratic accountability,* other government officials conduct the difficult process of oversight.

Accountability through the Presidency

Limits on presidential control of bureaucracy include: the nature of the presidency, (bureaucrats "outlast" and outnumber the president), their statutory authority and clientele support, and the president's inability to act alone to eliminate their jobs, funding, or programs. There are tools that the president can use to lead the bureaucracy. These are: reorganization, appointments, and the budget.

Presidents try, with limited success, to streamline the fragmentation and size of the bureaucracy that makes it hard for them to coordinate through reorganization. Presidents also use their appointees to try to reign in bureaucratic independence and promote their points of view. Presidents are more successful doing this to some agencies than to others. Regulatory agencies have much discretion; therefore, the appointed heads of these can act boldly on the president's agenda. Despite the hundreds of appointments that a president makes (and would have a hard time keeping track of), these officials are outnumbered by thousands of career service workers. The Executive Office of the President, particularly the Office of Management and Budget, helps the president control the bureaucracy. The OMB reviews agencies' budget requests and reviews their proposals and regulations.

Accountability through Congress and the Courts

Congress's greatest power over the bureaucracy is the responsibility of authorizing and allocating funds to programs. Congress can also use its oversight role to make sure that congressional intent is being executed. Because this is such a big job and only one of many congressional tasks, the General Accounting Office (GAO) and the Congressional Budget Office (CBO) do much of the legwork. When they find discrepancies in bureaucratic spending and policy implementation, legislators follow up. Congress can also constrain bureaucrats' discretion through making laws specific or including expiration dates to programs, called sunset laws. Yet there are disincentives to taking these actions.

Agencies can be sued when people think that laws have been followed inappropriately. Then judges can order agencies to change what they are doing. This is uncommon, because the courts recognize the need for agency flexibility. Lawsuits are used, however, against the most egregious administrative rules.

Accountability within the Bureaucracy Itself

Whistle-blowing is one way that bureaucratic wrongdoing is revealed from within. It entails an employee reporting problems such as mismanagement or deceptions. Although a law protects whistle-blowers from punishment for coming forward, it is a professionally risky act. Therefore, many whistle-blowers are ex-bureaucrats.

Another way that accountability to the public is encouraged within the bureaucracy is through the demographic representativeness of the people working in the executive branch. While not entirely reflective of the race and gender of the American public, especially at the top levels, it is more diverse than the other branches of government.

Reinventing Government

President Bill Clinton tried to update and improve the administrative structure of the federal government through the National Performance Review. In addition to cutting the size of the bureaucracy (the number of workers and the amount of money it spends), it decentralized authority and encouraged a more output-focused (results) orientation. Agencies had to monitor and evaluate themselves using effectiveness standards. More power was given to lower-level bureaucrats. George W. Bush did not adhere to the model and discontinued it. It was just one in a history of efforts to make the bureaucracy more efficient, responsive, and accountable.

TAKE NOTE

This chapter is of moderate importance to the AP exam. Focus your attention on understanding what the bureaucracy is, generally how it is organized, and how presidents, Congress, and interest groups try to control it.

Observations from Past Exams

Material in this chapter falls under the "Institutions of National Government" topic, which is supposed to make up between 35 percent and 45 percent of the multiple-choice test questions. Questions about the bureaucracy focus on the relationships among it and the other institutions and linkages among the bureaucracy and public opinion, voters, interest groups, parties, the media, and subnational governments. An examination of past tests reveals a few questions about the bureaucracy.

There was only one multiple-choice question on bureaucracy on the last two released exams. It asked which office provided the principal staff for the president (the WHO). This question could also be answered from material in Chapter 12.

On tests from the last six years, there were five free-response questions in which information about the bureaucracy was relevant to the answers. Students could choose the bureaucracy as a policymaking institution to discuss for a question on interest groups on the 1999 exam. Another question from that year's test dealt with the methods and failures of congressional oversight of bureaucracy. An illustration-based question about budgetary barriers to new policy initiatives could also have included information about the bureaucracy. For the 2003 exam, an understanding of the bureaucracy could have informed an answer about the factors that influence presidential approval ratings. The 2004 exam asked about the formal and informal powers of the president in foreign policy and how they contribute to presidential advantage over Congress. Acceptable answers included those that described presidential use of bureaucracy.

What to Do with the Boxes

A number of boxes in this chapter provide helpful summaries of important information. The Cabinet Executive Departments are listed in Figure 13-1 (p. 417). Other executive agencies, commissions, and corporations are listed on Table 13-1 (p. 419). Table 13-2 (p. 426) summarizes well the weaknesses and strengths of three approaches to managing the bureaucracy. "The Budgetary Process" box (p. 435) describes the steps in a process asked about often on the test.

A useful preparation for the illustration-based questions is to try to write a summary for Figure 13-2 (p. 423), Figure 13-3 (p. 430), Figure 13-4 (p. 431), and Table 13-3 (p. 438) before you read or review the one provided under the title.

Although the question of whether the CIA played politics with information about Iraq discussed in the "Debating the Issues" box (p. 425) is probably too specific to be the focus of an AP test question, the dual responsibilities of the bureaucracy (to objectively collect and evaluate information and to serve the president) should be understood. This example illustrates the tension well. The "Liberty, Equality & Self-Government" box (p. 432) addresses an important question: how to keep unelected officials responsive to the public. The "Why Should I Care?" box (p. 433) and the "Global Perspective" box (p. 439) help debunk stereotypes about bureaucrats that you should avoid using in your free-response answers.

Because of the focus of the AP test, you do not need to know specific data in the "States in the Nation" box (p. 416) and the "How the United States Compares" box (p. 428).

Key Terms

Don't just memorize these terms. Understand what they mean and how they compare to other concepts. Be able to give examples of each.

Bureaucracy (p. 415)
Hierarchical authority (p. 415)
Job specialization (p. 415)
Formalized rules (p. 415)

Cabinet (executive) departments (p. 417)
Independent agencies (p. 418)
Regulatory agencies (p. 418)
Government corporations (p. 418)
Presidential commissions (p. 419)
Taft-Hartley Act of 1947 (p. 420)
Hatch Act of 1939 (p. 420)
Policy implementations (p. 420)
Rulemaking (p. 421)
Patronage system (p. 422)
Spoils system (p. 422)
Merit (civil service) system (p. 423)
Pendleton Act of 1883 (p. 423)
Neutral competence (p. 423)
Executive leadership system (p. 424)
Agency point of view (p. 427)
Clientele groups (p. 429)
Bureaucratic accountability (p. 431)
Whistle-blowing (p. 437)
Demographic representativeness (p. 438)

Making Connections to Previous Chapters

While there is little connection between the "Mass Politics" section and bureaucracy chapter, there are some connections to make with material in the "Foundations" section. First, an understanding of bureaucracy will help you make more sense of Chapter 1's bureaucratic-rule theory of power (p. 31). The discussion of the growth of national authority (pp. 86–88) helps explain the growth in the bureaucracy and its power. While Chapter 13 conveys a sense of how large the bureaucracy is, it would be helpful to look at Figure 3-2 (p. 91) again to put this number in perspective.

It would be useful to revisit two sections of Chapter 9 after learning about the bureaucracy. Page 291 describes how interest groups lobby agencies. Pages 292–93 describe iron triangles and subgovernments in which bureaucratic agencies play an essential part. Chapter 10's discussion about the Federal Communication Commission (p. 312) provides a nice illustration of how Congress passes laws and then establishes regulatory agencies to administer those laws. From Chapter 11, it is important to understand how Congress works with, and sometimes against, the bureaucracy through its committee system (pp. 351–54), its own agencies (p. 360), and its oversight role (pp. 365–68).

Remember that the president's role as "chief executive" (p. 376) includes managing the bureaucracy. The role grew with the increased responsibilities of the federal government (pp. 380–81). The "Staffing the Presidency" section (pp. 391–97) could just as easily been placed in Chapter 13 because it deals with the part of the bureaucracy most closely controlled by the president, the Executive Office of the President. Many of Chapter 12's points about the cabinet and the difficulty presidents have controlling appointees (pp. 394–97) are elaborated on in this chapter.

SAMPLE QUESTIONS

Multiple-Choice Questions

1. Which of the following is a characteristic of bureaucracy?
   I.   hierarchical authority
   II. job specialization
   III. formalized rules
   IV. inaccountability

   a. Only I
   b. Only I and II
   c. Only I, II, and III
   d. I, II, III, and IV
   e. Only I, III, and IV

2. Which of the following groups in the executive branch would be least accountable to the president?
   a. Department of Defense
   b. cabinet
   c. National Security Council
   d. Securities and Exchange Commission
   e. Executive Office of the President

3. Which is the most common source of power for a lower-level bureaucrat?
   a. strikes or threats of striking
   b. threatening to quit
   c. the spoils system
   d. whistle-blowing
   e. policy expertise

4. What is the primary function of executive departments?
   a. to follow the president's orders
   b. to follow Congress's orders
   c. to follow electoral mandates
   d. to implement policies made by the president, Congress, and the courts
   e. to evaluate policies made by the president, Congress, and the courts

5. An unresponsive bureaucracy is most likely to result from which of the following?
   a. patronage system
   b. merit system
   c. executive leadership system
   d. presidential appointments
   e. spoils system

6. Which of the following is an example of a "clientele group"?
   a. Department of Agriculture
   b. Central Intelligence Agency
   c. Commission to Strengthen Social Security
   d. American Medical Association
   e. U.S. Postal Service

7. Which of the following is most helpful for keeping the bureaucracy accountable to Congress?
   a. Office of Management and Budget
   b. General Accounting Office
   c. regulatory agencies
   d. the Supreme Court
   e. periodic elections

8. What is the most likely cause for the change demonstrated in this figure?

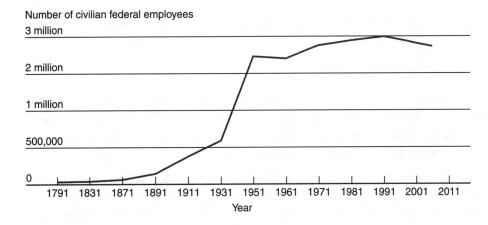

Number of civilian federal employees

   a. instituting the spoils system
   b. instituting the patronage system
   c. the increased role of White House staff
   d. a population explosion
   e. New Deal programs

Multiple-Choice Questions That Link Chapter 13 to Lessons in Earlier Chapters

9. The term "rule-making" refers to:
   a. the decisions about how laws will work in practice
   b. the entire process that a bill goes through to become a law
   c. executive orders of the president
   d. the work done in Congressional committees on proposed legislation
   e. the interaction between interest groups, Congress, and the bureaucracy

10. Which of America's core political ideals is least evident in bureaucracy?
   a. hard work
   b. equality
   c. self-government
   d. efficiency
   e. fairness

Multiple-Choice Answers

1. C; 2. D; 3. E; 4. D; 5. B; 6. D; 7. B; 8. E; 9. A; and 10. C

Free-Response Questions

1. There are five general forms of administrative organizations in the executive branch. They are: cabinet departments, independent agencies, regulatory agencies, government corporations, and presidential commissions.

   a. Provide examples of three of these, clearly identifying which kind of organization each is, and describe the role that each plays in policymaking. (3 points)

   b. Which of these three is most likely to be an instrument of presidential power? Explain why. (2 points)

   c. What are clientele groups? Describe an example of how a clientele group would affect one of the administrative organizations you described in "a." (2 points)

   This question is worth seven points.

   Part "a" is worth three points. Correctly naming an example of one of the forms and accurately describing its role earns each point. See pages 417 and 419 for acceptable examples. Note that the descriptions do not have to be extensive, but they need to convey the nature of the form of organization selected.

   Part "b" is worth two points. Identifying a cabinet or commission rather than independent agencies, regulatory agencies, or corporations is worth one point. Explaining why the president would have more influence over the former is worth another point. Acceptable explanations include: appointment process (without confirmation from Congress), ability to dismiss appointees, goals of the president to control the group and his ability to use the EOP to oversee those groups, and the type of issues dealt with (more presidential influence in foreign affairs than domestic policies).

   Part "c" is worth two points. One point is earned for correctly describing clientele groups (p. 429). The second point is earned by describing an example of how one would affect the administrative organization selected. This example can be hypothetical.

2. Patterson argues (p. 421) that bureaucracy has "two simultaneous but incompatible demands: that it administer programs fairly and competently and that it respond to partisan claims."

   a. Describe a feature of the bureaucracy that enhances its ability to administer programs fairly. Explain how the feature does this. (2 points)

   b. Describe a feature of the bureaucracy that enhances its ability to respond to partisan claims. Explain how the feature does this. (2 points)

   c. Over the last two hundred years, has the bureaucracy become more efficient or more partisan? Describe this change. (2 points)

   This question is worth six points.

   Part "a" is worth two points. One point is earned for identifying and correctly describing a feature. Acceptable features include: hierarchical authority, job specialization, formalized rules, independence from president and Congress (regulatory agencies, independent agencies), civil service with merit selection, neutral competence, congressional oversight of a nonpartisan nature, presidential reorganization of a nonpartisan nature, budgeting of a nonpartisan nature, whistle-blowing, and lawsuits. The second point is earned for explaining how it helps the bureaucracy administer programs fairly.

Part "b" is worth two points. One point is earned for identifying and correctly describing a feature. Acceptable features include: presidential appointments at the top, executive leadership system, presidential use of OMB, selection of facts to suit presidential preferences, Congressional oversight of a partisan nature, Congressional funding of a partisan nature, presidential reorganization of a partisan nature, and budgeting of a partisan nature. The second point is earned for explaining how it helps the bureaucracy respond to partisan claims.

Part "c" is worth two points. One point is awarded for saying that it has become more efficient. One point is earned by describing this change from a spoils system to a meritocracy.

CHAPTER FOURTEEN

The Federal Judicial System: Applying the Law

SUMMARY

This chapter describes the judiciary and its role in policymaking. The chapter illustrates how the U.S. judicial system is organized in the U.S., how cases come to and are evaluated by the courts, and the sources of and limitations on the court's discretion. Debates over how judges should execute their power and the proper role of courts in a democratic system are central to the chapter.

The Federal Judicial System

The U.S. Constitution says little about this branch of government. Article III established a Supreme Court and gave Congress the authority to set up lower courts. It established the process by which federal judges are selected (they are nominated by the president and confirmed by the Senate), but set no specific qualifications for their selection or dismissal.

The Supreme Court of the United States

The nation's top court is the Supreme Court of the United States. It has nine justices, including one chief justice. It has both *original* and *appellate jurisdiction*: some of the cases that the Court has authority to hear originate there, such as those involving foreign diplomats and including disputes between state governments, while others are appealed to the Supreme Court from lower federal courts or state courts. The vast majority of the cases heard by the Supreme Court fall under its appellate jurisdiction. Like other appellate courts, it does not hold trials. The Supreme Court evaluates cases by applying the Constitution, laws, and consulting its previous rulings, called precedents.

The Supreme Court has much discretion in selecting the cases it will hear, and the Justices choose to give full hearings to only a small percentage of the cases in which an appeal is sought (about 100 out of 7,000 annually). They decide another 100 or 200 cases without full hearings and issue *per curiam* decisions on those. A per curiam decision is one that is unsigned and delivers the facts and decision without elaboration. Three-fourths of the cases that receive a hearing are reversed, meaning that the lower courts' decision is changed. Losing parties in lower courts ask the Supreme Court to hear their cases. If four Supreme Court justices want to hear the case, the Supreme Court issues a *writ of certiorari* that tells the lower court to send up the documents. The Justices are more likely to issue a writ of certiorari if the U.S. government is a party in the dispute, the case involves a "substantial legal issue" or a "major constitutional issue," and if the lower courts are in disagreement over the issue.

After being given a writ of certiorari, the lower court sends up documents to the Supreme Court. Lawyers submit *briefs*, or written arguments, and each side presents its case to the Court in 30 minutes during *oral arguments*. Then the Supreme Court justices meet alone in a *judicial conference* to discuss and vote on the case. The decisions reached by the Court in conference are expressed through opinions. Opinions explain the rationale behind the decision. The "winning side" issues a *majority opinion* if there are a majority of justices who agree on the legal basis for the decision or a *plurality opinion,* when a majority does not agree with the reasoning but does agree with the decision. The person who will write the majority opinion is selected by the chief justice, when the chief justice is in the majority, or by the most senior member of the majority, when the chief is in the minority. Decisions can also have *concurring opinions,* which explain the rationale among members of the majority decision who have different reasons for voting that way, and *dissenting opinions,* in which members of the "losing side" explain their rationale. Until the decision and opinions are reported publicly, the justices may revise the opinions and can change their votes.

U.S. District Courts

The more than 90 federal district courts are located within states. Some states have as many as four district courts. Most federal cases begin and end in these courts. District courts are supposed to follow precedents established by the Supreme Court. Sometimes this does not happen because of misinterpretation, inapplicability of precedents, and ambiguity in precedents.

U.S. Court of Appeals

Appeals from district courts go to one of twelve general U.S. courts of appeals. One of these serves Washington, D.C., while each of the others hears cases from a "circuit" of more than one state. Each court of appeals has between four and twenty-six judges. Most cases are decided by panels of three; occasionally all of the judges in a circuit sit together (*en banc*) to resolve a case. Decisions are based on a review of the lower court's records, not by holding new trials. Fewer than 1 percent of these decisions are given another hearing by the Supreme Court.

Special U.S. Courts

Cases can also reach the Supreme Court through appeals from other federal specialty courts. These include the U.S. Claims Court, the U.S. Court of International Trade, and the U.S. Court of Military Appeals.

State Courts

Each state has its own court systems with hierarchies similar to the federal system. This is where 95 percent of the United States' legal cases are heard. Cases can sometimes move from the state system to the federal system if a constitutional issue is at stake. Therefore, the highest court in each state can still have its decisions reversed by the U.S. Supreme Court. This illustrates how the Supreme Court is the final authority and demonstrates the idea of national supremacy.

Federal Court Appointees

Federal judges and justices on the Supreme Court are political actors. This can be seen through the selection process and the discretion and authority of their decisions.

Selection of Supreme Court Justices and Federal Judges

Like all federal court appointments, the Supreme Court justices are nominated by the president and confirmed by the Senate. Within the Senate, the Judiciary Committee recommends confirmation or rejection of the president's nominees to the full Senate. For Supreme Court nominees, this process is typically more extensive and more visible than it is for other judicial appointments. The importance of the Supreme Court dictates that interest groups, the media, and the public will pay more attention to the qualifications and philosophies of these nominees. Although the Senate has rejected 20 percent of presidential nominees, most of these rejections occurred before 1900. The last nominee to be rejected in the Senate was in 1987. However, the recent case of Harriet Miers, which happened too recently to appear in the book, illustrates that some nominees who might have been rejected by the Senate withdraw from the process before this occurs.

Presidents now appoint hundreds of lower court judges. They rely on advisors and officials in the Justice Department to review their choices. When a district judgeship comes available in a state with a senator or senators of the same party as the president, the president will consult with them. If the president does not make this sort of consultation, then the other senators will not confirm the nomination out of courtesy to the senator from that state. This custom dates back to the mid-1800s; it is called *senatorial courtesy.*

Justices and Judges as Political Officials

There is no guarantee that appointees will make decisions that the president who appointed them would prefer. Yet, with some memorable examples to the contrary, this is typically what happens. There are visible partisan patterns to judicial decision making—Republican appointees vote differently than Democratic appointees. Democratic presidents Carter and Clinton appointed a higher percentage of female and racial minorities to courts than Reagan and the Bushes did. White males are still over-represented relative to their numbers in the general population. Although judges do not have to have any particular prior experience, today most have worked as judges or in the attorney general's office, or both.

The Nature of Judicial Decision Making

By constitutional design and because of the nature of legal institutions as well as political ones, judges have less discretion than elected officials. Judges can only make decisions on cases that come before them. They cannot request that cases be brought before them or give advisory opinions. Therefore, they do not initiate policy decisions. Their decisions are legally binding only on the litigants in that case. It is up to other political actors to take those decisions and apply them to other similarly situated people or groups. Judges must consider the facts of cases, laws, and previous decisions.

The *facts of a case* are the "relevant circumstances of the legal dispute or offense" (p. 462) as determined by trial courts. They determine which laws are relevant to the decision. The laws of a case also constrain judicial decision making. Judges cannot change the laws or intentionally misinterpret them in order to make decisions that they prefer. Instead, they interpret the Constitution, *statutory laws* (laws passed by legislatures), administrative laws (regulations from the executive branch) or treaties. Judicial discretion comes in when these are vague or in conflict with each other.

Whereas statutory laws are those passed by Congress or subnational legislators regarding illegal action (*criminal law*) or noncriminal disputes (*civil law*), *common law* are the previous court rulings. The *principle of stare decisis* is that previous decisions, called *precedents*, should be upheld so that people and institutions can reasonably predict what the laws mean when the courts apply them. This principle constrains judges' discretion.

Political Influences on Judicial Decisions

The Constitution and laws do not always provide clear answers to the myriad disputes that come before judges. Therefore, judges use their own judgments when deciding some cases. Precedents, too, are not absolute constraints, as the Courts can reverse them. Therefore, it is important to consider the factors outside and inside the courts that influence decision making.

Even though judges are not elected, they are not completely divorced from the public. The Court's reputation and concern with public compliance can influence their rulings. Interest groups bring lawsuits to the Court and file amicus curiae briefs on cases they support or oppose.

The public can also influence the judiciary through its elected federal officials: Congress and the president. Congress can establish federal courts and change the number of judges. It can pass new legislation that circumvents the Court's interpretation of previous laws. The executive branch can take an aggressive or lackadaisical approach to enforcing judicial decisions. It can bring cases to the Court. The appointment process is another way that elected officials have a hand in the Court.

Supreme Court decisions that are not unanimous tend to find Republican appointees voting against Democratic ones. The effect of partisanship can be seen in the *Bush v. Gore* decision that stopped recounts in Florida and ended the dispute over the outcome of the 2000 presidential election in favor of George W. Bush. Judges tend not to change their views over the course of their appointment. Therefore, the surest way to change the direction of the Court is to change its membership.

Judicial Power and Democratic Government

How much power and discretion should unelected judges have in a democratic system? On the one hand, we want the Court to keep politicians from getting out of control. On the other, we want power in a representative democracy to be in the hands of elected officials whom the public can dismiss rather than appointed politicians with life terms. The Court's power to declare congressional, executive, and state and local officials' decisions unconstitutional (*judicial review*) in a sense puts it above elected officials. Although the Supreme Court has used judicial review more than 1,000 times, it has rarely—less than 10 percent of the time—been used in opposition to federal elected officials. The question of the judiciary's legitimacy has become more heated as the judiciary has advanced broad policy reforms over time. As the role of government has increased, so has the judiciary's. This has been controversial. The two doctrines that disagree over the proper role of the Court are *judicial restraint* and *judicial activism.*

Those who believe in the doctrine of judicial restraint think that the judiciary should defer to elected officials by applying laws and precedents rather than looking for new ways to interpret them. They believe that this approach best reflects the principles of self-government and is the best way to preserve the *legitimacy* of the Court and *compliance* to its rulings. Those who believe in the doctrine of judicial activism think the judiciary should have a freer hand and can develop new legal principles even if they are at odds with decisions of elected officials. For example, social justice is not explicitly discussed in the Constitution, but some activist judges claim that the philosophy is implied and can be the basis for decisions.

There are three common misperceptions about judicial activism: first, that it originated in the 1960s during Chief Justice Earl Warren's Court; second, that it is inherently liberal; and third, that it indicates that judges are completely divorced from the laws and the Constitution. These are not correct. Judicial activism can be exercised by liberals or conservatives. While the activism during the Warren Court was generally liberal, in the late 1800s and early 1900s conservative activist judges reversed Congressional regulation of the economy. More recently, conservative justices have been activists on questions of federalism. It is also important to remember that all judges are constrained by laws and case facts. The differences between judges who are considered activists and those who are not lies in the degree to which they will challenge elected officials' judgments and exert their own judgments on what they believe is meant, but not precisely said, in the Constitution, laws, and precedents.

TAKE NOTE

This is an important chapter for the AP exam. It is essential to understand how and why the judiciary is both a legal and a political institution.

Observations from Past Exams

Material in this chapter falls under the "Institutions of National Government" topic, which is supposed to make up between 35 percent and 45 percent of the multiple-choice test questions. Questions about the judiciary focus on the relationships between the judiciary and other institutions and linkages among the judiciary and public opinion, voters, interest groups, parties, the media, and subnational governments. An examination of past tests reveals many questions about the judiciary.

There were seven questions on the judiciary on the most recently released multiple-choice AP U.S. Government and Politics test, from 2002. They asked about what typically happens when the lower court decisions are appealed, what amicus curiae briefs are, why most justices have political experience, what the doctrine of original intent holds, and on "checks" on federal courts' power. Two of the seven questions provided illustrations and asked for responses. One asked students to interpret a cartoon about presidential influence through appointment of justices. The other presented data on the race and gender of judicial appointments for four presidents. There were three multiple-choice questions about the federal judiciary on the 1999 exam. One of these was about why Supreme Court justices were given tenure "subject to good behavior." The other two dealt with the Court's caseload, one about jurisdiction and the other about its discretion.

Understanding this chapter would have helped students successfully answer free-response questions on four of the most recent exams. The 1999 and 2004 tests had similar questions that asked about how specific interest groups try to influence policymaking. Knowledge about the Court could have been used here. In the 1999 question, students could pick one "national-level policymaking institution," which could be the Court, and describe what characteristic or resource from this group would influence the choice. The 2004 question more specifically cued students to the Court by asking for a description of litigation as a technique for interest groups and why groups would use it. The 2000 exam asked about the Supreme Court nomination process. Specifically, it asked how three characteristics of nominees are politically relevant and how interest groups try to influence the appointment process. The 2005 exam asked how the Supreme Court is insulated from public opinion and what factors keep it from going too far from public opinion.

What to Do with the Boxes

The chapter includes helpful summaries of important information from the text. The first is the types of Supreme Court opinions (p. 451). The second is the "Sources of Law That Constrain the Decisions of the Federal Judiciary" (p. 463). The third is a table listing "Significant Supreme Court Cases" and their rulings (p. 468). The visual representation of the federal judicial system (p. 452) is a helpful illustration. The "Liberty, Equality & Self-Government" box on "Judicial Review" (p. 469) provides a nice review of an important concept and offers some questions that relate to lessons from earlier in the book. The "Is the Supreme Court Suited to the Making of Broad Social Policy?" box (p. 473) does a better job than the text of the chapter in evaluating the Court's capacity to advance policy changes and comparing that to the other two branches.

Other boxes include information that might help on the test, even though it is unlikely to be asked about specifically. First, the "How the United States Compares" box (p. 471) focuses on an important concept—judicial power. Even though you do not need to know about judicial systems in other countries, this box reviews features of the U.S. system that are essential to understand. While the detail in the "Debating the Issues: Should All the Florida Ballots Have Been Counted?" box (p. 447) is not likely to be required for the AP test, it is useful to see sections from a majority opinion and a dissenting opinion to get a better sense of how the justices express the reasoning behind their decisions.

The "Why Should I Care?" box about judicial appointments (p. 459) reviews some information about the role of the Court and judicial decision-making. The table naming the justices (p. 460) is out of date since the death of Chief Justice Rehnquist and the retirement of Sandra Day O'Connor. They have been replaced by Bush appointees John Roberts and Samuel Alito. More important than memorizing the justices' names is to observe that most of the members have served a long time on the Court, were appointed by Republican presidents, and had prior judicial experience. This is also true of the two newest appointees, both of whom previously served on U.S. Circuit Courts of Appeal. A useful preparation for the illustration-based questions on the test is to try to write a summary for Figure 14-1 (p. 449) and Figure 14-3 (p. 461) before you read or review the one provided under the title. Try to come up with arguments for why the data look the way they do.

Because of the focus of the AP test, you do not need to focus on the Global Perspectives box about the International Criminal Court (p. 454) or the state variation in selecting judges (p. 455). It is important to understand that state and federal court systems differ and that all federal judges are appointed.

Key Terms

Don't just memorize these terms. Understand what they mean and how they compare to other concepts. Be able to give examples of each.

Jurisdiction (p. 448)
Original jurisdiction (p. 448)
Appellate jurisdiction (p. 448)
Precedent (p. 448, 463–64, 464)
Writ of certiorari (p. 448)
Per curiam (pp. 448, 451)

Solicitor general (p. 449)
Oral arguments (p. 449)
Briefs (p. 449)
Judicial conference (p. 450)
Decision (p. 450)
Opinion (p. 450)
Majority opinion (p. 450, 451)
Plurality opinion (p. 450, 451)
Concurring opinion (p. 450, 451)
Dissenting opinion (p. 451)
U.S. district courts (pp. 451–52)
U.S. court of appeals (pp. 452–53)
En banc (p. 453)
Special U.S. courts (p. 453)
Senatorial courtesy (p. 458)
Facts (of a court case) (p. 462)
Laws (of a court case) (p. 462)
Criminal law (p. 462)
Civil law (p. 462)
Statutory law (p. 463)
Administrative law (p. 463)
Philosophy of stare decisis (p. 463)
Amicus curiae (p. 465)
Equal-protection clause (p. 467; review this on p. 162)
Judicial review (p. 467, 469, review this on p. 58)
Legitimacy (of judicial power) (pp. 468, 470)
Judicial restraint (p. 469)
Compliance (p. 470)
Judicial activism (p. 471)

Making Connections to Previous Chapters

The chapter does a good job of reminding you that the federal judicial system is part of a larger political system. To reinforce this lesson, it is useful to think about material in this chapter in relation to information you have already learned about the executive branch (Chapter 12 and Chapter 13), interest groups (Chapter 9), and the constitutional foundations (Chapter 2 and Chapter 3).

Consider how "Factors in Presidential Leadership" (pp. 397–409) relate to the judicial appointment process (pp. 456–60) and political influences on Court decisions (pp. 464–67). Think about the ways that the president can try to influence the Court and how and why these approaches are limited. For example, the solicitor general (p. 449) in the Department of Justice brings cases that coincide with the president's agenda to the Court, but the Court still decides whether to hear the cases.

The judicial appointment process (pp. 446–47, 459) is a nice example of checks and balances among the three branches of government set up by the Constitution (p. 54). *Judicial review,* discussed in Chapter 2 (pp. 54–58) is explained in more detail in this chapter. It is essential to understand how judicial review works, how and when it originated, why it is important for judicial power, and how it illustrates "separated institutions sharing power" (pp. 53–56).

You can also see connections between the section on "Judicial Power and Democratic Government" (pp. 467–74) and civil liberties (Chapter 4) and civil rights (Chapter 5). Many of the Court decisions included in this chapter should be familiar to you. More information is provided here on must-know cases like *Gideon v. Wainwright* and *Miranda v. Arizona*. Use the table on page 468 to review some of these.

The small section on "Lobbying the Courts" in Chapter 9 (pp. 291–92) is fleshed out in the discussion on pages 465–66. Missing from the list of lobbying techniques from Chapter 9 are two described here: filing *amicus curiae* briefs and litigating. Excerpts from amicus curiae briefs are found in the box about gerrymandering (p. 343) in Chapter 11. It is also important to think about the role that interest groups can play in influencing the appointment process.

SAMPLE QUESTIONS

Multiple-Choice Questions

1. The *Bush v. Gore* decision illustrates:
   a. the Supreme Court's power of judicial review over the president
   b. the Supreme Court's power of judicial review over the Congress
   c. the Supreme Court's power of judicial review over state legislatures
   d. the Supreme Court exercising judicial restraint
   e. the Supreme Court exercising judicial activism

2. The Supreme Court selects most of the cases that it hears. What is an exception to this?
   a. cases that the solicitor general appeals to the Court
   b. cases that deal with constitutional issues
   c. cases in which the opposing parties are state governments
   d. cases in which the presidential candidates are parties
   e. cases in which there are no precedents

3. What is the difference between a per curiam decision and a majority decision?
   a. Per curiam is unanimous and a majority opinion might not be.
   b. Per curiam is unanimous and a majority opinion never is.
   c. Per curiam is unsigned and a majority opinion is signed by a single justice (the one who wrote it).
   d. Per curiam is unsigned and a majority opinion is signed by the justices who agreed with the opinion.
   e. Per curiam expresses the reasoning behind the minority's opinion and the majority opinion expresses the reasoning behind the majority's opinion.

4. Which of the following is true of U.S. Courts of Appeals?
   a. They are where most federal court cases end.
   b. They hold new trials for cases appealed from the district courts.
   c. There is at least one in every state and as many as four in some states.
   d. Their jurisdiction is defined in the U.S. Constitution.
   e. They correct legal errors made by district courts.

5. Senatorial courtesy:
   a. is the process described in the Constitution in which the Senate must approve presidential judicial nominations for them to get appointed
   b. is the process (not described in the Constitution) in which the Senate must approve presidential judicial nominations for them to get appointed
   c. is the term used to describe the tradition in which Senators consider the president's preferences when they appoint judges
   d. is the term used to describe the tradition in which Senators defer to the president's preferences when they confirm his judicial nominations
   e. is the term used to describe the tradition in which president defers to specific senators when nominating district court judges

6. The figure below indicates that:

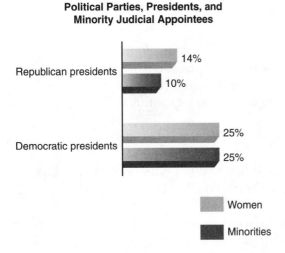

a. there are more women and more blacks in the Democratic Party than there are in the Republican Party
   b. prior to the election of Jimmy Carter, there was no sizable difference in the demographics of presidential judicial appointees
   c. Republican presidents have appointed fewer women to the Supreme Court than Democrats have
   d. Democratic presidents are more susceptible to interest-group pressure than Republicans are
   e. Republican presidents appoint more women than racial minorities to federal judgeships

7. A Supreme Court ruling is:
   a. binding on the parties involved in the case and all other parties in similar disputes
   b. binding on the parties involved in the case and some other parties in similar disputes
   c. binding on the parties involved in the case and no other parties
   d. not binding unless the president or Congress agrees with the ruling
   e. not binding even when the president or Congress agrees with the ruling

8. Why do votes on the Supreme Court often divide along political or ideological lines?
   a. Ambiguity in existing laws permits justices the discretion to use their own political beliefs in deciding cases.
   b. The justices are responsive to the president who appointed them because they are worried about impeachment.
   c. The justices are responsive to the president who appointed them because they feel like they "owe him."
   d. The justices disagree about the proper role of the Court, with some adhering to judicial activism and others to judicial restraint.
   e. The justices are responsive to public opinion because they worry about reelection.

Multiple-Choice Questions That Link Chapter 14 to Lessons in Earlier Chapters

9. Which of the following cases demonstrates judicial activism in the area of procedural due process?
   a. *Gideon v. Wainwright*
   b. *Marbury v. Madison*
   c. *McCulloch v. Maryland*
   d. *Gitlow v. New York*
   e. *Scalia v. Souter*

10. Amicus curiae briefs are:
   a. a form of inside lobbying that attempts to influence the Court's agenda
   b. a form of inside lobbying that attempts to influence the Court's decisions
   c. a form of outside lobbying that attempts to influence the Court's reputation
   d. a form of outside lobbying that attempts to influence the Court's decisions
   e. a form of outside lobbying that attempts to influence the Court's agenda

Multiple-Choice Answers

1. E; 2. C; 3. D; 4. E; 5. E; 6. E; 7. C; 8. A; 9. A; and 10. B

Free-Response Questions

1. Supreme Court justices are political actors, yet their power is constrained in some ways.

   a. Identify and describe two legal constraints on justices' discretion. (2 points)

   b. Identify and describe a political constraint on justices' discretion. (1 point)

   c. Identify and describe a factor that allows justices to exercise discretion. Provide an example of a decision that demonstrates this power and explain how it demonstrates this. (3 points)

   The question is worth six points.

   Part "a" is worth two points. One point is earned for each of the constraints. Acceptable constraints include: stare decisis and legal precedents, standing, civil laws, criminal laws, the Constitution and constitutional laws, and administrative regulations.

Part "b" is worth one point. One point is earned for identifying and describing a political factor that constrains judicial discretion. Acceptable constraints include: public expectations, concerns for institutional legitimacy, ability of Congress to alter laws that decisions are based on, and concern for enforcement.

Part "c" is worth three points. One point is earned for each factor that allows for judicial discretion. Acceptable factors include: ability to reverse precedent, ability to interpret ambiguous laws, can choose among cases dealing with different aspects of a decision to use as precedent, judicial activism (developing new legal principles), lack of fear of reprisal since they are appointed for life and not typically impeached on the basis of the decisions they make. The second point is earned for identifying a case that demonstrates judicial power. The third point is earned for explaining how the case illustrates judicial power. Acceptable cases are found in Chapters 2, 3, 4, and 14. NOTE: Answers cannot earn the third point without having the second.

2. a. Describe the formal, constitutionally defined process by which justices are selected for the Supreme Court. (1 point)

    b. Describe the way that interest groups, media, or public opinion try to influence this process. (1 point)

    c. Explain how the goal of self-government is manifest in the process of selection. (2 points)

    d. Explain how the goal of limited government is manifest in the process of selection. (2 points)

This question is worth six points.

Part "a" is worth one point for accurately describing the process of presidential nomination and Senate confirmation.

Part "b" is worth one point for correctly describing the way that one of these factors influences the process. Acceptable answers include: advertising, letter-writing campaigns, or media's watchdog role, all of which persuade the public to pressure politicians through demonstrations, letters, calls, etc.; advertising, letter-writing campaigns, or the media's watchdog role, all aimed at persuading Congress or the president directly; public opinion expressed through polls that persuade politicians.

Part "c" is worth two points. Points are awarded for correctly applying the concept of self-government from Chapter 2 to the appointment process. Acceptable answers need to demonstrate an understanding of the term "self-government" by including any explanation of the indirect effect of the public on who is nominated and/or confirmed. A general explanation is worth one point; a more detailed explanation is worth two.

Part "d" is worth two points. Points are awarded for correctly applying the concept of limited government from Chapter 2 to the appointment process. Acceptable answers need to demonstrate an understanding of the term "limited government" by including an explanation of how responsibility for appointment is shared rather than being in the hands of the president or Congress alone. A general explanation is worth one point; a more detailed explanation is worth two.

CHAPTER FIFTEEN

Economic and Environmental Policy: Contributing to Prosperity

SUMMARY

Chapter 15 begins the section on government policy. Economic and environmental policy areas are discussed first, with an emphasis on how the *policy process* works. A major lesson from this section is that policy is piecemeal and tends to react to problems rather than be overarching and forward-thinking. The policy process involves interaction among many different political actors who develop, change, and ultimately accept or reject policy proposals. The economic policy process is played out through fiscal and monetary policies.

Through economic policy, the government promotes business interests. Government also places restrictions on businesses through regulations that protect the environment. Through taxing and spending (fiscal policy) and decisions about the money supply (monetary policy), the government tries to promote economic prosperity, growth, and stability.

Government as Regulator of the Economy

In many ways, the government regulates the *economy* ("a system of production and consumption of goods and services that are allocated through exchange" among producers and customers, p. 482). As a regulator of the economy, government acts to promote both *efficiency* and *equity*. Today's economic system is a mixture of public and private controls, somewhere between Adam Smith's *laissez-faire doctrine*, which advocated predominantly private control of the economy, and Karl Marx's collective economy, in which workers own production and control the economy through their government. In the current mixed economic system, government *regulation* puts restrictions on how private businesses act but does so within limits.

Efficiency through Government Intervention

The degree of *efficiency* can be understood in these terms: the greater the output (goods and services) from a given amount of input (labor), the more efficient the process. Government strives to make the economy more efficient through regulations on business. Restraint of trade is one area that government regulates to promote efficiency. This began with the Interstate Commerce Act (1887), which regulated railroads. Today, many agencies, including the Food and Drug Administration and Federal Trade Commission, regulate business competition. These agencies strive to maintain market incentives for businesses while protecting the public from abuse. For example, government may prohibit mergers or require large companies to divest, or it may regulate marketing practices that stifle competition. Most penalties that government issues to firms that violate restraint of trade practices are financial penalties.

Government also strives to reduce inefficiencies by trying to prevent businesses from burdening society by wasting society's resources. A business that fails to pay the entire cost of production (*externalities*) is burdening society. One externality is the cost of damaging the environment. The Clean Air Act of 1963 and the Water Quality Act of 1965 are efforts to discourage corporate polluting and to pass the cost of this damage on to the companies. The Environmental Protection Agency was created in 1970 to monitor compliance with environmental regulations. Government can add to inefficiency at times through *overregulation.* Excessive burdens on business from the government can increase the cost of producing goods. *Deregulation* is a response to overregulation. The Airlines Deregulation Act in 1977 lifted government controls on airfares and resulted in more competitive ticket prices. This success led to instituting deregulation measures on other types of businesses, such as the banking and trucking industries. Deregulation can have unintended consequences, such as the Enron scandal. Enron was able to falsely inflate its earnings and drive up the price in its stock partly because of the lack of government regulation on accounting procedures and practices.

Equity through Government Intervention

Equity can be defined as a situation in which all parties involved in a transaction receive fair outcomes. The Food and Drug Administration, created in 1907, was an early example of an agency created to protect the public. The New Deal instituted other protections for investors, savers, and labor through the Securities and Exchange Act of 1934, the Banking Act of 1934, and the Labor Standards Act of 1938. The greatest number of reforms involving equity occurred in the sixties and seventies when ten federal agencies were created to protect the public and workers from business abuses. An example was the Consumer Product Safety Commission.

The Politics of Regulatory Policy

In response to changing national conditions, there have been three eras of regulation in the twentieth century: the Progressive Era, the New Deal era, and the "new social regulation" era of the sixties and seventies. The regulatory agencies created during the first two eras tended to be narrow in scope and regulated specific industries such as trucking and banking. Early regulatory agencies often worked together with the industries that they supervised, developing policies that greatly benefited business. The later regulatory agencies, such as the Environmental Protection Agency (EPA), have much broader scopes of control and cover more than one industry. It is much harder for industries regulated by an agency like the EPA to influence agency policy because so many types of businesses are targeted.

Government as Protector of the Environment

Pages 492–95 discuss ways in which government acts as a protector of the environment. Environmental protection by the government is a relatively recent phenomenon, beginning in the 1960s with the 1963 Clean Water Act and the 1965 Water Quality Act and continuing with the creation of the EPA in 1970.

Conservationism: The Older Wave

Early government protections of the environment concentrated on land preservation. The national park system, managed by the National Park Service, and the creation and management of national forests by the U.S. Forest Service are examples of this type of effort. Even though the government acted to preserve parks and forests, these lands are still managed according to a "dual use" policy that allows private interests to harvest resources on land owned by the government. For example, the government leases the timber rights in forests.

Environmentalism: The Newer Wave

The 1960s saw a new wave of environmentalism, culminating in 1970 with Earth Day and the creation of the Environmental Protection Agency. The EPA initially raised the ire of businesses because of the number of regulations it was issuing. As the economy slumped in the early 1970s, the public and the government recognized that there was a substantial cost in having so many environmental regulations. Thus, the focus of the agency shifted to ensuring compliance with existing laws and regulations rather than advocating for or creating new ones. Environmental regulation today enjoys strong public support, but there is still controversy over the extent of problems, the economic cost, and the potential of domestic policies to address worldwide problems.

Government as Promoter of Economic Interests

Even government agencies that are supposed to regulate business often promote their interests. They do this by providing services such loans and tax breaks. The most help government gives businesses is providing them with an educated workforce and transportation infrastructure such as roads, waterways, and airports.

Labor interests received little promotion by the government in the nineteenth century, as seen in court rulings and government action to break up strikes. This changed during the Roosevelt administration. For example, the National Labor Relations Act of 1935 gave workers the right to bargain collectively with employers and barred discrimination against unions. Other significant assistance to labor included minimum-wage laws and nondiscriminatory hiring practices. However, due to the individualistic culture of the United States, the U.S. government does not promote labor as much as its European counterparts.

As the major business in America, agriculture was assisted by government policies with the Homestead Act of 1862. It opened government lands to settlement, provided that the land was farmed for five years. Most assistance has occurred in the form of crop subsidies, which artificially raise crop prices, and crop allocations, which place limits on the amounts of a crop which can be raised in a given year. Legislation was passed in 1996 to decrease crop subsidies, and the resultant slump in the farm economy led to the reinstatement of many subsidies in the 2002 Farm Bill.

Fiscal Policy: Government as Manager of Economy, I

Fiscal policy involves the process of formulating policies and applying them. Before the Great Depression, government made no attempt to stabilize the economy. New Deal programs instituted by the Roosevelt administration marked the beginning of the government's role as a fiscal manager.

Taxing and Spending Policy

Fiscal policy refers to the decisions made by government about taxing and spending. The federal budget is the main expression of fiscal policy. The federal budget is not only government's allocation of fiscal resources, but also a device to regulate economic growth. Federal fiscal policy has been influenced by John Maynard Keynes, who advocated increasing government spending during economic recessions and depressions to an amount greater than the amount of tax revenues it takes in, a policy known as *deficit spending*. Keynes believed that by placing more money in the hands of consumers, the economy would be stimulated. Therefore, deficit spending should increase as the economy worsens.

One way to stimulate the economy is using *demand-side economics*, focusing on consumer demand. Deficit spending is an example of demand-side economics, but it does not always work because of budget deficits and the *national debt* (the amount government owes to creditors). The national debt and budget deficits tend to restrain government's ability to use demand-side economics. Demand-side economics has served to reduce the severity of economic declines because government spending has remained high and continuous through programs like social security.

Supply-side economics simulates the economy by focusing on businesses (the supply side). Supply-side economic theory states that tax breaks for businesses and wealthy individuals will stimulate the economy. The implementation of this type of economic stimulation has led to economic growth, but it has also increased the national debt because of the lower tax revenues the government receives from cutting taxes. Supply-side policies were used by Presidents Ronald Reagan (when the policies were also called "Reaganomics") and George W. Bush.

Government also deals with *inflation*, which is an increase in the prices of goods and services over time. Cutting spending or increasing taxes, which reduce demand and stabilize pricing, can decrease inflation.

The Process and Politics of Fiscal Policy

Fiscal policy is mainly determined by the budgetary process, which involves the president and Congress. The Office of Management and Budget (OMB) in the executive branch starts the process by issuing general guidelines to federal agencies. The agencies develop their budgets based on the guidelines and then submit them to the OMB. The OMB reviews and compiles the budgets with the president, and the president submits the proposed budget to Congress. Because almost two-thirds of the budget involves *mandatory spending* such as Social Security and Medicare, the president directly influences only the third of the budget that involves *discretionary spending*, such as defense or the national parks system.

Congress uses the Congressional Budget Office (CBO), which is similar to the OMB, to review the proposed budget. The CBO notifies the budget committees of both chambers of errors in the costs of administering agencies and programs and of errors in receipts (tax revenues). The House and Senate budget committees draft budget resolutions, which estimate spending and revenues, and detail the allocation of funds to federal programs and agencies. The House Appropriations Committee and its 13 subcommittees review the budget, hold hearings at which members ask questions of the federal agencies, and make changes to the budget. The budget is then submitted to the full House for a vote. The Senate undergoes a similar but less thorough process. Differences in appropriations bills between the House and Senate are worked out in conference committee. The final bill is sent to the president for approval or veto.

The budget process and fiscal policy are subject to partisan politics. Historically, Democrats favor increased government spending during periods of economic slumps, while Republicans tend to favor stimulating business activity as a means of lifting the economy. Democrats also tend to favor a *graduated personal income tax*, sometimes called a *progressive tax*, which increases tax rates as income increases.

Monetary Policy: Government as Manager of Economy, II

Monetary policy is the manipulation of the money supply. It determines how much money is in circulation. Increasing and lowering the money supply is a method of influencing the economy.

The *Federal Reserve System,* created by the Federal Reserve Act of 1913, controls the money supply in the United States. The Fed's board of governors is appointed by the president and approved by the Senate. The Fed regulates national banks and certain state banks. It manipulates the money supply in two ways: by raising or lowering the amount of money it requires banks to have on deposit in the Federal Reserve and by raising or lowering the interest rate it charges member banks to borrow from the Reserve. Monetary policy's big advantage over policy is that it can be deployed quickly, resulting in quicker results, both concrete and psychological.

Even though its effects are relatively modest, the Fed has much power over the economy. Yet there is debate over two major issues regarding the Fed: whom it serves and the amount of unchecked power. It serves both the public and member banks but tends to be protective of bank interests, raising the question of whom it benefits the most. In terms of independence, members of the Fed are not subject to removal once appointed by the president and their meetings are held behind closed doors.

TAKE NOTE

This chapter is of limited importance for the AP test. The most essential information is about the budgetary process, the distinction between mandatory and discretionary spending, and the meaning of the terms *public policy* and *deregulation.* Environmental protection laws have been useful examples for free-response questions.

Observations from Past Exams

This chapter falls under the "Public Policy" section of the AP curriculum, which is supposed to make up between 5 percent and 15 percent of the multiple-choice questions. Specifically, it addresses the policymaking process and the role of government institutions and the bureaucracy in it. Linkages among policy processes and institutions, federalism, parties, interest groups, public opinion, elections, and policy networks are important foci of the test.

Material from this chapter was relevant to one question, on mandatory spending, on the 2002 multiple-choice test. One multiple-choice question on the 1999 exam asked about federalism and public policy.

Information from this chapter would have been useful in answering a free-response question on the 2005 exam about changes in the federal government's power based on taxing and spending. The second part of this question allowed students to choose the Clean Air Act to illustrate how laws expanded federal power. There was an illustration-based response question on the 1999 exam that demonstrated the growth in mandatory spending in the federal budget and one on the 2002 exam that showed the relative distribution of benefits to the young and old over time. An understanding of the budget and spending from Chapter 15 might have assisted in answering these questions. The 2000 exam had a free-response question that allowed students to choose environmental policy to illustrate that tensions between decentralization and centralization continue.

What to Do with the Boxes

"The U.S. Policy Process" box (p. 483) provides a useful overview of the policy process and an interesting explanation for when policy change is likely to occur. Figure 15-1 (p. 495),

Table 15-2 (p. 498), Figure 15-5 (p. 504), and Table 15-3 (p. 508) are summaries of information central to the chapter.

The "Liberty, Equality & Self-Government" box (p. 491) does a good job of discussing economic policy in terms of American values of freedom, equality, and economic security, reminding you that politics is essentially about competing values. Although the specifics in the "Debating the Issues" box (p. 496) and the "Global Perspective" box (p. 510) are unlikely to be the focus of an AP test question, they reinforce the lesson in the text about the global context in which U.S. policy operates.

A useful preparation for the illustration-based questions on the test is to try to write a summary for Figure 15-1 (p. 495), Figure 15-3 (p. 501), and Figure 15-4 (p. 503) before you read or review the one provided under the title. Try to come up with arguments for why the data look the way they do.

Because of the focus of the AP test, you do not need to concentrate on the biographical information about Adam Smith (p. 484) and John Maynard Keynes (p. 500), "How the United States Compares" (p. 488), specifics about deregulating long-distance services (p. 490), and state comparisons (p. 507).

Key Terms

Don't just memorize these terms. Understand what they mean and how they compare to other concepts. Be able to give examples of each.

Policy process (pp. 481–82)
Economy (p. 482)
Laissez-fare doctrine (p. 482)
Regulation (p. 484)
Efficiency (p. 484)
Externalities (p. 486)
Deregulation (p. 487)
Equity (in relation to economic policy) (p. 488)
Fiscal policy (p. 499)
Deficit spending (p. 499)
Economic depression (p. 500)
Economic recession (p. 500)
Demand-side economics (p. 500)
Budget deficit (p. 500)
National deficit (p. 500)
Balanced budget (p. 501)
Budget surplus (p. 501)
Supply-side economics (p. 501)
Capital-gains tax (p. 502)
Inflation (p. 502)
Mandatory spending (p. 504)
Discretionary spending (p. 504)
Graduated personal income tax (progressive tax) (p. 506)
Monetary policy (p. 508)
Federal Reserve System (p. 508)

Making Connections to Previous Chapters

This chapter primarily connects with the section of Chapter 11 that deals with Congress (pp. 358–62) and the section in Chapter 13 about bureaucracy's roles (pp. 420–21, 435) in the policy process. This chapter's evaluation of economic intervention using the goals of efficiency and equity is reminiscent of the discussion of bureaucratic accountability (pp. 430–38). Chapter 15 also reiterates and expands on information about the Office of Management and Budgeting found in three different chapters (pp. 360, 392–93, and 434–35). This chapter also provides many concrete examples of bureaucratic organizations described more generally in Chapter 13. Other sections to review in light of this chapter are those on the expansion of federal power in Chapters 3, 12, and 13. Checks and balances introduced in Chapter 2 are illustrated here.

SAMPLE QUESTIONS

Multiple-Choice Questions

1. According to the figure below, in which years was the United States closest to having a balanced budget?

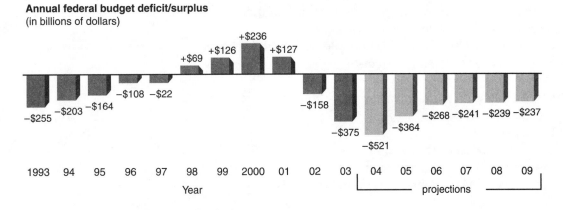

Annual federal budget deficit/surplus
(in billions of dollars)

a. years when Republicans were in the White House
b. 2000 and 2001
c. 1997 and 1998
d. 2004 and 2005
e. The figure does not have data appropriate for answering the question.

2. Which of the following is an institution through with government regulates trade?
   I. Food and Drug Administration
   II. Interstate Commerce Commission
   III. Federal Trade Commission

a. I
b. III
c. II and III
d. I and II
e. I, II, and III

3. Which period saw the greatest increase in the number of reforms designed to promote equity in economic programs?
   a. 1940s and 1950s
   b. 1950s and 1960s
   c. 1960s and 1970s
   d. 1970s and 1980s
   e. 1980s and 1990s

4. Which of these groups has as its primary mandate the quality of America's air and water?
   I. National Park Service
   II. Department of Agriculture
   III. Environmental Protection Agency

   a. I
   b. II
   c. III
   d. I, II, and III
   e. I and III

5. Supply-side fiscal policy may include:
   a. increases in government spending that increases the deficit
   b. increases in government spending that do not increase the deficit
   c. increases in money in consumers' hands
   d. a tax break for businesses and people with high incomes
   e. a cash rebate for most taxpayers

6. Which organization is most concerned with monetary policy?
   a. the U.S. Congress
   b. the president
   c. the Federal Reserve System
   d. the Federal Trade Commission
   e. the Office of Management and Budget

7. Which exerts the greatest limits on presidential power over the budget?
   a. the Office of Management and Budget
   b. the Congressional Budgeting Office
   c. public opinion
   d. Congress's opposition to programs introduced by the president
   e. mandatory spending

8. When did the U.S. government take on the responsibility of stimulating and stabilizing the economy?
   a. after the Constitution was ratified
   b. after the Industrial Revolution
   c. after the Great Depression
   d. after the civil rights movement
   e. after the dollar was taken off the gold standard

Multiple-Choice Questions That Link Chapter 15 to Lessons in Earlier Chapters

9. If Congress did away with the equal-time provision, this would be an example of:
   a. overregulation
   b. deregulation
   c. conservationism
   d. globalization
   e. fiscal policy

10. Which is the least likely to exhibit agency capture?
    a. Federal Communication Commission
    b. Environmental Protection Agency
    c. Nuclear Regulatory Commission
    d. Department of Agriculture
    e. National Aeronautics and Space Administration

Multiple-Choice Answers

1. C; 2. E; 3. C; 4. C; 5. D; 6. C; 7. E; 8. C; 9. B; and 10. B

Free-Response Questions

1. The federal budgetary process illustrates how separation of power works.

   a. Describe a formal advantage that the president has in the budgetary process. (1 point)

   b. Describe an informal advantage that the president has in the budgetary process. (1 point)

   c. Describe a formal or informal advantage that Congress has in the budgetary process. (1point)

   d. Describe a way that the budgetary process could be reformed and explain how the reform would affect the power of the president or Congress. (2 points)

   This question is worth five points.

   Part "a" is worth one point for correctly describing a formal advantage of the president. Acceptable answers include: role of initiating the budget, use of OMB to establish guidelines, use of OMB to guide agency budget preparations, and ability to veto budget passed by Congress.

   Part "b" is worth one point for correctly describing an informal advantage of the president. Acceptable answers include: public expectation that the president should lead, national mandate, ability to spin the media coverage, power to persuade, and president's role as leader of this party (especially when president's party is in the majority).

   Part "c" is worth one point for correctly describing a formal advantage that Congress has. Acceptable answers include: Congress has the constitutional power to appropriate funds, expertise from standing committee specialization, use of the CBO to estimate costs, use of the CBO to review agency requests, representational role (closeness to the state or district) and oversight role provide insights into the programs and spending, longevity on the Budget and Appropriation Committees gives Congress experience and insights, subcommittees' ability to hold hearings with agencies, and ability to override veto of president.

Part "d" is worth two points. The first point is earned for describing a reform. The second is earned for explaining how that reform would affect the president or Congress. Acceptable answers include: changes in entitlement programs to limit mandatory spending, thereby allowing the president and Congress more control over spending; balanced-budget amendment would limit amount that could be spent; balanced-budget amendment would also result in less interest to pay on borrowed money, allowing for more discretionary spending choices, return to Congress initiating the process, as was the process years ago; and line-item veto, which would enhance the president's power.

2. Patterson says that "the U.S government plays a substantial economic role through regulation of privately owned businesses."

   a. Describe what this statement means. (1 point)

   b. Provide an example of how privately owned businesses are regulated. (1 point)

   c. For that example, identify the organization that regulates that type of business. (1 point)

   d. Explain how regulation can promote a core American value. (1 point)

   e. Explain how regulation can undermine a core American value. (1 point)

   This question is worth 5 points.

   Part "a" is worth one point for correctly describing what this statement means. It needs to be clear from the answer that the student understands what the terms "economic role" and "regulation" mean. The student needs to make clear that the government is putting restriction on the economic practices of a business.

   Part "b" is worth one point for correctly providing an example of regulation. This example may be hypothetical. Examples may include: restricting trade, prohibiting mergers, regulating fees, lawsuits against practices that threaten competition, financial penalties for price-fixing, fines for externalities, requirements and rules for safety, prohibiting certain products or practices.

   Part "c" is worth one point for correctly identifying the organization that regulates the example provided in "b." The organization cannot be hypothetical. It must be one of the executive-branch agencies such as the Interstate Commerce Commission, Federal Trade Commission, Food and Drug Administration, Federal Communication Commission, various cabinet departments (such as Justice, Agriculture), Environmental Protection Agency, Consumer Product Safety Commission.

   Part "d" is worth one point for correctly identifying a core American value and how it is promoted by regulation. The easiest one to make a case for is equality.

   Part "e" is worth one point for correctly identifying a way that regulation undermines a core American value. The easiest one to make a case for is freedom.

CHAPTER SIXTEEN

Welfare and Education Policy: Providing for Personal Security and Need

SUMMARY

Welfare policy in the United States has been greatly influenced by different philosophies. Some policy-makers believe that government should have a leading role in giving assistance to those in economic need. Others feel that welfare acts as a disincentive for needy Americans to work and better themselves. America's federal system also invites debate because federal guidelines and funding can conflict with state goals in administering welfare (and education) policies. Despite these disagreements, welfare programs have helped to reduce the poverty level in the United States.

Education policy is a responsibility traditionally reserved to the states. Recent federal intervention has been a source of controversy and debate. Education policy in the United States reflects the principle of "equality of opportunity" because it gives people tools to succeed. Therefore, a large amount of money is spent on providing education through public schools and universities.

In the United States, *social insurance programs,* such as social security or Medicare, are more prevalent than *public assistance programs,* such as food stamps or rent vouchers. In part, this is because welfare programs are designed to push people towards self-reliance. As a result, the neediest Americans receive less government assistance than others.

Poverty in America: The Nature of the Problem

Poverty is a significant problem that social welfare policy attempts to minimize through efforts to help people receive necessities such as food and shelter. The *poverty line* is the annual cost to an urban family of four for food, clothing, shelter, and other basic necessities. Although America's poor are distributed across all ages, races, and religions, certain groups tend to have more needy individuals. The impoverished disproportionately include children, single-parent families, and minority-group members. Geographic concentrations exist as well: rural and urban areas tend to have more poverty than suburbs. Many Americans are unaware of the poverty problem in the United States. In fact, the country has the highest level of poverty (and twice the level of child poverty) among industrialized nations.

Although many people think that poverty is a matter of choice, most poverty-stricken individuals are victims of circumstance. Most poor people are poor temporarily—for example, because of job loss—and full-time employment does not mean that a family of four will be above the poverty line.

The Politics and Policies of Social Welfare

Republicans and Democrats differ in their views on social welfare policy. Democrats, because of their ideology and constituency (labor, poor, minorities), have introduced most welfare programs.

Republicans have come to accept welfare but seek to keep programs as small as possible. Three types of social welfare programs are discussed in this chapter: job training, special education, and income redistribution plans.

Job Training

Since President Franklin Roosevelt combined job programs with social security during the Great Depression, employment and welfare policies have been linked. Job programs receive more support from the public because they reinforce the values of hard work and individualism, the idea that people can and should "pull themselves up" rather than be given a "free ride." Despite successes in the early 1970s, job-training programs were cut because they were viewed as too expensive. The less-ambitious programs that followed have failed to move many people into permanent jobs.

The 1996 Welfare Reform Act was a major change in how federal welfare assistance was provided. It required recipients to find jobs within two years and limited the total time that people could receive welfare to five years. To fund this act, federal money was given to states in the form of block grants. This means that states determined how to distribute money and train recipients. The goal was to reduce dependency on welfare and train recipients to be productive members of the workforce. Its effectiveness has not yet been determined.

Rather than provide incentives to the people on welfare, the Workforce Investment Act of 1998 provides incentives to local communities and businesses to create job training. One part of this bill, the Youth Opportunity Grants, focuses on training people ages fourteen to twenty-one.

Education Initiatives and Redistribution Initiatives

Education programs have been included in social welfare efforts. The most visible is Head Start, established in the 1960s to provide preschool opportunities to underprivileged children. The aim was to give them a better chance to succeed in school. Head Start was cut substantially in the 1980s.

The United States has considerable income inequality. Income taxes do not redistribute wealth as much as in other democratic countries. The result is that the *effective tax rate* is about the same for high-income families as low-income families. To the extent that well-off Americans contribute the greatest absolute amount to government and some of the revenue goes toward social welfare programs, we can see a redistribution of wealth.

Another way income is redistributed to poor people is through the Earned Income Tax Credit (EITC). EITC is a *transfer payment,* one that is given directly to an individual. It gives low-income families up to four thousand dollars per year. Eligibility is determined at the time taxes are filed. The U.S. Census Bureau estimates that the EITC is responsible for 6 percent more families living above the poverty line.

Individual-Benefit Programs

The majority of welfare programs are *individual-benefit programs* that provide *transfer payments* such as the EITC directly to recipients. Individual-benefit programs, also called *entitlement programs,* attempt to assist people experiencing such circumstances as unemployment or poverty. Individual-benefit programs fall into two categories: social insurance and public assistance. It is important to remember that most federal funding that intends to improve the general welfare, such as construction of schools and hospitals, is not distributed in the form of individual-benefit programs.

Before the Great Depression, the federal government did not get involved in social welfare programs; this was reserved to the states. The prevailing theory was of *negative government:* that government works best when it encourages self-reliance by staying out of the lives of people. Since the Great Depression, the federal government has taken on a much greater role in social welfare programs and policy. This reflects the attitude of *positive government:* that government works best when it steps in with economic help to individuals when necessary, enhancing their freedom.

Social Insurance Programs

Social insurance programs are the most popular type of social welfare program. Social security, Medicare, and unemployment benefits are examples of this type of program. They are available only to people who "pay in" to the programs through payroll taxes.

Social security is the biggest social insurance program. It is aimed primarily at the elderly. The Social Security Act of 1935 established it. Eligibility is determined by individual contributions through payroll taxes and benefits are based on the amount "paid in" by the recipient. The long-term viability of social security is questionable based on its current financing structure: today's workers pay for the benefits of yesterday's workers so the increase in the number of elderly and the smaller number of current workers paying into the system is reason for concern.

The Social Security Act also had provisions for *unemployment insurance,* with benefits that are payable after involuntary job loss. Unemployment insurance is a joint program between the federal government and the states. States set the payroll tax rates, while the federal government sets minimum standards. Unemployment insurance is not as highly supported as Social Security because people assume that those who lose their jobs are at fault or lack a work ethic.

Since World War II, Democratic presidents have proposed a government-funded health care system. Their success has been limited by accusations of promoting "socialized medicine." In 1965, the *Medicare* program was enacted. It is a medical insurance program for seniors, funded by payroll taxes. The program pays for medical care, but the patient also contributes. It is a popular program, but rising medical costs and shrinking payroll contributions present challenges to funding. In 2003, a prescription drug benefit was added. This benefit took effect in 2006.

Public Assistance Programs

Public assistance programs are funded by tax revenues, and eligibility is determined solely by financial need. A *means test* is used to determine eligibility, meaning that applicants must prove their financial need of assistance. These are the programs commonly referred to as "welfare," and they are not terribly popular with Americans because they tend to be considered "hand-outs." Americans do not support public assistance programs as much as Europeans, and welfare policies reflect this. The government spends much more on social insurance programs than it does on public assistance programs.

An early example of a public assistance program is the *Supplemental Security Income* program. It was enacted as part of the Social Security Act of 1935 to provide assistance to the blind and to poor older Americans. *Aid to Families with Dependent Children (AFDC)* was started in the 1930s and continued until the Welfare Reform Act of 1996 discontinued it. AFDC was a controversial entitlement program that gave money to single parents with dependent children in their households. The Temporary Assistance for Needy Families (TANF) block grants replaced AFDC in 1996. This change limited the length of time recipients could receive cash assistance and placed other restrictions on receiving funds.

The *food stamp program* started in 1961. It provides an *in-kind benefit* in the form of coupons or vouchers for items such as rent or food instead of cash. The program aims to provide poor families with better nutrition, but it is costly and abuse is fairly common. The Welfare Reform Act allows states to limit the length of time that recipients may receive benefits. *Subsidized housing* is another in-kind benefit program, providing rent assistance to the poor via rent vouchers. *Medicaid,* enacted in 1965, gives health care to those already on welfare. It is considered a public assistance program with funds coming from tax revenues. The program is controversial because it is expensive.

Education as Equality of Opportunity: The American Way

Relative to other values, European democracies tend to put a higher value on economic security than the United States, as evidenced by health care systems and retirement funds that are available to all their citizens. The United States gives benefits to some but not all citizens because of one of its core values—*equality of opportunity*, which holds that individuals have an equal chance to succeed, but success is up to the individual. Education policy is a good example of this.

The United States spends more on education than any other country. It attempts to broadly educate all children, regardless of class and income. Because schools are a major vehicle for creating equal opportunities for all citizens, their inadequacies cause alarm. When standardized test scores fell in recent years, cries for education reform followed. One proposed reform would create a *voucher system* allowing students to attend private schools using public tax dollars. Other reforms allow parents to send their children to public schools of their choice. Advocates of school choice emphasize the opportunity they provide and opponents criticize the lack of equality. In 2002, the Supreme Court decided that vouchers were constitutional in the case of *Zelman v. Simmons-Harris.*

The Federal Role in Education: Political Differences

Responsibility for education has traditionally been given to state and local governments. Local communities tend to resist federal involvement. Early federal education policy was concentrated in the area of secondary education. The Morrill Act (which provided free land for the establishment of colleges), the GI Bill (which assisted veterans wanting to get a college education), and the National Defense Education Act of 1958 (which provided loans and set up institutes for students studying in science fields) are three examples of early policies. Federal involvement in and funding of higher education increased dramatically in 1965 with the Higher Education Act, which introduced Pell grants, and the Elementary and Secondary Education Act, which authorized funds for such items as school construction and teacher training. Since this time, federal funds have been split evenly between colleges and local school systems.

One of the most controversial pieces of legislation concerning education was the No Child Left Behind Act of 2001, which tied federal education funds to students' test scores in reading, math, and science. The debate over this law was divided along lines very similar to those that have been drawn over welfare policies. Democrats tended to oppose the law, preferring instead to increase funding to improve schools. Republicans supported the program because they seek nonmonetary reforms.

Culture, Politics, and Social Welfare

The American value of individualism has resulted in public attitudes toward welfare policies that have stifled the programs' success. The current welfare system is both inefficient and inequitable. Welfare policy in the United States is based on the principle that recipients must prove their need to earn their benefits. This makes the system *inefficient* because the people the funds are intended for often do not receive them and *inequitable* because the neediest people often do not get assistance.

Because the welfare system is complex, bureaucratic, and expensive, with separate programs designed to meet various needs, it is inefficient. Yet attempts to provide simpler, more universal programs, such as a guaranteed annual income, have failed because they run counter to core American values.

Although most Americans support programs to help the poor and others in need of assistance, they underestimate the amount of assistance needed. The underprivileged and programs to help them do get much less political support than programs that help the majority, such as social security and Medicare. As a result, there is much inequality. In fact, the wealthiest Americans, those whose income is in the top 20 percent nationally, receive more benefits from social insurance programs than poor people do from all public assistance programs combined.

TAKE NOTE

This chapter is not extremely important for the AP test. It does have some important terminology and it helps to illustrate some lessons about federalism.

Observations from Past Exams

This chapter falls under the "Public Policy" section of the AP curriculum, which is supposed to make up between 5 percent and 15 percent of the multiple-choice questions. Specifically, it addresses the policymaking process and the role of government institutions and the bureaucracy in it. Linkages among policy processes and institutions, federalism, parties, interest groups, public opinion, elections, and policy networks are important foci of the test.

Past multiple-choice exams reveal that little is drawn from this chapter. There was one question related to welfare and education policy on the 2002 multiple-choice test. It referred to a table that demonstrated changes in income over time. The 1999 multiple-choice test used the term "entitlement spending" in a question that asked about the largest contributor to "uncontrollable spending" and block grants in another.

The 1999 exam had a free-response question with a figure illustrating the relative amount of government spending for the young and poor. The 2001 exam had a figure that showed the relative distribution of government benefits for children and the elderly that this chapter might have helped students make sense of. The 2002 exam had a free-response question asking about the growth in mandatory spending. Understanding of the term "entitlement" was essential to interpreting the pie charts on this question. The 2003 exam asked how block grants contributed to the difference between the increased number of state and local government officials compared to the number of federal government employees.

What to Do with the Boxes

Some boxes include information that might help prepare for the test, even though it is unlikely to be asked about specifically. For example, the "Debating the Issues" box (p. 526) applies concepts from Chapter 15 to a specific issue. The "Why Should I Care?" box (p. 529) provides examples that might make social security easier to understand. The "Political Culture" box (p. 535) and the "Liberty, Equality & Self-Government" box (p. 541) illustrate how American core values are promoted and obstructed in public policies. Figure 16-6 (p. 540) illustrates what is meant in the text by "bureaucratic" and inefficient.

A useful preparation for the illustration-based questions on the test is to try to write a summary for Figure 16-1 (p. 518), Figure 16-2 (p. 524), Figure 16-3 (p. 525), Figure 16-4 (p. 531), and Figure 16-5 (p. 537) before you read or review the one provided under the title. Try to come up with arguments for why the data look the way they do.

Because of the focus of the AP test, you do not need to focus on the "States in the Nation" box (p. 517), the "How the United States Compares" box (p. 519), and the biographical information about Franklin Roosevelt (p. 527).

Key Terms

Don't just memorize these terms. Understand what they mean and how they compare to other concepts. Be able to give examples of each.

Social welfare programs (p. 516)
Poverty line (p. 518)
Social Security Act of 1935 (pp. 520, 528–29, 531)
Social Security (p. 520, 528)
1996 Welfare Reform Act (pp. 522, 532)
Head Start (p. 522–23)
Effective tax rate (p. 524)
Earned Income Tax Credit (p. 525)
Transfer payment (p. 525)
Entitlement program (p. 526)
Negative government (p. 527)
Positive government (p. 527)
Social insurance (p. 527)
Medicare (p. 530)
Public assistance (p. 530)
Means test (p. 530)
Supplemental Security Income (p. 531)
Aid for Families with Dependent Children (AFDC) (p. 532)
Temporary Assistance for Needy Families (TANF) (p. 532)
In-kind benefit (p. 533)
Medicaid (p. 533)
Equality of opportunity (p. 534)
School vouchers (p. 537)
No Child Left Behind Act of 2001 (p. 538)

Making Connections to Previous Chapters

Chapter 1's discussion of politics being about conflict between values and how to define them is illustrated well in this chapter. The distinction between equality and equality of opportunity (p. 13) has clear consequences for education and welfare policy.

This chapter is best understood in relation to Chapter 3. The consequences of federalism for policymaking are illustrated well through welfare and education policy. It would be useful to reread the section on categorical and block grants (p. 93) when studying the policies in this chapter, particularly Temporary Assistance for Needy Families and No Child Left Behind. Changes in the responsibilities between national and state and local government in the area of education illustrate models of federalism presented in Chapter 3.

Chapter 6's discussion of the influence of public opinion on policy is enlivened by the examples from this chapter. Consider how welfare policy illustrates how the "public's views place a boundary on what policymakers can reasonably do" (p. 208). Patterson describes the Welfare Reform Act as illustrating the majoritarian model of power (p. 28) because of the influence of public opinion.

Consider how class bias in voting and participation (Chapter 7) and interest-group involvement (Chapter 9) relate to welfare and education policies. Also review ideological thinking (Chapter 6) and party coalitions (Chapter 8) to better understand the partisan differences that draw battle lines on welfare and education issues. Think about what implication media roles and biases (Chapter 10) have on reporting on poor people and welfare programs. Which of the standing committees (listed in Table 11-2, p. 352) and Cabinet departments (listed in Figure 13-1, p. 417) would have jurisdiction over education policies and which would have it over welfare policies?

The "Debating the Issues" box (p. 526) uses terminology introduced in Chapter 15. Evaluating welfare policy on the basis of efficiency and equity (Chapter 16, pp. 539–42) resonates with lessons about both goals introduced explicitly in Chapter 15 (pp. 484–89) and the discussion of bureaucratic accountability (Chapter 13, pp. 430–38). Review the federal budget pie chart (Figure 15-2, p. 499) in light of what you learned about welfare policies and entitlement programs in this chapter.

SAMPLE QUESTIONS

Multiple-Choice Questions

1. Which of the following is true of the 1996 Welfare Reform Act?
   a. It declared that caring for the poor was no longer the government's responsibility.
   b. It switched the responsibility of caring for the poor from the federal government to the states.
   c. It switched the responsibility of caring for the poor from the state governments to the federal government.
   d. It switched the responsibility of caring for the poor from government to government-funded private organizations such as charities.
   e. It switched the responsibility of caring for the poor from federal and state government to local governments.

2. Social security is:
   a. a transfer payment because it transfers money directly from one group of people (young) to another (old)
   b. a transfer payment because government gives benefits directly to people
   c. a public assistance program because government helps people in need
   d. a public assistance program because it is funded by taxes
   e. a supply-side program because it gives money to where the needs are

3. Which of these does the federal government have the most control over?
   a. unemployment benefits
   b. Social Security
   c. Medicare
   d. AFDC
   e. education

4. The approach taken in No Child Left Behind Act of 2001:
   a. is unconstitutional
   b. is popular among public school teachers
   c. was supported by both political parties
   d. has primarily benefited poor schools and the students in them
   e. has tied federal funds to test performance

5. Which of the following programs has had the greatest amount of public support?
   a. Medicare
   b. Medicaid
   c. food stamps
   d. Aid for Families with Dependent Children
   e. Temporary Assistance for Needy Families

6. Which of the following is indicated in the figure?

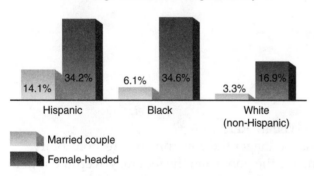

Percentage of Families Living in Poverty

   I. There are fewer white families below the poverty level than there are Hispanic and black families.
   II. Regardless of race, female-headed families are more likely to be below the poverty level than couples headed by married families.
   III. The nature of the family (married or female-headed) has less of an impact on poverty for Hispanics than it does for blacks.

   a. I
   b. II
   c. III
   d. II and III
   e. I, II, and III

7. Funding for welfare programs for the poor:
   a. makes up a third of the federal budget
   b. makes up a larger part of the federal budget than defense spending does
   c. makes up a smaller part of the federal budget than Social Security and Medicare do
   d. makes up a larger part of the federal budget now than it did in the 1960s
   e. is part of the mandatory spending

Multiple-Choice Questions That Link Chapter 16 to Lessons in Earlier Chapters

8. According to the Supreme Court, school vouchers that allow public funds to be used to pay for parochial school tuition:
   a. violate the establishment clause
   b. violate the free exercise of religion clause
   c. violate the equal-protection clause
   d. do not violate any clause in the Constitution
   e. need to be evaluated by state courts because of the Tenth Amendment

9. What is the consequence of the Temporary Assistance for Needy Families using block grants?
   a. It gives the federal government official total control of the policy.
   b. It gives state and local government officials total control of the policy.
   c. It gives the federal, state, and local government officials equal control of the policy.
   d. It gives the federal government control over setting guidelines and state governments over the specifics.
   e. It gives the federal government veto power over programs designed and funded by the states.

10. In-kind benefits are most consistent with which American value?
    a. equality
    b. justice
    c. freedom
    d. self-government
    e. patriotism

Multiple-Choice Answers

1. B; 2. B; 3. B; 4. E; 5. A; 6. D; 7. C; 8. D; 9. D; and 10. A

Free-Response Questions

1. Examine the figure below.

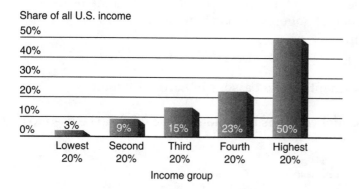

Share of all U.S. income

Lowest 20% (3%)	Second 20% (9%)	Third 20% (15%)	Fourth 20% (23%)	Highest 20% (50%)

Income group

a. Describe the major findings from this figure. Refer specifically to data from the figure. (1 point)

b. Identify a feature of U.S. political culture that contributes to this trend. Explain how it contributes. (2 points)

c. Identify a feature of elections that contributes to this trend. Explain how it contributes. (2 points)

d. Describe a policy that seeks to change this trend. Explain how it attempts to do this. (2 points)

This question is worth seven points.

Part "a" is worth one point for correctly describing the figure as showing that there is a great deal of economic disparity in the United States, with people at the top 20 percent income level having 50 percent of the wealth and people in the lowest 20 percent having only 3 percent of the wealth.

Part "b" is worth two points. One is earned for identifying a feature of political culture that contributes to the trend. The second is earned for explaining how it contributes. Acceptable answers include: equality of opportunity instead of economic equality, freedom, individualism, capitalism, free-market system, self-reliance, and personal responsibility.

Part "c" is worth two points. Answers that identify a way in which elections maintain economic inequality are worth one point. Two points are earned for answers that clearly explain how elections contribute to this inequality. Acceptable answers include: the impact of income on voting, impact of income on campaign participation, the upper-class bias of interest groups, the effect of campaign rhetoric that demonizes the poor, the lack of issue voting, the lack of choices in the two-party system, and the impact of the media's coverage of the horse-race aspect of campaigns rather than social policy issues.

Part "d" is worth two points. One is earned for describing a policy that tries to change this finding. The second is earned for explaining how it tries to do that. Acceptable answers include: education policies that try to provide tools for upward mobility, the Earned Income Tax Credit, social security, unemployment insurance, public assistance programs, Supplemental Security Income, Temporary Assistance for Needy Families.

2. Choose one of the following policies: No Child Left Behind Act of 2001, 1996 Welfare Reform Act, or the Social Security Act of 1935.

   a. Describe the policy and the problem it attempts to solve. (2 points)

   b. Describe the pluralist model and explain how or why it helps explain this law or why it passed. (2 points)

   c. Describe the majoritarian model and explain how or why it helps explain this law or why it passed. (2 points)

   d. Describe the bureaucratic-rule model and explain how or why it helps explain this law or why it passed. (2 points)

   This question is worth eight points.

   Part "a" is worth two points. One point is awarded for describing the problem that the policy was trying to solve. One point is for describing the policy. The threshold for describing the problem is high; for example that the Welfare Reform Act was to end abuses of the welfare program, not to help poor people. The threshold for describing the policy is low. A general sense of what the law did will suffice; see descriptions in the chapter.

   Part "b" is worth two points. One point is awarded for correctly describing the pluralist model (see Chapter 1). The second point is awarded for explaining how or why it helps explain the law or why it passed. Acceptable answers need to be focused on interest-group advocacy and how the law reflects that.

   Part "c" is worth two points. One point is awarded for correctly describing the majoritarian model (see Chapter 1). The second point is awarded for explaining how or why it helps explain the law or why it passed. Acceptable answers need to be focused on public opinion or political culture and how the law reflects these.

   Part "d" is worth two points. One point is awarded for correctly describing the bureaucratic rule model (see Chapter 1). The second point is awarded for explaining how or why it helps explain the law or why it passed. Acceptable answers need to be focused on administrators within the government and how the law reflects their actions or interests.

CHAPTER SEVENTEEN

Foreign and Defense Policy:
Protecting the American Way

SUMMARY

The United States has two major foreign policy goals: physical protection of the country and its people, and protection of the country's economic interests by participating in international policies that help the economy and assure international stability. The president takes the lead role in formulating foreign and defense policies. He uses the military, diplomacy, intelligence information, and economic organizations to formulate and execute policies. Economic interests have become more important and influential on foreign policy as the economy has become more globalized and dependent on the economies of other countries.

The Roots of U.S. Foreign and Defense Policy

Pages 548–57 give background information on U.S. foreign policy since World War II. The defense policy between World War II and 1990 dealt mainly with concern over the Soviet Union. Since 1990, foreign and defense policies have changed to meet new challenges such as terrorism and economic globalization. What has not changed is the United States' level of military preparedness, which continues to be maintained at high levels.

The United States as Global Superpower

Before World War II, the United States was *isolationist*; it did not take a large role in the affairs of other countries. After the war, the U.S. became an *internationalist* country, much more concerned and involved in other countries' affairs. The Soviet Union and United States emerged from the war as global superpowers, and the *lesson of Munich,* that Europe's appeasing of Hitler did not deter his aggressiveness, was applied in foreign policy towards the Soviets. The United States embraced the idea of *containment* towards the Soviet Union, in the belief that the Soviets were aggressors and had to be stopped by the United States.

The Cold War and Vietnam

The *Cold War* lasted from 1945 to 1990. The term refers to the fact that although the United States and the Soviet Union did not directly fight, they were hostile towards each other. The international power structure during this time featured the United States and the Soviet Union as the only superpowers, a *bipolar* power structure. United States foreign policy included support of governments in danger of being taken over by communists.

The Vietnam War helped to change the United States' view towards a policy of containment. The *lesson of Vietnam* was that applying this policy had limits, particularly after public opinion turned against the war.

Détente and Disintegration of the "Evil Empire"

An era of *détente* began after the Vietnam War, marked by Nixon's journey to China in 1972 and Strategic Arms Limitation Talks (SALT) with the Soviets. Détente refers to an increase in cooperation and communication between the United States and the Soviet Union. The era of détente ended after the Soviet invasion of Afghanistan in 1979. President Reagan promoted a tougher stance toward the Soviet Union, calling it an "evil empire." What Reagan and other U.S. policymakers did not know was how close the Soviet economy was to collapsing. Pro-democracy movements in satellite countries helped to speed the collapse of the Soviet Union in 1991. The United States was left as the world's only superpower, a power structure called *unipolar.*

A New World Order

After the collapse of the Soviet Union, the idea of *multilateralism* (nations acting together to solve problems) influenced U.S. foreign policy. The first war in Iraq (1990) and the Balkan wars (1992) are examples of uses of multilateralism. Continuing problems reveal that military intervention did not provide permanent solutions.

The War on Terrorism and the Iraq War

The September 11 attacks in 2001 changed foreign policy views again. They heralded a focus on terrorism. The War on Terrorism is unique in that it is waged against people and organizations rather than nations. President Bush used the *preemptive war doctrine*, the idea that the U.S. can attack a threatening country, to justify aggression in countries that supported terrorist actions against the U.S. but had not yet attacked. In the past, the nation had issued "first strikes" but only when the threat was "serious and immediate" (p. 553). The first example of Bush's less-constrained use of this doctrine was the Iraq War in 2002. Although the Iraqi army was quickly defeated, weapons of mass destruction (WMDs) were not found, and the post-combat phase has been more expensive and dangerous than was anticipated. As in the Vietnam War, domestic public opinion turned against Bush's policy. World opinion, with the exception of Great Britain, was unsupportive from the beginning, in part because the United States acted without the general consent of the United Nations. Nevertheless, fighting terrorism abroad has remained a high priority as reflected in the 2005 federal budget's allocations.

The Process of Foreign and Military Policymaking

Because national security involves relations with other countries, the main tools used to develop and implement policies differ from those used to implement domestic policies. The president, using executive-branch agencies, takes the lead in foreign policy. The tools, or policymaking instruments, are: diplomacy, military force, economic means, and use of intelligence.

Diplomacy, the tool preferred by most countries, can be bilateral (between two countries) or multilateral (among more than two). This is the method of relations preferred by most countries. The second tool of foreign policy is *military power*, which is usually used defensively and can also be *unilateral*, with one country acting alone. The United States has used military force often in its history, both unilaterally (Grenada, 1982) and multilaterally (Iraq, 1991, and Afghanistan, 2002). The third and fourth policymaking instruments are economic exchange and intelligence gathering. *Economic exchange* involves either trade or assistance, with trade being the more important instrument. *Intelligence* involves guarding and monitoring information.

The Policymaking Machinery

The president and Congress share responsibility for foreign and military policy, but the president directs the policymaking machinery because of the powers granted by the Constitution as commander in chief, chief diplomat, and chief executive. From within the White House Office of the President, the president relies on the National Security Council for advice and to help keep other bureaucrats in line with the administration's goals. The president's national security advisor, who directs the NSC, helps to formulate foreign policy using access to diplomatic, military and intelligence information.

Defense organizations are both internal (Department of Defense, the Joint Chiefs of Staff, and the Department of Homeland Security) and external (the military alliance of the North Atlantic Trade Organization). *Intelligence organizations* seek to keep the president informed about what is going on in the world. They include the Central Intelligence Agency, the National Security Agency, and agencies within the State and Defense Departments. Since the end of the cold war, intelligence has concentrated on drug trade and terrorism. The failure of these groups to detect the attacks of September 11 led Congress to investigate and recommend structural and process changes.

Diplomatic organizations provide aid in many areas, including negotiating with other countries, protecting U.S. citizens abroad, and gathering intelligence. The Department of State, which includes ambassadors to other countries, conducts most diplomatic activities. International organizations, including the Organization of American States and the United Nations, are also vehicles for American diplomatic actions.

Economic organizations include domestic agencies such as the Agriculture and Labor Departments, which promote U.S. products abroad, and international organizations such as the World Trade Organization. The World Bank and International Monetary Fund provide long- and short-term loans to nations in need of assistance.

The Military Dimension of National Security Policy

The United States' national security policy relies heavily on the military. The amount spent on defense is far greater in the United States than in allied countries. The expense and effectiveness of the military was clear in the Iraq war.

The United States' role as the only superpower is partly due to the strength of its conventional military forces, as well as to the advanced technology of weapons systems. Older systems such as nuclear weapons, the number of which greatly increased under the policy of deterrence during the Cold War, are still a part of defense strategy.

There are six types of military action: unlimited nuclear warfare, limited nuclear warfare (such as the detonation of a single nuclear bomb), unlimited conventional warfare, limited conventional warfare, counterinsurgency (defending countries that are useful to America's political and economic interests against insurgency), and police-type action (including drug trafficking and terrorism). The possibility of unlimited nuclear and conventional warfare has been reduced since the end of the Cold War. Limited conventional warfare (used, for example, during the Iraq War of 2002) is generally used after other resolution methods have failed. It has been the most productive use of military power over time.

Although policy debates are usually among political elites, public opinion can influence policy, as in the decision to withdraw troops from Vietnam. Business interests also influence defense policies because of the economic benefits a strong military can provide, such as the design and manufacturing of advanced weaponry systems. Business interests help to form the *military-industrial complex,* which consists of the military branches, the arms industry, and Congressional representatives from areas that include companies.

The Economic Dimension of National Security Policy

Pages 567–75 describe the role of economics in formulating national security policy and make the point that a strong and prosperous economy is necessary to build and maintain military strength.

Economic benefits are often realized through America's national security policy. One example is the *Marshall Plan,* enacted in 1947 to help rebuild Europe after World War II. The plan was designed to help Europe recover economically and politically from the war. The Marshall Plan also benefited the U.S. economy by opening up new markets for American products.

Today, the world is economically tri-polar: power is concentrated in the United States, east Asia, and the European Union. The United States is both the weakest (for example, it has the worst trade imbalance) and the strongest (its agricultural sector) of the three power centers. It is also more competitive, as evidenced by its strong growth and low inflation as compared to Europe or Japan.

America's Global Economic Goals

The United States is not self-sufficient. It needs other countries for trade (to improve the economy at home), energy, and other resources. It also needs a stable global economy to meet these goals. International trade is much more important today than in the past, which has forced businesses to think in global terms to succeed. For example, only half of the oil used by the U.S. is produced domestically. U.S. goals in the world economy include maintaining a stable and open trade system, maintaining access to resources the U.S. economy needs, and keeping the world economy stable.

Economic globalization refers to the complex interactions among nations' economies. It both benefits and threatens the economic goals of the United States. More markets for U.S. goods and lower prices for consumers from imports are among the benefits of economic globalization. However, foreign firms may compete in the same markets and may have competitive advantages over U.S. firms (such as cheap labor) and threaten their economic interests. Multinational firms are one result of economic globalization.

The two major sides on trade issues are *free-trade position* (the belief that economic goals are easier to obtain when trade barriers are low) and *protectionism* (the belief that domestic businesses must be protected from foreign competition, or at least be allowed to do business in a fair-trade environment). The executive branch tends to favor free trade because free trade tends to help the economy as a whole over time, while the legislative branch tends to find protectionism more agreeable because free trade could make it more difficult for businesses from their home districts to be successful). One example of the opposing views colliding was in the 1993 debate over the North American Free Trade Agreement (NAFTA). NAFTA, which proposed lowering trade barriers between participating countries, was promoted by President Bill Clinton and passed Congress after side deals were worked out to protect domestic interests from some of the potential adverse effects of the agreement. Another example that reflects the current prevailing attitude towards the free-trade position is the United States' support of the World Trade Organization (WTO), which promotes global trade. The WTO has been criticized by protectionists as compromising the environment and human rights. The loss of domestic jobs has also put the free-trade position under fire.

Because the world economy can be destabilized by the gap between rich and poor countries, policies to help developing countries are essential. Developmental assistance is provided to poorer countries through the International Monetary Fund and the World Bank. The United States is a leading contributor to both organizations. These countries provide markets for American goods.

The United States has inconsistently tied foreign aid with human rights. Protecting human rights is not always the priority. Two examples of when human rights lagged behind other concerns were when the United States supported repressive anticommunist regimes during the Cold War and its current trade relationship with China, despite China's high rate of human-rights violations. Although the United States has made more efforts since the Cold War to provide trade and assistance to developing democracies, when these goals clash with economic ones the more immediate self-interest tends to win out. Even though economic goals are important, the United States' biggest policy goal today is stopping terrorism.

TAKE NOTE

This chapter is not extremely important for the AP test.

Observations from Past Exams

The chapter falls under the "Public Policy" section of the AP curriculum that is supposed to make up between 5 percent and 15 percent of the multiple-choice questions. Specifically, it addresses the policymaking process and the role of government institutions and the bureaucracy in it. Linkages among policy processes and institutions, federalism, parties, interest groups, public opinion, elections, and policy networks are important foci of the test.

Past exams reveal little coverage of material from this chapter. There were no multiple-choice questions on this on the 2002 exam. The 1999 multiple-choice test had a question about the increase in presidential power since 1945 that included factors related to foreign policy.

The 2004 exam had a free-response question that asked about the formal and informal powers of the president that enhance his role in foreign policy over Congress. Although material covered in Chapter 12 would enable students to answer this question, this chapter might also help.

What to Do with the Boxes

None of the boxes contain information essential for the AP test.

Some boxes include information that might help prepare for the test, even though it is unlikely to be asked about specifically. "How the United States Compares" (p. 563) reinforces the point made in the text about the large financial commitment the United States has to the military. The "Liberty, Equality & Self-Government" box (p. 568) highlights the tension between the values of liberty and security already discussed in Chapters 1 and 4.

A useful preparation for the illustration-based questions on the test is to try to write a summary for Figure 17-1 (p. 555), Figure 17-2 (p. 569), Figure 17-3 (p. 574), and Figure 17-4 (p. 575) before you read or review the one provided under the title. Try to come up with arguments for why the data look the way they do.

Because of the focus of the AP test, you do not need to focus on "Debating the Issues" (p. 554), "Why Should I Care?" (p. 556), "Global Perspective" (p. 560), and "States in the Nation" box (p. 572).

Key Terms

Don't just memorize these terms. Understand what they mean and how they compare to other concepts. Be able to give examples of each.

Isolationist (p. 549)
Internationalist (p. 549)
Containment (p. 549)
Cold War (p. 549)
Bipolar power structure (p. 549)
Détente (p. 551)
Multilateralism (p. 551)
Preemptive war doctrine (p. 553)
Weapons of Mass Destruction (WMDs) (pp. 553–55)
Diplomacy (p. 557)
Unilateralism (p. 557)
Deterrence (p. 564)
Insurgency (p. 566)
Military-industrial complex (p. 567)
Marshall Plan (p. 568)
Multinational corporations (p. 570)
Economic globalization (p. 570)
Free-trade position (p. 571)
Protectionism (p. 571)
North American Free Trade Agreement (p. 571)

Making Connections to Previous Chapters

This chapter relates primarily to Chapter 12's discussion about presidential power, (particularly pp. 378–80. Page 558 provides an example of how the White House Office of the President (discussed on pp. 392–97) helps keep the bureaucracy in line with the president's goals. The example of post-September 11 congressional investigations (p. 561) provides a nice illustration of congressional oversight introduced in Chapter 11 (pp. 365–68). Various bureaucratic agencies and departments introduced in Chapter 13 are given closer attention here.

SAMPLE QUESTIONS

Multiple-Choice Questions

1. Which of the following had the strongest impact on the United States' withdrawal from Vietnam?
   a. European diplomatic efforts
   b. Chinese diplomatic efforts
   c. public opinion
   d. a budgetary crisis in the United States in the early 1970s
   e. accomplishing its long-term goals in the region

2. What part of the executive branch acts as a coordinator among foreign, defense, and intelligence organizations?
   a. the National Security Agency
   b. the Joint Chiefs of Staff
   c. the Department of Defense
   d. the National Security Council
   e. the Department of Foreign Policy

3. Which of the following is true about the Department of State?
   I. It directs day-to-day relations with other countries.
   II. It gathers foreign intelligence.
   III. It is part of the executive branch and reports to the National Security Council.

   a. I, II, and III
   b. I and II only
   c. I and III only
   d. I only
   e. II only

4. What are the World Trade Organization and the International Monetary Fund examples of?
   a. international organizations headed by the United States
   b. international organizations that promote United States interests abroad
   c. international organizations that the United States works with to promote economic aspects of its foreign policy
   d. international organizations created in response to the interdependence of nations' economies
   e. subnational organizations

5. United States' counterinsurgency activities have diminished in part because of:
   a. increased global political stability since World War II
   b. the lesson of Vietnam
   c. the lesson of Munich
   d. a decrease in the number of conventional ground forces in the United States military
   e. the inability of the government to pay for such operations

6. Which type of military action has historically produced the most satisfactory results over the long term?
   a. counterinsurgency
   b. police-type action
   c. limited conventional warfare
   d. unlimited conventional warfare
   e. unlimited nuclear action

7. Support for the World Trade Organization has generally come from:
   a. protectionists
   b. labor unions
   c. the Republican Party
   d. those in favor of free trade
   e. isolationists

8. According to the figure below:

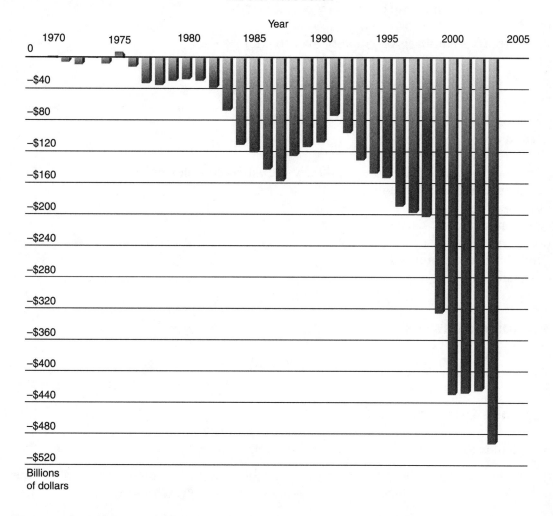

The U.S. Trade Deficit

a. between 1970 and 2003, there were no years in which the U.S. exported more than it imported
b. between 1970 and 2003, there were no years in which the U.S. imported more than it exported
c. during the George W. Bush administration, the U.S.'s trade imbalance improved dramatically
d. during the Bill Clinton administration, the U.S.'s trade imbalance grew substantially worse
e. the party of the president has significant impact on the trade deficit

Multiple-Choice Questions That Link Chapter 17 to Lessons in Earlier Chapters

9. What helps explain the Democratic Party's opposition to free-trade policies?
    I. the economic makeup of the party's coalition
    II. the position of unions on the issue
    III. the party's emphasis on equality over freedom

    a. I
    b. II
    c. III
    d. I and II
    e. I, II, and III

10. The relationships among the actors in military-industrial complex most closely approximates which of the following?
    a. subgovernments
    b. regulatory agencies
    c. cooperative federalism
    d. political action committees
    e. iron triangles

Multiple-Choice Answers

1. C; 2. D; 3. B; 4. C; 5. B; 6. C; 7. D; 8. D; 9. E; and 10. E

Free-Response Questions

1. The president is the lead actor in the making of foreign policy.

    a. Identify and describe a formal power that contributes to this. Explain how it contributes to the president's advantage over Congress in foreign policy. (2 points)

    b. Identify and describe a bureaucratic organization that the president can use to help him lead in foreign policy. Explain how it contributes to the president's advantage over Congress in foreign policy. (2 points)

    c. Describe a way that Congress can exert its influence in the area of defense policy or diplomatic policy. Be sure to identify which of these two you are describing. Explain why it is unlikely that Congress will challenge the president in this way. (2 points)

    This question is worth six points.

    Part "a" is worth two points. The first point is earned by describing a formal power that contributes. The second point is for explaining how it contributes. Acceptable answers include: responsibilities identified in Article II of the Constitution (commander-in-chief role, chief diplomat, and chief executive).

    Part "b" is worth two points. The first point is earned by describing a bureaucratic organization that contributes. The second point is for explaining how it contributes. Acceptable answers include: National Security Council, Department of Defense, State

Department, Central Intelligence Agency, Joint Chiefs of Staff, Department of Homeland Security.

Part "c" is worth two points. The first point is earned by describing a way that Congress can exert its influence in one of these areas. It is essential that the method identified is appropriate for the type of policy identified. The second point is earned by explaining why Congress would be unlikely to do this. Acceptable answers for defense policy are: appropriations for defense, use of the media to undermine public support for the president's action or build support for alternative action, War Powers Act, ability to declare war, oversight of defense department, override presidential veto of defense policies initiated by Congress, and approval of department secretaries. Acceptable answers for diplomatic policy include: approval of ambassadors, approval of treaties, use of the media to undermine public support for the president's action or build support for alternative action, override presidential veto of diplomatic policies initiated by Congress, and state department oversight.

2. Defense policy can be understood in terms of the different theories of power.

   a. Describe the majoritarian theory. Explain how, when, or why defense policy best illustrates this model. (2 points)

   b. Describe the pluralist theory. Explain how, when, or why defense policy best illustrates this model. (2 points)

   c. Describe the elitist theory. Explain how, when, or why defense policy best illustrates this model. (2 points)

   This question is worth six points.

   Part "a" is worth two points. The first point is awarded for correctly describing majoritarianism. The second point is awarded for explaining how, when, or why defense policy illustrates this theory. Acceptable answers convey the role of public opinion in constraining or dictating defense policy on issues of broad national concern. Examples may include the role that public opinion played in ending U.S. involvement in Vietnam or accelerating the pace of withdrawal from Iraq.

   Part "b" is worth two points. The second point is awarded for explaining how, when, or why defense policy illustrates this theory. Acceptable answers convey the role that interest groups play in constraining or dictating routine and less-publicized defense policy. For example, students might write about the military-industrial complex and the impact of the arms industry within it.

   Part "c" is worth two points. The second point is awarded for explaining how, when, or why defense policy illustrates this theory. Acceptable answers convey the role that a powerful few play in constraining or dictating routine and less-publicized defense policy. For example, students might discuss the role of the National Security Council or specific elites, such as the director of the CIA.

PRACTICE TEST I

United States Government and Politics

Two hours and twenty-five minutes are allotted for this examination: 45 minutes for Section I, which consists of multiple-choice questions; and 100 minutes for Section II, which consists of four mandatory essay questions. Section I is printed in this examination booklet. Section II is printed in a separate booklet.

SECTION I

Time – 45 minutes
Number of questions – 60
Percentage of total grade – 50

UNITED STATES GOVERNMENT AND POLITICS

Section I
Time—45 minutes
60 Questions

Directions: Each of the questions or incomplete statements below is followed by five suggested answers or completions. Select the one that is best in each case and then fill in the corresponding oval on the answer sheet.

1. The federal structure of the U.S. government is most evident in
   A. the separation of powers
   B. checks and balance
   C. free elections
   D. the process of amending the Constitution
   E. the Bill of Rights

2.

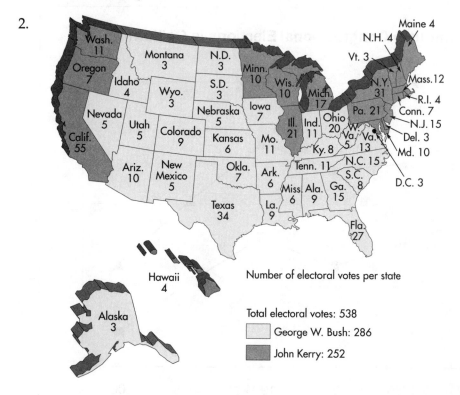

Number of electoral votes per state

Total electoral votes: 538

George W. Bush: 286

John Kerry: 252

Based on the data above, which of the following would have changed the outcome of the 2004 presidential election?
   I. If John Kerry had won the Western states with larger margins
   II. If John Kerry had won Alabama instead of George W. Bush
   III. If John Kerry had won Arizona and New Mexico instead of George W. Bush
   IV. If John Kerry had won Indiana and Kentucky instead of George W. Bush

A. I
B. II or III
C. III or IV
D. IV
E. I, II, III, IV

3. In the last 50 years, Congress has "checked" federal courts' power by
   A. changing the number of justices on the Supreme Court
   B. changing the jurisdiction of the Supreme Court
   C. impeaching a justice for making political decisions
   D. passing a constitutional amendment to make a decision moot
   E. passing laws that rewrite legislation that the Court has interpreted

4. The theory that a small number of people in key political and economic positions control politics is
   A. majoritarianism
   B. pluralism
   C. elitism
   D. bureaucratic rule
   E. capitalism

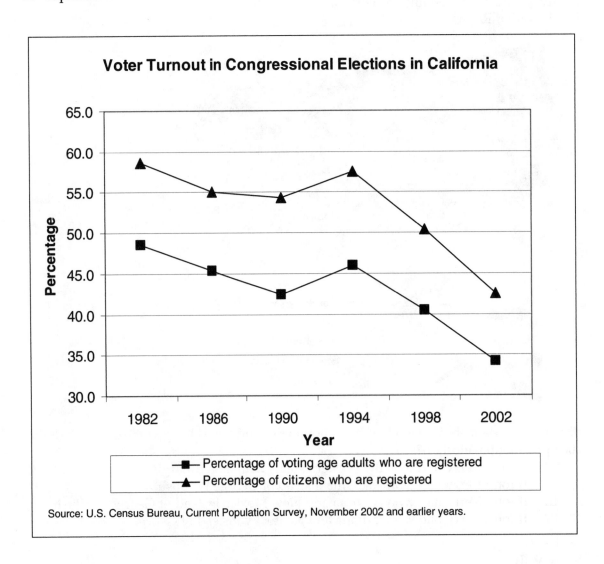

Voter Turnout in Congressional Elections in California

Source: U.S. Census Bureau, Current Population Survey, November 2002 and earlier years.

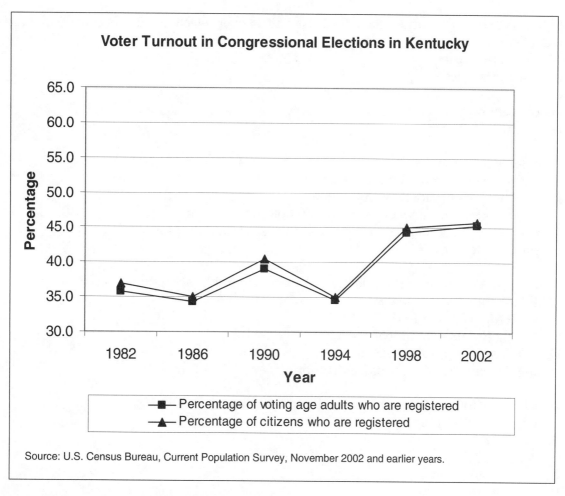

Voter Turnout in Congressional Elections in Kentucky

Source: U.S. Census Bureau, Current Population Survey, November 2002 and earlier years.

5. The data in the figures above support which of the following statements?
   A. Turnout in off-year elections is lower than turnout in presidential elections.
   B. Turnout has dropped since the mid-1960s.
   C. Kentucky has more contested congressional elections than California does.
   D. Turnout in congressional elections is higher in Kentucky than it is in California.
   E. From 1982 to 1994, turnout in congressional elections was higher in California than it was in Kentucky, but it was lower in 1998 and 2002.

6. What is the best explanation for the larger gap between the two lines in the California figure compared to the size of the gap between the two lines in the Kentucky figure?
   A. California has a higher level of education than Kentucky does.
   B. California has a greater number of legal and illegal aliens than Kentucky does.
   C. California has a younger population than Kentucky does.
   D. From 1994 until 2002, California had greater economic problems than Kentucky had.
   E. The legacy of the Voting Rights Act remains in Kentucky but not in California.

7. Political party organizations have the least control over selecting party nominees in which of the following processes?
   A. closed primaries
   B. open primaries
   C. patronage
   D. conventions
   E. caucuses

8. A conference committee
   A. is responsible for marking up legislation
   B. is only necessary for some legislation
   C. oversees the executive departments by holding hearings
   D. consists of the leaders of each party in the Senate and the House
   E. defines the rules for debate

9. Which of the following bars racial discrimination in public accommodations?
   A. Fourteenth Amendment
   B. Civil Rights Act of 1964
   C. Voting Rights Act of 1965
   D. the *Plessy v. Ferguson* decision
   E. the *Brown v. Board of Education* decision

10. Which of the following has the greatest impact on vote turnout?
    A. party identification
    B. race
    C. sex
    D. education
    E. religion

11. The White House Office
    A. is another name for the executive branch of government
    B. includes 15 departments with heads that serve as the president's cabinet
    C. is composed of civil servants who got their jobs based on their merit
    D. is composed of staff appointed directly or indirectly by the president
    E. is composed of staff appointed by the president with approval by the Senate

12. The "commerce clause" of the Constitution
    A. has given the national government great power over private businesses since the founding of the country
    B. gives private businesses great power over national government intrusion
    C. gave the national government power to regulate businesses in the states through incorporation of the Fourteenth Amendment
    D. increased the national government's power to regulate business once it began to be interpreted broadly by the Supreme Court
    E. spells out the ways that Congress can regulate commerce

13. Which of the following is a formal (or constitutional) power of the president?
    A. "pack the Supreme Court" by adding to the number of justices on it
    B. declare war
    C. appropriate money to programs and executive agencies
    D. make treaties with other countries with the approval of the Senate
    E. make treaties with other countries with the approval of the Senate and the House of Representatives

14. Which right or rights of accused criminals were relevant in the *Miranda v. Arizona* ruling?
    A. those expressed in the Fourth Amendment
    B. those expressed in the Fifth Amendment
    C. those expressed in the Sixth Amendment
    D. those expressed in the Fourth and Fifth Amendments
    E. those expressed in the Fifth and Sixth Amendments

15. What restricts the role that public opinion plays in policymaking?
    A. the general public's lack of knowledge and interest in politics
    B. politicians lack of interest in the public's opinions
    C. the fact that most of the public lacks opinions on political issues
    D. the ideological nature of the public's opinions
    E. the limitations of polls for accurately measuring public opinion

16. One of the reasons presidents have become more powerful since World War II is that
    A. they are more popular with the public
    B. divided government has become less frequent
    C. they were given the line-item veto
    D. the federal government's responsibilities have grown
    E. the president is commander-in-chief

17. To serve as a justice on the Supreme Court, a person needs to
    A. have some experience as a federal judge
    B. have some experience as a federal or state judge
    C. have some experience as a lawyer, but does not need to have judicial experience
    D. have some experience in politics, but not necessarily as a lawyer or judge
    E. have no particular job experience.

18. The term "agenda setting" refers to
    A. how the public sets the government's priorities
    B. how the public sets the news media's priorities
    C. how the government sets the public's priorities
    D. how the news media sets the government's priorities
    E. how the news media sets the public's priorities

19. Which of the following techniques is most likely to be used by the American Medical Association?
    A. a letter-writing campaign by members
    B. protest outside Congress
    C. wine and dine Congress
    D. bribe members of the executive branch
    E. provide information about medical issues to Congress

20. Which of the following welfare programs is run entirely by the federal government?
    A. Social Security
    B. Temporary Assistance for Needy Families
    C. Food Stamps
    D. Medicaid
    E. Aid for Families with Dependent Children

21. When did state governments have to stop restricting the freedoms identified in the Bill of Rights?
    A. immediately after the Bill of Rights was added to the Constitution
    B. immediately after the Fourteenth Amendment was passed
    C. slowly over time, after the groundbreaking Supreme Court ruling in the case of *Barron v. Baltimore*
    D. slowly over time, after the groundbreaking Supreme Court ruling in the case of *Gitlow v. New York*
    E. Slowly over time, after Congress passed the "selective incorporation" law

22. Which of the following is true about political socialization?
    A. It is rare because most children are not interested in politics.
    B. It is rare because most parents are not interested in politics.
    C. One pattern is that there is more similarity between children and their parents than there are differences.
    D. Because it works differently for each person, it lacks predictable patterns.
    E. It ends when a child turns 18.

23. The following are consequences of candidate-centered campaigns EXCEPT:
    A. they weaken officeholder and party accountability for policymaking
    B. they strengthen the relationship between voters and candidates
    C. they increase the power of interest groups
    D. they provide clearer issue platforms
    E. they increase the power of campaign consultants, pollsters, and media managers

24. Which of the following has resulted in Congress successfully curtailing the president's power?
    A. the War Powers Act
    B. the Budget and Impoundment Control Act
    C. executive privilege
    D. the line-item veto
    E. the Twenty-seventh Amendment

25. The issue of whether the Boy Scouts of America had the right to deny membership to gays demonstrates a tension between
    A. the values of freedom and equality
    B. self-government and limited government
    C. the role of Congress and the Supreme Court
    D. pluralism and elitism
    E. democracy and republic

26. The "equal protection" clause of the Fourteenth Amendment has been interpreted by the Supreme Court to mean that
    A. federal laws must treat all people the same in all circumstances
    B. state laws must treat all people the same in all circumstances
    C. federal and state laws must treat all people the same in all circumstances
    D. federal and state laws and private parties must treat all people the same in all circumstances
    E. that all people do not have to be treated the same in all circumstances

27. Which of the following techniques is the president most likely to use to try to control the executive bureaucracy?
    A. invoking executive privilege to obtain confidential documents from the bureaucracy
    B. ordering Congress to conduct investigative hearings
    C. blowing the whistle on official misconduct by alerting the media
    D. coordinating information and activities through reorganization and staff oversight
    E. withholding appropriations from programs that are not consistent with his objectives

28. The U.S. House of Representatives and the U.S. Senate differ in which of the following ways?
    A. There are more standing committees in the Senate.
    B. There are more formal rules in the Senate.
    C. Standing committees play a more important role in the House.
    D. The Senate deals with national issues and the House deals with local issues.
    E. "Logrolling" occurs in the House but not in the Senate.

U.S. Supreme Court Caseload

Year	Number of Cases Filed	Number of Cases Argued	Number of Cases with Signed Opinions
2004	7496	87	74
2003	7814	91	73
2002	8255	84	71
2001	7924	88	76
2000	7852	86	77
1999	7377	83	74

Source: 2001, 2003, 2005 Chief Justice's Year-End Reports on the Federal Judiciary

29. What does the difference between the numbers in the first and second columns in the table above demonstrate?
    A. that the *Marbury v. Madison* decision has had a long-term impact
    B. that the recent Court has adhered to the doctrine of judicial activism
    C. that the recent Court adheres to the doctrine of judicial restraint
    D. that the Court has much discretion over which cases it hears
    E. that the Constitution gives the Supreme Court both original and appellate jurisdiction

30. Which of the following most accurately characterizes the trend in voter turnout in presidential elections since the 1960s?
    A. Although voter turnout has gone up and down in the last 20 years, it has consistently been lower than it was in the 1960s.
    B. Voter turnout has continued to drop in every presidential election since 1960.
    C. Voter turnout dropped but returned to the level it was in 1960 during the Reagan years.
    D. Voter turnout dropped but returned to the level it was in 1960 in 1992.
    E. Voter turnout has no discernable pattern. Some years it is high and other years it is low.

31. Critical elections that change party coalitions and shift voter support strongly in favor of one party
    A. were common in the 1990s
    B. were common in the 1960s and 1970s
    C. are called dealigning elections
    D. undermine the influence of voters on public policy
    E. reduce split-ticket voting

32. When were women given the right to vote for president?
    A. after Congress and then three-quarters of the state legislatures approved the right
    B. after Congress and then all of the state legislatures approved the right
    C. after a law was passed by the House and the Senate and signed by the president
    D. after state legislatures passed laws establishing the eligibility rules in their states
    E. after a national constitutional convention called by two-thirds of the states approved the right

33. The Articles of Confederation
    A. established a national Congress appointed by state governments
    B. established a national Congress elected by the people in each state
    C. did not establish a national Congress to compete with state governments
    D. established both a national Congress and state congresses
    E. established a national Congress that appointed state congresses

34. All of the following contribute to the power of "iron triangles" EXCEPT:
    A. the public's limited knowledge of political issues
    B. the media's focus on personalities over issues
    C. specialization
    D. incumbency advantage
    E. competing interest groups

35. Presidential approval ratings
    A. tend to go up when foreign policy crises break out
    B. tend to go up as the presidential term continues
    C. tend to go up and down based on the degree of opposition the president has in Congress
    D. tend to go up as the president gains more experience in office
    E. fluctuate randomly

36. Social-regulation policies instituted in the 1960s and 1970s
    A. have primarily been eliminated by subsequent deregulation policies
    B. focused on protecting the environment, consumers, and workers
    C. focused on constraining unfair business practices
    D. focused on stimulating the economy and saving industries
    E. were largely unsuccessful because regulatory agencies were controlled by the industries they were supposed to regulate

37. Affirmative action programs that give preferential treatment to women and racial minorities
    A. are supported by the public
    B. emphasize the value of freedom over the value of equality
    C. are considered unconstitutional by the Supreme Court because they discriminate based on race or gender
    D. are considered unconstitutional by the Supreme Court when they set up strict quotas
    E. are considered constitutional by the Supreme Court when they are established by private companies

38. *Griswold v. Connecticut* was a precedent for deciding *Roe v. Wade* because
    A. they both dealt with sex
    B. they both dealt with issues of equality for women
    C. they both were activist
    D. they both related to equal rights protection
    E. they both dealt with the right of privacy

39. Political candidates may have direct control over spending which of these funds?
    I. soft money
    II. 527 money
    III. hard money
    IV. PAC contributions
    V. federal matching funds

    A. I, II, III, IV, and V
    B. I, II, and IV
    C. III, IV, and V
    D. I, II, V
    E. I, III, and IV

40. Cases that have one of the following characteristics are more likely than others to be given a *writ of certiorari* EXCEPT:
    A. when the Solicitor General requests a hearing
    B. when lower court decisions are inconsistent
    C. when constitutional issues are involved
    D. when justices want to clarify or reverse a precedent
    E. the lower court has made a mistake

41. When evaluating laws that treat women differently than men, the Supreme Court
    A. uses the strict-scrutiny test to almost always strike down the law
    B. uses the strict-scrutiny test to sometimes strike down the law
    C. uses the intermediate-scrutiny test to sometimes strike down the law
    D. uses the reasonable-basis test to sometimes strike down the law
    E. uses the Fourteenth Amendment to always strike down the law

42. Congress's oversight tools include all of the following EXCEPT:
    A. committee and subcommittee hearings to investigate how policies are executed
    B. the ability to cite executive branch officials for contempt if they fail to answer questions
    C. dismissal of civil servants who fail to properly execute policies
    D. reducing or threatening to reduce appropriations for programs
    E. restricting ways that funds can be spent for programs

43. What is the difference between the political beliefs of a libertarian and those of a conservative?
    A. Nothing; they share the same political beliefs.
    B. A conservative is in favor of deregulation and a libertarian is not.
    C. A conservative is opposed to a national health care system and a libertarian is not.
    D. A conservative is opposed to decriminalizing marijuana and a libertarian is not.
    E. A conservative is in favor of increasing spending for welfare programs and a libertarian is not.

44. Only a minority of U.S. citizens ever participates in politics by:
    I.   voting
    II. campaigning
    III. lobbying
    IV. protesting

    A. I, II, III, IV
    B. II, III, IV
    C. I, II, and IV
    D. III and IV
    E. IV

45. The power of judicial review entails
    A. the ability of the Supreme Court to review cases and set precedents
    B. the ability of the Supreme Court to review and reverse its own precedents
    C. the ability of the Supreme Court to declare government actions unconstitutional
    D. the ability of the Supreme Court to determine its own caseload
    E. the ability of the Supreme Court to exercise its appellate jurisdiction

46. Today, political speech can be censored when
    A. it damages the reputation of a public official
    B. it is particularly offensive to the community
    C. it passes the "clear-and-present-danger" test
    D. it passes the "imminent-lawless-action" test
    E. it is accompanied by flag burning

47. Categorical grants
    A. allow states and localities to spend federal money as they see fit
    B. allow states and localities to spend state money as they see fit
    C. allow states to fund local programs with grants
    D. allows the federal government to designate how states and localities can spend federal money
    E. allows the federal government to designate how states and localities can spend state money

48. Labor unions
   A. are primarily made up of unskilled workers
   B. can provide material incentives to members
   C. are prohibited from forming political action committees
   D. cannot overcome the free-rider problem
   E. have grown in political strength over the last 30 years

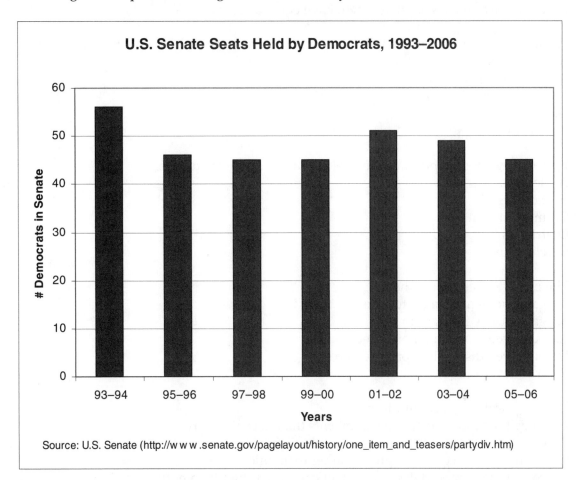

U.S. Senate Seats Held by Democrats, 1993–2006

Source: U.S. Senate (http://w w w .senate.gov/pagelayout/history/one_item_and_teasers/partydiv.htm)

49. Based on data in the chart above, when was there "divided government"?
   A. 1993–94 and 2001–02
   B. 1993–94, 2001–02, and 2003–04
   C. 1995–96, 1997–98, 1999–2000, 2003–04 and 2005–06
   D. 1995–96, 1997–98, 1999–2000, 2001–02
   E. 1993–94, 2003–04, and 2005–06

50. What is an advantage of the current system for appointing bureaucrats over the "spoils system" used in the past?
   A. Today's system keeps the bureaucracy more accountable to the president.
   B. Today's system keeps the bureaucracy more accountable to the mass public.
   C. Today's system guarantees demographic diversity.
   D. Today's system provides for more turnover, which brings in new ideas.
   E. Today's system provides more skilled and experienced workers.

51. According to the Constitution, which of the following has the most authority in the American system?
    A. the president
    B. the Supreme Court
    C. the Congress
    D. the states
    E. the three branches of government have equal authority

52. White people of which of the following religions are most likely to vote for Democrats?
    A. Catholics
    B. Protestants
    C. born-again Christians
    D. Jews
    E. Mormons

53. Which is the most important source of children's political attitudes?
    A. schools
    B. families
    C. mass media
    D. friends
    E. churches

54. The Equal Rights Amendment
    A. gave women the right to vote
    B. gave blacks the right to vote
    C. outlawed discrimination based on race
    D. outlawed discrimination based on sex
    E. was never ratified

55. Most political action committees
    A. contribute more money to incumbents than to challengers
    B. contribute some of their money to officials in the executive branch
    C. are funded by corporate profits rather than union dues
    D. contribute to candidates of one political party rather than both
    E. contribute a greater proportion of their money to presidential elections than Congressional campaigns

56. A social movement had the greatest impact on bringing about which of the following?
    A. *Brown v. Board of Education*
    B. the "exclusionary rule"
    C. No Child Left Behind law
    D. Voting Rights Act
    E. the end to racial profiling

57. Which of the following committees plays an important role in the greatest number of bills?
    A. Rules Committee in the Senate
    B. Rules Committee in the House of Representatives
    C. Judiciary Committee in the Senate
    D. Ways and Means Committee in the Senate
    E. Government Reform Committee in the House of Representatives

58. The primary way that the public influences the Supreme Court is by
    A. forcing it to hear cases on issues the people consider important
    B. electing justices they agree with
    C. recalling justices who overstep their authority
    D. electing officials who appoint and confirm appointments of justices
    E. persuading Senators to impeach justices whose rulings they disagree with

59. The Office of Management and Budget does which of the following?
       I. reviews and adjusts agency budget proposals
      II. evaluates the costs and benefits of major regulations
     III. ensures that the executive branch's budget proposal is consistent with the president's priorities

    A. I
    B. II
    C. III
    D. I and III
    E. I, II, and III

60. An "executive agreement" is
    A. an agreement between the U.S. and another nation that is arranged by the president and approved by the Senate
    B. an agreement between the U.S. and other nations that is arranged by the president and does not have to be approved by the Senate
    C. an agreement between different departments in the executive branch
    D. any reprieve or pardon that the president issues for those convicted of crimes
    E. the right of the president to withhold confidential information affecting national security

UNITED STATES GOVERNMENT AND POLITICS

SECTION II
Time—100 minutes

Directions: You have 100 minutes to answer all four of the following questions. It is suggested that you take a few minutes to plan and outline each answer. *Spend approximately one-fourth of your time (25 minutes) on each question.* Illustrate your essay with substantive examples where appropriate. Make certain to number each of your answers as the question is numbered below.

JEANNE PAINTER JOHNSON

1. Imagine that the cartoon above appeared in a newspaper during the week after George W. Bush won the 2004 election.

    A. Describe a point that the cartoon makes about the news media's coverage of elections and how it is made in the cartoon.

    B. Identify and describe another feature (not identified in the cartoon) that characterizes the news media's coverage of campaigns.

    C. Using an explanation that focuses on the media, explain why the media covers elections in one of the ways you described in your answers to "A" or "B."

    D. Using an explanation that focuses on campaigns, explain why the media covers elections in one of the ways you described in your answers to "A" or "B."

2. Civil liberties are not absolute. The Supreme Court balances them against competing rights and the interests of society.

   Select one of the following issues.

   • Parents of a student in a California public school claim that the school should not start the day with the Pledge of Allegiance to the flag even if their daughter is not required to say the pledge.

   • A Native American challenges his arrest for violating a state drug law by smoking peyote during a ceremony.

   For the issue you select, do each of the following:

   A. Identify the civil liberty that is at issue and the constitutional clause and amendment in which this liberty appears.

   B. Describe a competing value and how it is on the other side of the litigant's case.

   C. Explain how the Fourteenth Amendment and the way that the Supreme Court has interpreted it in the past are relevant to this issue.

   D. Identify and describe a technique that interest groups concerned about this case could try to influence the outcome of this issue.

   E. Identify and describe a technique that Congress could use to "check" the Court's power on this issue.

3. American politics has a "class bias."

   A. Describe what is meant by a "class bias" in American politics.

   B. Describe how this bias is evident in political participation.

   C. Identify two factors that contribute to this bias in political participation. Explain how or why each factor contributes.

   D. Identify a specific example that shows the effect of "class bias" on public policy. Describe the process through which the class bias affected public policy.

4. Two of the major goals of the Framers of the Constitution were to create limited government that would not threaten personal liberty and to create self-government in which decisions are based on popular consent.

   A. Define two of these Constitutional features and explain how they promote limited government in terms of Congressional power.

      • grants of power
      • denials of power
      • checks and balances

   B. Describe two ways that the Constitution promotes self-government through Congress.

   C. Describe one of the functions of Congress listed below and explain how it is exercised in a way that promotes limited government.

   D. Describe another one of the functions of Congress listed below and give an example of how it is exercised in a way that promotes self-government.

      • lawmaking function
      • oversight function
      • representative function

PRACTICE TEST I ANSWERS

Answers to Section I (Multiple Choice)

1. The correct answer is (D). Federalism is a system of government in which authority is divided between national and state governments. The amendment process for the Constitution requires passage by a two-thirds majority of both chambers of Congress and approval by two-thirds of the states. See page 73 for a discussion of federalism and page 52 for the Constitution's amendment process.

2. The correct answer is (D). Kerry had 252 Electoral College votes compared to Bush's 286. If Kerry had won Indiana's eleven votes and Kentucky's eight, he would have had 271 and Bush would have had 267. Neither Alabama's eight Electoral College votes nor Arizona and New Mexico's combined fifteen Electoral College votes would have been enough to give Kerry more Electoral College votes than Bush. The margin of victory in a Western state does not influence the number of Electoral College votes awarded from those states, so (A) is incorrect.

3. The correct answer is (E). One of the checks on power that Congress has over the courts is to rewrite laws that the Court has interpreted. Although Congress can change the number of justices and restrict the Court's appellate jurisdiction, it has not done so. Congress cannot pass constitutional amendments by itself. Amendments require ratification by the states before taking effect. None of the amendments in the last 50 years have "checked" the Court's power. See pages 54–56 and page 466 for more information.

4. The correct answer is (C). Elitism refers to the view that the government is run by a few privileged individuals. See pages 27–31 for a discussion on the theories of power.

5. The correct answer is (E). This is the only answer for which there is relevant supporting data on the figure.

6. The correct answer is (B). The gap between the two lines is greater in California because there California has a greater number of noncitizens who are old enough to vote. The implication of calculating turnout for assessing its level is discussed briefly on page 215.

7. The correct answer is (B). Open primaries (or direct primaries) allow voters of any party affiliation to directly choose a party's candidate. Closed primaries limit participation to members of the political party. Caucuses limit participation to partisans who are willing to spend time and effort to participate. Conventions are composed of party activists. Patronage involves appointments, not elections. See pages 256–57 for more information.

8. The correct answer is (B). Conference committees are necessary only when House and Senate versions of a bill are different. About 10 percent of bills require conference committees. See pages 357–58 for more information.

9. The correct answer is (B). The Civil Rights Act of 1964 provides protection against discrimination in businesses that serve the general public, such as restaurants and gas stations. See pages 163–64 for more information.

10. The correct answer is (D). Education is the most important predictor of voter turnout. Other predictors include age and economic class. See pages 223–24 for more information. Party identification influences vote choice more than voter turnout.

11. The correct answer is (D). The White House Office consists of the president's close personal advisers, who are hired and fired by the president as he sees fit. See pages 392–94 for more information.

12. The correct answer is (D). The commerce clause gave Congress the power to regulate commerce but did not specify which powers were granted. The Supreme Court limited the power of Congress to regulate commerce until 1937, when it began to interpret the clause more broadly. See pages 85–88 for more information on the commerce clause and the reasons for the Court's broader interpretations after 1937.

13. The correct answer is (D). Congress, not the president, has the authority to change the number of justices on the Supreme Court. The president needs approval of the Senate, not the House, to make treaties. Congress is responsible for appropriating funds and declaring war. See the box on page 376 for more information.

14. The correct answer is (E). *Miranda v. Arizona* dealt with self-incrimination, expressed in the Fifth Amendment, and the right to counsel expressed in the Sixth Amendment. See table 4-2 on page 126 for more information.

15. The correct answer is (A). Because the general public is not knowledgeable about policy formation and alternatives, public opinion plays a limited role in the formation of policy. See pages 185–87 for more information.

16. The correct answer is (D). The president has always been commander-in-chief. The line-item veto has never been granted to the president. Choices (A) and (B) are false. Since 1945, the president's power has grown as the United States has become more of a global leader, especially in areas of foreign policy. Congress is unable to respond quickly to foreign policy matters because of its size and responsibilities.

17. The correct answer is (E). Though Supreme Court justices are chosen because of prior judicial experience, other professional qualifications, and agreement with the president's views, there are no specific job experience requirements. See pages 457–58 for more information.

18. The correct answer is (E). Agenda setting is a term that refers to the ability of the press to focus the public's priorities by what it reports on. See page 322 for more information.

19. The correct answer is (E). An interest group with a relatively small and affluent membership is likely to use inside lobbying techniques. The most common inside lobbying focuses on providing information about issues important to the interest group. See page 289 for more information.

20. The correct answer is (A). Social security is funded and run by the federal government. Choices (B), (C), and (D) are administered jointly by the federal government and states. Choice (E) is no longer a federal program. See pages 528 and 532–33 for more information.

21. The correct answer is (D). The Fourteenth Amendment prohibited states from denying due process rights to individuals. *Gitlow v. New York* was the Court's first use of selective incorporation, when it used the Fourteenth Amendment to apply the freedom from government restrictions of expression to state governments. See page 112 and Table 4-1 on page 113 for other cases that used selective incorporation.

22. The correct answer is (C). The family is one of the strongest agents of political socialization, and early-childhood influences from the family tend to remain throughout life. See pages 193–95 for more information on agents of political association.

23. The correct answer is (D). The other choices are all consequences of candidate-centered campaigns. Political party power is not affected by candidate centered-campaigns. Such campaigns focus more on personal characteristics than on issues, compared to party-centered campaigns. See pages 264–72 for more information.

24. The correct answer is (B). The Budget and Impoundment Control Act, passed in 1974, prohibits the president from withholding funds authorized by Congress indefinitely. The War Powers Act was designed to limit presidential authority but has been largely unsuccessful. Executive privilege enhances the power of the president, as would the line-item veto if it were passed. The Twenty-seventh Amendment refers to compensation for members of Congress. See page 405 for more information on the Budget and Impoundment Control Act.

25. The correct answer is (A). The Boy Scouts of America has the freedom to pick its members, but the equality of gays is compromised through their exclusion. See pages 9 and 10 for discussions on freedom and equality and the box on page 164 for a discussion about the Boy Scouts of America excluding gays from the organization.

26. The correct answer is (E). The "equal protection clause" states that individuals must be treated equally under the law, but it does not say that all people must be treated the same in all circumstances. Minimum-age drinking laws are an example of this. See pages 162–63 for more information, and Table 5-1 (p. 162) for the tests used to enforce the Fourteenth Amendment's equal protection clause.

27. The correct answer is (D). Reorganization, appointments, and budgeting are the three management tools the president has over the bureaucracy. However, he cannot violate the Budget and Impoundment Control Act to try to discipline the bureaucracy (see p. 405). See pages 431–34 for more information on the three presidential tools.

28. The correct answer is (C). Table 11-2 indicates that the Senate has fewer standing committees. House members specialize more through their standing committee membership on only two committees, compared with four for senators. To become law, bills need to go through both the Senate and the House; therefore, they deal with the same issues. There are fewer formal rules in the Senate because there are fewer members and they operate under more of a mutual-consent system. See the discussion of Senate leadership on pages 347–48.

29. The correct answer is (D). The small percentage of cases that the Supreme Court accepts demonstrates that it has great discretion. Recall that the Court needs to issue a writ of certiorari for lower-court cases to be heard. See pages 448–49.

30. The correct answer is (A). This question refers to Figure 7-1 on page 216. Voter turnout in the last 20 years has fluctuated, but it has never reached the 62 percent turnout of 1960.

31. The correct answer is (E). Realignments are rare, with just three since the 1850s. Realignments result in enduring changes in party coalitions and solidify the standing of the dominant political party. Split-ticket voting, in which voters vote for one party's candidate for president and the other party's candidate for Congress, is reduced because of the strong support for the dominant political party. See page 247 for more information on split-ticket voting and pages 244–46 for more information on realignments.

32. The correct answer is (A). The question is referring to the process of amending the Constitution, which requires that amendments be proposed by a two-thirds majority in both chambers of Congress or by a constitutional convention called by two thirds of the states, which has never occurred. See page 52 for more information on amending the Constitution.

33. The correct answer is (A). The Articles of Confederation created a weak national government that was subordinate to the states. State legislators appointed and paid members of the national Congress. See page 43 for a discussion on the Articles of Confederation.

34. The correct answer is (E). Iron triangles are informal groups of like-minded government agencies, members of Congress and lobbyists that come together to promote a specific interest. There are no competing interest groups in iron triangles. Issue networks often have competing interest groups as members. See pages 292–93 for more information.

35. The correct answer is (A). The president's approval ratings tend to go up when foreign policy crises occur, although they erode when the issues are not resolved. See pages 406–09 for more information on the public's support of the president.

36. The correct answer is (B). The 1960s and 1970s were a period of regulatory reform. It has been called the "era of new social regulation." See pages 491–92 for more information.

37. The correct answer is (D). The decision in *University of California Regents v. Bakke* (1978) stated that strict quotas could not be used in affirmative action policies. See pages 169–72 for information on affirmative action laws and Supreme Court rulings.

38. The correct answer is (E). *Griswold v. Connecticut*, a case in which a state law prohibiting the use of birth control was ruled unconstitutional, dealt with the privacy rights of Americans. The right of privacy was central to the case of *Roe v. Wade*, in which abortion rights were upheld. See pages 121–22 for more information on both cases.

39. The correct answer is (C). Soft money and 527 money cannot be given directly to a candidate. Hard money and federal matching funds go directly to candidates. PAC contributions can be given to candidates, within limits. See page 262 for more information.

40. The correct answer is (E). The Supreme Court tends to take cases that involve broad legal questions and does not try to correct all mistakes made by lower courts. See pages 448–49 for more information.

41. The correct answer is (C). There are three tests developed by the Court in its application of the Fourteenth Amendment's equal protection clause. The intermediate-scrutiny test applies to gender and is classified as an "almost-suspect" category, which assumes that a law discriminating by sex is unconstitutional unless it meets a clearly justified purpose. See Table 5-1 on page 162 and pages 162–63 for a discussion on the tests used to apply the equal protection clause.

42. The correct answer is (C). Congress has no power to remove civil servants who fail to properly execute policies. See pages 365–68 for more information on the oversight functions of Congress.

43. The correct answer is (D). Libertarians want government to stay out of personal affairs, including drug use.

44. The correct answer is (B). Just over half of U.S. citizens eligible to vote participate in elections. Only a small minority ever get involved in campaigning, lobbying, or protesting. See page 235 for more information.

45. The correct answer is (C). Judicial review was first asserted by the Court in *Marbury v. Madison* in 1830. Judicial review allows the Court to decide whether a government action is constitutional. See pages 56–58 and 467–68 for more information.

46. The correct answer is (D). The "imminent lawless action" test states that government can only censor speech when it aims to produce, and is likely to produce, imminent lawless action. See page 113 for more information.

47. The correct answer is (D). Categorical grants can be used only for a specific activity designated by the federal government. These are more restrictive than block grants, which allow state and local governments more freedom to choose how to spend federal funds. See page 93 for more information.

48. The correct answer is (B). Material incentives are economic benefits such as high-paying jobs that attract group members. See pages 281–82 for more information.

49. The correct answer is (D). Divided government refers to times when the presidency and a chamber of Congress are controlled by different parties. This occurred when Democratic President Clinton faced a Republican Senate in 1995–96, 1997–98, and 1999–2000 and when Republican President Bush faced a Democratic Senate in 2001–02.

50. The correct answer is (E). The current system used for appointing bureaucrats is the executive leadership system, which uses management tools and leadership by the president to manage the bureaucracy. It does not guarantee accountability, demographic diversity, or turnover. See page 422 for more information on the spoils system and page 424 for more information on the executive leadership system.

51. The correct answer is (C). Although the three branches of government operate in a system of divided powers, Congress has the most constitutional authority. See pages 401–06 for a good discussion on this topic.

52. The correct answer is (D). Jewish people are more likely to be Democratic than any of the other religious groups. See Figure 8-4 on page 252 for more information.

53. The correct answer is (B). The family has the greatest impact on socialization, and early-childhood influences from the family tend to remain throughout life. See pages 193–95 for more information on agents of political socialization.

54. The correct answer is (E). Congress approved the Equal Rights Amendment in 1973, but it was never ratified by the states. See pages 148–49 for more information.

55. The correct answer is (A). Political action committees (PACs) contribute more money to incumbents than to challengers because incumbents are more likely to win elections. PACs contribute to both political parties, primarily to members of Congress, and their funds must be obtained voluntarily and not through profits or union dues. See pages 296–99 for more information.

56. The correct answer is (D). The Civil Rights Act of 1964 and the Voting Rights Act of 1965 were both responses by Congress to the civil rights movement of the early 1960s. None of the other answers were a result of social movements. *Brown v. Board of Education* preceded the movement. See page 234 for more information.

57. The correct answer is (B). The Rules Committee in the House of Representatives decides when and how bills will be voted on. It also decides whether amendments will be allowed. The Rules Committee in the Senate has much less power. See pages 356–57 for more information.

58. The correct answer is (D). The public cannot directly influence the Supreme Court because justices are not elected officials. It can indirectly influence the Court through its election of officials responsible for appointing and confirming justices. Justices typically behave as the president appointing them expected (see p. 458 and the box on p. 459). Although Congress can impeach justices (see p. 61), this is rarely done and not based on unpopular rulings. Therefore, this is not the primary way that the public influences the Court.

59. The correct answer is (E). The Office of Management and Budget is an executive agency created to help the president coordinate the budgetary process. Its functions include the actions described in all three of these statements. See page 424 for more information.

60. The correct answer is (B). Executive agreements with other countries are made by the president. The Supreme Court has ruled that they have the same legal status as treaties. Although approval from the Senate is not required, Congress can cancel executive agreements. See pages 375–76 for more information.

Answer Guidelines for Section II

Question 1 is worth seven points.

Part "A" is worth one point. Acceptable answers include: preoccupation with horse race (focus on winning or losing), heavy reliance on polls, continuous coverage of elections (starting to cover 2008 the day after 2004), lack of issue coverage, candidate-centered coverage, descriptive coverage rather than evaluative, objective (rather than partisan) press, reliance on official sources, extensive coverage of politics, and media as "signaler" of important developments. These features are evident from pointing to one or more of the headlines.

Although the cartoon does not emphasize the skeptical view of government or the spin that reporters can put on a story, students can get credit for this if they point to the line "By I know it all." Students can only get credit for "attention-grabbing" if they point to the size of headlines.

Unacceptable answers are references to watchdog journalism, strategy-focused coverage, negativity bias, liberal or conservative bias, partisan bias, or two-party bias because there is no evidence of these in the cartoon.

Part "B" is worth two points. The first is awarded for identifying a correct feature. The second is for correctly describing it. Acceptable answers include: a feature of the news media that is listed above that was not used to answer "A." They can also include watchdog journalism, strategy-focused coverage, negativity bias, two-party bias, short soundbites, image-centered coverage, scandal coverage (feeding frenzies), superficial issue coverage, conflict coverage, following agendas set by the campaigns, and coverage of advertising.

For students to get a point for ideological bias they need to point to specific news organizations that promote a point of view, such as Fox News, New Republic, American Spectator, not to ABC, CBS, NBC, CNN, major newspapers or newsmagazines. If they make a general statement about the news being liberally biased, the answer does not get a point.

Part "C" is worth two points. The first is earned by identifying a factor that contributes to the media covering the election in a particular way that focuses on the media itself. The second is for correctly explaining how this feature contributes to the coverage. Acceptable answers include: it is easier this way (to take news, use polls that are available, go to official sources, etc.), pack journalism (others are doing it this way), the goal of objective journalism, organizational norms and need to make a profit (give the people what they are perceived to want), and the needs and desires of the public audience (not ideological, not issue-focused). NOTE: The student cannot earn any points for explaining why the media do something that the media do not in fact do.

Part "D" is worth two points. The first is earned by identifying a factor that contributes to the media covering the election in a particular way that focuses on the media itself. Acceptable answers include: campaigns, specifically ads or candidates or consultants; focus on candidates rather than issues or ideologies; campaigns start early; candidates feed the media certain types of information (short repetitive slogans, vague ideas, etc.); and the rules of the game hurt third-party candidates. NOTE: The student cannot earn any points for explaining why the media do something that the media do not in fact do.

Question 2 is worth six points.

Part "A" is worth one point. The acceptable answer for the first issue is: religious freedom found in the "establishment clause" of the First Amendment. The acceptable answer for the second issue is: religious freedom found in the "free-exercise clause" of the First Amendment. No point is awarded unless the clause and the amendment are specified.

Part "B" is worth one point. Acceptable answers for the first issue are patriotism, community, or unity. A case might be made for free speech if the answer points out that other students would be prohibited from saying the pledge voluntarily. Acceptable answers for the second issue are order or security. A case might be made for equality if the answer points out that other groups are not permitted to use the drug.

Part "C" is worth two points. The first point is awarded for saying that the Fourteenth Amendment has been used to apply the Bill of Rights to the actions of state governments or referring to "incorporation." The second point is awarded for explaining how this is relevant to this issue.

Part "D" is worth one point. Acceptable answers include: filing amicus curiae (friend of the court) briefs, supporting the litigants in the case by supplying lawyers and financial backing, filing a class-action suit for similarly situated litigants, and lobbying Congress to pass a law that clarifies the issue.

Part "E" is worth one point. Acceptable answers include: change the number of Supreme Court justices to change the balance of power on the Court and influence the decision, impeach and remove judges to change the balance of power on the Court and influence the decision, write legislation that prohibits or protects the right so the Court will need to interpret that, and initiate a constitutional amendment that prohibits or protests the right so the Court will need to interpret that.

Question 3 is worth seven points.

Part "A" is worth one point. Students must convey the idea that higher-income people have an advantage over lower-income people.

Part "B" is worth one point. Students need to say that upper-class or higher-income groups vote, campaign, join groups, or lobby government at higher rates than lower-income groups. No points are awarded for saying that class affects which party, vote, or issue position a person takes.

Part "C" is worth three points. One point is awarded for identifying two factors; no point for identifying only one. One point is awarded for explaining how or why one factor contributes to the class bias in political participation. One point is awarded for explaining how or why a second factor contributes to the class bias in political participation. Acceptable reasons for lower-income groups participating less than higher groups include: fewer resources (time and money) to expend on politics, weaker civic attitudes, weaker sense of civic duty, more apathy, more alienation because of low level of trust, less political knowledge, less political interest, America lacks class-based parties that mobilize these groups, and a system that assumes personal initiative to participate (registration laws, no holidays for elections, etc.).

Part "D" is worth two points. One point is awarded for describing the impact of class bias in a specific example. The example can be hypothetical. It simply needs to illustrate that lower-income groups didn't "get something" from government or didn't keep something from happening or that upper class groups did "get something" from government or kept something from happening. The second point is awarded for describing the process by which the group was or was not effective (through electing advocates, lobbying Congress, etc.).

Question 4 is worth eight points.

Part "A" is worth three points. One point is awarded for correctly describing both constitutional features that promote limited government in terms of Congress. The second is awarded for explaining how one promotes limited government. The third point is awarded for explaining how the second promotes limited government. Acceptable answers for grants of powers is the idea that the scope of Congress's authority is limited to the section listed powers granted in Article I, Section 8 (e.g., to tax, establish army and navy, declare war, regulate commerce, create currency, borrow money); denial of power is the idea that authority not granted to Congress is denied to Congress; Congress is prohibited from passing ex post facto laws; it is hard to amend the Constitution to give Congress more power; powers are reserved to the states in Amendment 10; the Bill of Rights prevents the federal government from infringing on specified liberties; checks and balances limit Congress by allowing the Court to interpret legal disputes arising under Congressional acts and by allowing the president to veto bills and interpret laws.

Part "B" is worth one point. Students must identify two ways to get one point. These include: representative democracy established by having the people directly elect members of the House of Representatives; indirectly electing their senators through their appointments by popularly elected state legislatures; the six-year terms for senators, which allow for reelection or rejection; two-year terms for the House of Representatives, which allow for reelection or rejection; apportionment, or establishing and maintaining "one person, one vote" through House districts; filling vacancies between elections by the president, who is indirectly elected; and residency requirements.

Part "C" is worth two points. One is earned by describing the function of Congress. The second point is earned by explaining how the function is exercised in a way that promotes limited government. It is easiest to earn the second point by selecting "oversight role" and explaining how it constrains the executive branch from overstepping its power. The second point can also be earned for "lawmaking function" if the focus is on passing laws that constrain government action or features of the system that make it difficult to exercise power. The second point can be earned for "representational function" if the focus is on how constituency service helps constrain government actions, how committee service on behalf of local interests helps limit government action, or how representing diverse people through pluralism or partisanship acts as a check on government action.

Part "D" is worth two points. One is earned by describing a different function of Congress than the one discussed in "C". The second point is earned by explaining how the function is exercised in a way that promotes self-government. It is easiest to earn the second point by selecting "representation role" and explaining how it empowers the public through parties, groups, or mass opinion. Specific discussions may focus on: efforts to measure the public's interests through polls, service, mailings, telephone calls; constituency service; logrolling; pork-barrel legislation; delegate-role orientations; committee assignments that help district interests; and party leadership reflecting the public will. The second point can be earned for "oversight function" if the discussion of checking the executive branch comes from a public demand or interest. The second point can also be earned for "lawmaking function" if the focus is on passing laws that represent the people, discussing delegate-role orientation, logrolling, or pork-barrel legislation.

PRACTICE TEST II

United States Government and Politics

Two hours and twenty-five minutes are allotted for this examination: 45 minutes for Section I, which consists of multiple-choice questions; and 100 minutes for Section II, which consists of four mandatory essay questions. Section I is printed in this examination booklet. Section II is printed in a separate booklet.

SECTION I

Time – 45 minutes
Number of questions – 60
Percentage of total grade – 50

UNITED STATES GOVERNMENT AND POLITICS

Section I
Time—45 minutes

60 Questions

Directions: Each of the questions or incomplete statements below is followed by five suggested answers or completions. Select the one that is best in each case and then fill in the corresponding oval on the answer sheet.

1. The Supreme Court's ruling in *McCulloch v. Maryland* was important because it established the precedent for
    A. how checks and balances work
    B. the Court's judicial review authority
    C. expanding national authority
    D. selective incorporation
    E. dual federalism

2. How do interest groups typically lobby the Supreme Court?
    A. They organize their members to write letters to justices.
    B. They file "amicus curiae" briefs that defend their position on pending cases.
    C. They contribute money to justices' campaigns.
    D. They hire lobbyists to advocate their positions on pending cases with justices.
    E. Interest groups do not lobby the Supreme Court.

3. The role of parents in political socialization of children is
    A. not as great as the role of schools, which provide explicit political information
    B. not as great as the mass media, which monopolize children's attention
    C. not as great as friends, who exert social peer pressure
    D. not great because children rebel against their parents
    E. great because children learn their values from their parents

4. Which of these interest groups is most likely to fight for collective goods?
    A. United Steelworkers Union
    B. American Medical Association
    C. U.S. Chamber of Commerce
    D. AFL-CIO
    E. Greenpeace U.S.A

Voter Turnout in Presidential Elections

Age Group	1988	1992	1996	2000	2004
18–24	48.2%	52.5%	48.8%	45.4%	51.5%
25–44	63.0	64.8	61.9	59.6	60.1
45–64	75.5	75.3	73.5	71.2	72.7
65 and over	78.4	78.0	77.0	76.1	76.9

Source: "Statistics of the Presidential and Congressional Election of November 2, 2004", www.clerk.gov
Internet Release date: May 26, 2005

5. The data displayed in the table above support which of the following statements?
   A. Old people are more likely to vote for Republicans than to vote for Democrats.
   B. Old people were increasingly likely to vote from 1988 to 2004
   C. The impact of age on voter turnout was the same from 1988 to 2004.
   D. The impact of age on voter turnout was the same from 1988 to 2004, with the exception of 1992.
   E. Regardless of age, voter turnout increased from 1988 to 1992.

6. During the last few decades, the greatest limit to presidents' power over the federal budget has been
   A. an uncooperative Congress that insists on passing its own version of the budget
   B. a vigilant public that resists presidential leadership on budgetary matters
   C. constraints placed on presidential power by Supreme Court rulings
   D. existing laws that authorize extensive mandatory spending
   E. a reluctance of the president to propose budget initiatives or cuts

7. Which of the following had the greatest immediate impact on increasing voter turnout?
   A. the 1993 Motor Voter law making it easier to register to vote
   B. the Fifteenth Amendment giving blacks the right to vote
   C. the Twenty-fourth Amendment banning the poll tax
   D. the Twenty-sixth Amendment allowing eighteen-to-twenty-one-year-olds to vote
   E. the Voting Rights Act of 1965

8. Why does the cabinet have a limited influence on the president's decisions?
   A. because cabinet officials lack experience and expertise
   B. because cabinet officials lack a "big picture" point of view, focusing instead on their particular agencies' objectives
   C. because the cabinet is too large to be useful to the president
   D. because the president has no control over who is on the cabinet
   E. because the cabinet considers its primary constituency to be the people who selected them

9. Which of the following are examples of retrospective voting?
    I.   voting for the incumbent because the incumbent has lowered taxes
    II. voting against the incumbent because the incumbent has supported school vouchers
    III. voting for the incumbent because the economy is healthy

    A. I
    B. II
    C. III
    D. I and III
    E. I, II, and III

10. Rather than amend the Articles of Confederation, a new constitution was written at a constitutional convention. Why?
    A. The Articles provided no amending process to fix their weaknesses.
    B. Most Americans agreed that the Articles were beyond repair.
    C. The Revolutionary War rendered the articles obsolete.
    D. There was not the required unanimous agreement among states to amend the Articles.
    E. The Constitutional Convention was instructed by the states to write a new constitution.

11. Which of the following is true about standing committees?
    A. They resolve differences between the House and Senate versions of bills.
    B. They analyze bills introduced to Congress by the president.
    C. They appropriate funds for government programs annually.
    D. They serve both lawmaking and oversight roles in particular issue areas.
    E. Their jurisdictions are determined by committee chairmen or chairwomen.

12. For the most part, the following statements about voting turnout are true EXCEPT:
    A. Voting is more common in general elections than in primaries.
    B. Voting is more common in presidential elections than in midterm elections.
    C. Voting was more common during the 1960s than it is today.
    D. Voting is more common in other Western democracies than in the United States.
    E. Voting is more common among those people who cannot afford to influence politics in other ways.

13. "Senatorial courtesy" refers to
    A. the tendency of senators to defer to the president by confirming justices he nominates to the Supreme Court
    B. the tendency of senators to defer to the president by confirming judges he nominates to district courts
    C. the tendency of senators to defer to other senators when deciding whether to confirm justices nominated to the Supreme Court
    D. the tendency of senators to defer to other senators when deciding whether to confirm judges nominated to district courts
    E. the tendency of senators to defer to their constituents

14. What are the primary roles of the Democratic National Committee and the Republican National Committee?
    A. They provide services such as funds and training for party candidates.
    B. They control the nominating process, choosing candidates.
    C. They control the campaigns of party candidates.
    D. They write party platforms that candidates campaign on.
    E. They organize their party's programs in Congress.

15. What political institution has the responsibility of redistricting after a reapportionment?
    A. the Census
    B. the U.S. House of Representatives
    C. the U.S. Senate
    D. state governments
    E. the federal judiciary

Political Action Committee Contributions to Selected Pennsylvania House of Representative Candidates (2004)

Congressional District	Major Candidates	Amount Raised
01	**Robert A. Brady (D)** * Deborah L. Williams (R)	$ 654,746 $ 0
02	**Chaka Fattah (D)** * Stewart Bolno (R)	$ 353,968 $ 14,710
03	**Phil English (R)** * Steve Porter (D)	$1,338,016 $ 235,126
04	**Melissa Hart (R)** * Stevan Drobac Jr. (D)	$1,445,691 $ 11,279
07	**Curt Weldon (R)** * Paul Scoles (D)	$ 894,581 $ 23,957
08	**Michael G. Fitzpatrick (R)** Virginia Waters Schrader (D)	$1,271,864 $ 619,605
09	**Bill Shuster (R)** * Paul I. Politis (D)	$1,269,369 $ 16,382
13	**Allyson Schwartz (D)** Melissa Brown (R)	$4,597,032 $1,953,561
16	**Joe Pitts (R)** * Lois K. Herr (D)	$ 542,444 $ 87,646
18	**Tim Murphy (R)** * Mark Boles (D)	$1,229,326 $ 160,003

*Incumbent
Winner is in bold

Source: Federal Elections Commission, www.fec.gov

16. The data displayed in the table above support which of the following statements about political action committees' contributions?
   - I. Candidates who are already in the House of Representatives get more contributions than those who are not.
   - II. Candidates who are competing for open seats get more contributions than those who are not.
   - III. Winners get more contributions than losers.

   A. I
   B. II
   C. III
   D. I and III
   E. I, II, and III

17. Which group is most likely to say that government should stay out of economic matters but should be active in promoting certain values in society through public policies?
   A. liberals
   B. conservatives
   C. free riders
   D. libertarians
   E. populists

18. Which of the following officials are appointed by the president without Senate approval?
   A. the U.S. Ambassador to Mexico
   B. the Attorney General
   C. the Chief Justice of the U.S. Supreme Court
   D. the White House Chief of Staff
   E. replacements for governors who die in office

19. Which of the following is the American Civil Liberties Union most likely to do?
   A. file lawsuits against the government
   B. hold up protest signs at Congressional hearings
   C. wine and dine key congressmen
   D. contribute money to congressional campaigns
   E. pass state legislation

20. In which of these situations is a "legislative veto" being used?
   A. when an executive agency is required to approve Congressional actions
   B. when the president is required to approve Congressional actions
   C. when Congress is required to approve what executive agencies and the president do
   D. when voters are permitted to negate congressional actions
   E. when the Supreme Court rules that a congressional action is unconstitutional

21. The "revolving door" in government
   A. helps the mass public learn about government
   B. results in incremental policymaking
   C. illustrates that "it's not what you know but who you know"
   D. illustrates that "it's not who you know but what you know"
   E. illustrates that "it's both who you know and what you know"

22. In *Federalist* No.10, James Madison claimed that government is most dangerous when
    A. factions compete for power
    B. leaders are physically far away from the people
    C. a single group gains control
    D. a constitution lacks a Bill of Rights
    E. decisions are not made democratically

23. Which of the following is a "reserved power" derived from the Tenth Amendment to the Constitution?
    A. the power of Congress to declare war
    B. the power of U.S. laws to be supreme over state laws
    C. the power of states in areas not delegated to the national government or prohibited to the states
    D. the power of the federal government to regulate interstate commerce
    E. the power of the states to regulate interstate commerce

24. Most cases in the federal court system
    A. begin in district courts and end there
    B. begin in district courts and end at a U.S. court of appeals
    C. begin in a U.S. court of appeals and end there
    D. begin in a U.S. court of appeals and end at the Supreme Court
    E. begin in district courts and end at the Supreme Court

Popular Votes for Presidential Candidates, 2004

Name of Party	Number of Votes	Percentage of Votes
Democratic	58,894,584	48.14%
Republican	61,872,711	50.57%
Independent	155,966	0.13%
Libertarian	369,308	0.30%
Constitution	130,322	0.11%
Green	115,670	0.09%
Reform	58,212	0.05%
Populist	23,094	0.02%
All other parties	729,613	0.60%

Compiled from Official Sources by Jeff Trandahl, Clerk of the House of Representatives

25. Which of the following is not necessarily true based on the data in this table?
    A. The Republican candidate wins the presidency.
    B. The Republican candidate and the Democratic candidate compete in a runoff.
    C. Third-party candidates cost the Democratic candidate the election.
    D. This is evidence of a two-party system.
    E. This is evidence of a multiparty system.

26. The news media's attention to public-opinion polls during campaigns
    A. is infrequent
    B. is focused on liberal issues
    C. is used to fulfill a watchdog role
    D. is focused on political issues
    E. is focused on voters' preferences among the candidates

27. Which of the following has not changed over time?
    A. the process for electing U.S. House of Representatives
    B. the process of electing U.S. senators
    C. the process of electing the president.
    D. the process of selecting presidential party nominees.
    E. the number of terms a president can serve.

28. Which of the following is both accurate and an indication of the weakening of political parties?
    A. The number of people who vote Republican has grown.
    B. National party fundraising has decreased since the 1960s.
    C. Candidate-centered campaigns have replaced party-centered campaigns.
    D. Third-party candidates have been increasingly successful at getting elected to the House of Representatives.
    E. The dealignment of the 1970s and 1980s has ended.

29. Who is most likely to participate in a filibuster?
    A. members of the majority party in the House of Representatives
    B. members of the majority party in the Senate
    C. members of the minority party in the House of Representatives
    D. members of the minority party in the Senate
    E. There is no consistent pattern.

30. Why didn't racial segregation in schools end after the *Brown v. Board of Education* decision?
    I. The decision held that as long as schools were of equal quality they could be separate.
    II. Many southern and border-state schools did not enforce the decision.
    III. The decision did not require integration of schools that were racially segregated because of housing patterns.

    A. I
    B. II
    C. III
    D. II and III
    E. I and III

31. An interest group is most likely to lobby
    A. all legislators
    B. a simple majority of legislators
    C. legislators who oppose their preferred legislation
    D. legislators who are likely to support their preferred legislation
    E. legislators who are undecided regarding their preferred legislation

32. Which of the following conditions must be met for the government to stop the press from publishing a story?
    A. if it contains information that is false and will damage a public official's reputation, regardless of whether the reporter knew the information was false
    B. if it contains information that is false and will damage a public official's reputation but only if the reporter knew the information was false
    C. if it contains information that appeals to "prurient interest" and has no "redeeming social significance"
    D. if it contains information that was obtained illegally
    E. if it contains information that the government has proved to a court that the story will harm national security

33. The power of the presidency increased most dramatically during the administration of which president?
    A. Theodore Roosevelt
    B. Franklin D. Roosevelt
    C. Harry Truman
    D. Ronald Reagan
    E. George W. Bush

34. People who are alienated are most likely to
    A. vote for Democrats
    B. vote against incumbents
    C. vote for women
    D. vote for independents
    E. not vote

35. Presidential scholar Richard Neustadt claimed that the true power of the president is "the power to persuade." Which of the following is the best indicator that a president has failed to do this effectively?
    A. when he gives a State of the Union address
    B. when he uses the Office of Legislative Affairs
    C. when he conducts press conferences
    D. when he vetoes bills
    E. when he proposes a budget

36. Today, delegates to the national party conventions are selected
    A. through primaries by the voters of each state
    B. through conventions by the party leaders of each state
    C. through caucuses by the congressional leaders of each state
    D. through either primaries or caucuses by voters in each state
    E. through the national party organizations

37. The rights of gays and lesbians
    A. are protected by the Fourteenth amendment
    B. are protected by the Equal Rights Amendment
    C. are determined primarily by federal statutory law
    D. are determined primarily by state laws and common law
    E. are determined primarily by civil laws

Practice Test II:
United States Government and Politics

38. What is the difference between grassroots lobbying and lobbying that is not grassroots?
    A. Grassroots lobbying does not require money.
    B. Grassroots lobbying promotes environmentalism rather than other issues.
    C. Grassroots lobbying is not organized or preplanned.
    D. Grassroots lobbying entails the public contacting government officials.
    E. There is no difference. Grassroots lobbying is simply another name for lobbying.

39. The "free-exercise clause" of the First Amendment refers to
    A. the division between church and state
    B. the freedom of speech
    C. the freedom to assemble
    D. the freedom to choose and practice religion
    E. the freedom to petition the government

40. The following statements about the Declaration of Independence are true EXCEPT:
    A. it was a call for revolution
    B. it contained the fundamental values expressed later in the Constitution
    C. it claimed that men had national rights that government could not take away
    D. it described a form of government with separation of government and checks and balances
    E. it was written by Thomas Jefferson, who was inspired by John Locke.

41. Why is voter turnout lower in midterm elections than in presidential elections?
    A. There is more media coverage of presidential elections.
    B. There are more frequent midterm elections than there are presidential elections.
    C. They involve candidates from the same party competing against each other.
    D. They have more stringent voter-registration requirements.
    E. There are only local candidates competing for positions with limited power.

42. Which of the following best characterizes the relationship between interest groups and bureaucratic agencies?
    A. The relationship is adversarial because interest groups protest bureaucratic agencies' actions.
    B. The relationship is adversarial because agencies implement policies that interfere with interest-group objectives.
    C. The relationship is sometimes adversarial and sometimes it is not because agencies selectively cooperate or oppose interest groups depending upon what suits agency objectives.
    D. The relationship varies, with regulatory agencies being adversarial and independent agencies being cooperative.
    E. There is no relationship between interest groups and agencies because bureaucrats are not elected officials.

Advanced Placement* Test Preparation Guide • The American Democracy   **211**

43. Which of these is most consistent with the way that Americans define equality?
    A. affirmative action programs that include quotas
    B. affirmative action programs in companies guilty of having used discriminatory hiring practices.
    C. Medicaid
    D. subsidized housing
    E. government-funded schools

44. All of the following organizations were created to improve the effectiveness of the president EXCEPT
    A. Executive Office of the President
    B. General Accounting Office
    C. Council of Economic Advisers
    D. Office of Management and Budget
    E. Office of Legislative Affairs

45. The Civil Service Commission and the merit system were established by
    A. the Pendleton Act
    B. the Civil Rights Act
    C. the Budget and Impoundment Act
    D. the Sherman Antitrust Act
    E. the Fourteenth Amendment

46. The term "dual federalism" refers to
    I. a form of federalism that no longer dominates intergovernmental relations
    II. a form of federalism in which national, state, and local policymakers cooperate to solve problems
    III. a form of federalism in which states are dependent upon the federal government

    A. I
    B. II
    C. III
    D. I and II
    E. II and III

47. Presidents can be removed from office by
    A. a national recall election
    B. recall elections in two-thirds of the states
    C. a vote of two-thirds of the Senate and a simple majority of the House of Representatives
    D. a vote of impeachment in the House of Representatives
    E. a vote of five justices on the Supreme Court

48. "Iron triangles" illustrate
    A. the power of checks and balances for controlling factions
    B. the limitations of checks and balances for controlling factions
    C. the nature of federalism
    D. the power of executive leadership
    E. the power of public opinion

49. Which of the following was a Supreme Court precedent that was later reversed?
    A. *Gideon v. Wainwright*
    B. *Miranda v. Arizona*
    C. *Plessy v. Ferguson*
    D. *Marbury v. Madison*
    E. Supreme Court precedents cannot be reversed

50. All of the following make it harder for third-party candidates to win EXCEPT:
    A. single-member districts
    B. the way the news media cover campaigns
    C. split-ticket voting
    D. the rules for receiving federal matching funds
    E. the public's attachment to the Democratic and Republican parties

51. Which of the following characteristics more accurately describes the U.S. party system than those in European democracies?
    A. U.S. political parties are more ideologically polarized.
    B. U.S. political parties are more class-based.
    C. U.S. political parties are more effective at stimulating voter turnout.
    D. U.S. political parties have overlapping coalitions and programs.
    E. U.S. political parties are more plentiful.

52. How do most of the cases at the Supreme Court get there?
    A. They have original jurisdiction
    B. The cases are appealed from U.S. courts of appeals
    C. The cases are appealed from district courts
    D. The cases are appealed from state supreme courts
    E. The cases are brought directly to the Court by the attorney general.

53. When were states required to respect the procedural rights of criminals and those accused of being criminals?
    A. after the Supreme Court interpreted the "due process clause" of the Fourteenth Amendment in a way that incorporated these rights
    B. after the Supreme Court interpreted the "equal protection clause" of the Fourteenth Amendment in a way that incorporated these rights
    C. after the Supreme Court interpreted the "supremacy clause" of the Fourteenth Amendment in a way that incorporated these rights
    D. after the Supreme Court interpreted the procedural rights listed in the Fourteenth Amendment as applying to the states
    E. after Congress passed laws requiring states to respect these rights

54. Most lobbying is focused on
    A. maintaining business-related interests and benefits
    B. increasing poor people's benefits
    C. maintaining middle-class interests and benefits
    D. reforming government processes
    E. promoting the moral agenda of the "religious right"

55. Which of the following is generally true of party identification?
    A. It changes frequently during a person's lifetime as the person's political attitudes change.
    B. It is measured by looking at who people vote for.
    C. It is a choice based upon a person's ideology.
    D. It is usually acquired during childhood.
    E. It is only meaningful for the small percentage of people highly active in politics.

56. The approach to welfare reform in the 1996 Welfare Reform Act
    A. empowered states by giving them block grants
    B. empowered states by giving them categorical grants
    C. empowered states by giving them unfunded mandates
    D. burdened states by giving them categorical grants
    E. burdened states by giving them block grants

57. What makes civil rights different from civil liberties?
    A. Civil rights are the freedoms of racial minorities.
    B. Civil rights are inalienable rights that are protected by limitations placed on government.
    C. Civil rights are rights of groups that the government actively protects.
    D. Civil rights are not inalienable rights; they are privileges earned by groups.
    E. Civil rights were created by social movements in the 1950s and 1960s.

58. Most political activists
    A. work for national party organizations
    B. work for state party organizations
    C. work for local party organizations
    D. serve as delegates to their national party conventions
    E. are appointed through the merit system

59. People in which of the following groups are more likely to be Republicans than Democrats?
    A. white Protestant men who live in the Midwest and suburbs
    B. white Protestant men who live in the Northeast and cities
    C. white Protestant women who live in the Midwest and suburbs
    D. white Protestant women who live in the Northeast and cities
    E. white Jewish men

60. The cartoon above features two members of the House of Representatives: one Republican and one Democratic. What is the message of the cartoon?
    A. The franking privilege is good for legislators but bad for the economy.
    B. Partisan conflict in Congress is good for legislators but bad for the economy.
    C. Democratic legislators and Republican legislators do not care about economic security because they are too busy bickering.
    D. The trading of votes between legislators so that each gets benefits for their districts has negative consequences.
    E. Filibusters put the time and attention of legislators on each other instead of on larger issues.

UNITED STATES GOVERNMENT AND POLITICS

SECTION II
Time—100 minutes

Directions: You have 100 minutes to answer all four of the following questions. It is suggested that you take a few minutes to plan and outline each answer. *Spend approximately one-fourth of your time (25 minutes) on each question.* Illustrate your essay with substantive examples where appropriate. Make certain to number each of your answers as the question is numbered below.

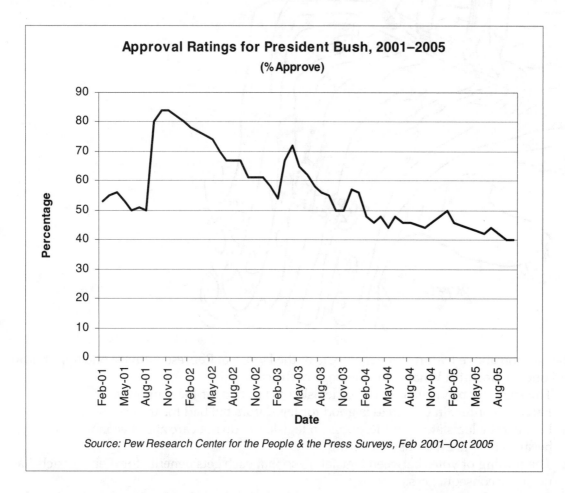

Source: Pew Research Center for the People & the Press Surveys, Feb 2001–Oct 2005

1. The figure above shows public approval ratings for President George W. Bush. Using the information in the figure and your knowledge of American politics, perform the following tasks.

    A. Identify the major trend in the graph that is typical of presidential popularity and not particular to George W. Bush. Identify a factor that contributes to that trend and explain how or why it contributes.

    B. Identify a key turning point in President Bush's popularity. Describe how this illustrates a phenomenon that is typical of presidential popularity. Be sure to describe the phenomenon.

    C. Identify a characteristic of public opinion and explain how it contributes to the limited effect public approval has on presidential decision-making.

2. Parties, interest groups, and mass media are thought of as "linkage institutions" that link the public and politicians to one another. In your answer below, be sure to discuss at least two of these three groups.

   A. Choose one of these linkage institutions and explain how it connects the mass public with politicians. Identify a technique used by this linkage institution that is not used by the others and explain how it helps facilitate this connection. Explain how or why this linkage institution is limited in its ability to connect the mass public to politicians.

   B. Choose one of these linkage institutions and explain how it connects nonmajoritarian groups with politicians. Identify a technique used by this linkage institution that is not used by the others and explain how it helps facilitate this connection. Explain how or why this linkage institution is limited in its ability to connect the mass public to politicians.

   C. Choose one of these linkage institutions and explain how it helps politicians connect to the public. Identify a technique used by this linkage institution that is not used by the others and explain how it helps facilitate this connection. Explain how or why this linkage institution is limited in its ability to connect politicians to the mass public.

3. Since the mid-1960s, there has been an incumbency advantage for members of the House of Representatives.

   A. Describe what is meant by "incumbency advantage."

   B. Identify and describe two factors that have contributed to this advantage. Explain how they contribute.

   C. Identify a consequence of the incumbency advantage for policymaking and explain how the incumbency advantage results in this.

4. There is currently a gay, lesbian, bisexual, and transsexual (GLBT) movement for equal rights. Like equal rights movements before it, federalism provides it with opportunities and obstacles for achieving movement goals.

   A. Describe a reform sought by GLBT movement for equal rights. Explain how opponents evoke core American values to oppose this reform.

   B. Explain how federalism provides an opportunity for equal rights movements.

   C. Explain how federalism presents an obstacle for equal rights movements.

   D. The Supreme Court has three tests that it uses to review laws that treat people differently. They are: strict-scrutiny test, intermediate-scrutiny test, and reasonable-basis test. Identify which of these you think are appropriate for sexual orientation, what the implications are for decisions, and another group that this test applies to.

PRACTICE TEST II ANSWERS

Answers to Section I (Multiple Choice)

1. The correct answer is (C). *McCulloch v. Maryland* established the precedent for national authority when it ruled that the federal government could establish a national bank. See pages 80–81 for more information on this important case.

2. The correct answer is (B). Though interest groups do not directly lobby the Supreme Court, they let the Court know their opinions by filing lawsuits or filing amicus curiae (friend of the court) briefs that defend their position on pending cases. See page 465 for more information.

3. The correct answer is (E). The family is one of the strongest agents of political socialization, and values—which are not directly political but influence political views—are taught through family interactions from early childhood on. See pages 193–95 for more information on agents of political socialization.

4. The correct answer is (E). Greenpeace, U.S.A. is most likely to fight for collective goods—those benefits that people share—because it fights to protect the environment. Unions offer individual goods, while the AMA is a professional group that lobbies for doctors. See pages 281–83 for more information.

5. The correct answer is (C). The relationship was the same for all the years. The older age groups showed a larger turnout than younger groups.

6. The correct answer is (D). More than two-thirds of the federal budget involves mandatory spending measures and is not controlled by the president. See pages 504–05 for more information.

7. The correct answer is (E). The Voting Rights Act of 1965 was an exception to most civil rights legislation affecting voting, including the Fifteenth and Twenty-fourth Amendments, in that it had a large and immediate impact on voter turnout. See page 165 for a discussion on civil rights legislation related to voting behavior. See page 218 for a discussion on the Motor Voter law, which increased voter registration but failed to increase voter turnout. See page 223 and the box on page 226 for discussions of age as a reason for not voting. Among eighteen-to-twenty-four-year-olds, voter turnout has declined by almost a third since the passage of the Twenty-sixth Amendment.

8. The correct answer is (B). Cabinet officials tend to have two traits that make it difficult to influence presidential decisions on a large scale. The first is an agency point of view, in which the officials place the interests of their office or agency over the interests of other offices. The second is that most officials are specialized in the policy area that they oversee. See page 427 for more information on both the agency point of view and the power of expertise.

9. The correct answer is (E). Retrospective voting is a term used when voters support incumbents when they are happy with what the incumbents are doing and oppose incumbents when they disagree with what they are doing. I, II and III are examples of this type of voting. See pages 226–27 for information on prospective and retrospective voting.

10. The correct answer is (D). The Framers of the Constitution recognized that the national government was too weak to hold the nation together, but the Articles of Confederation allowed any state to block amendments. Because there was disagreement between states, the Framers decided to write the Constitution to strengthen the national government. See pages 45–47 for a fuller discussion of the development of the Constitution.

11. The correct answer is (D). Standing committees have responsibility for a specific area of public policy. Standing committees are responsible for both lawmaking and oversight in the area they specialize in. See page 351 for more information.

12. The correct answer is (E). People with higher incomes are more likely to vote.

13. The correct answer is (D). Senatorial courtesy refers to the tradition that a senator from the state in which a federal judge is to be appointed has a say in who gets the appointment. Both the president and other senators tend to defer to the "home-state" senator. See page 458 for more information.

14. The correct answer is (A). The Democratic National Committee and the Republican National Committee have little power and do not control nominating processes, campaigns, party policies, or platforms. They provide services such as campaign funds and training to party candidates. See pages 260–62 for more information.

15. The correct answer is (D). State governments have responsibility for redistricting House election districts. See page 342 for more information.

16. The correct answer is (E). Open seats are contests in which there are no incumbents. Incumbents are people who are already in the office and are seeking reelection. Data in the table supports all three statements.

17. The correct answer is (B). Conservatives believe that government should limit its involvement in economic areas but should uphold traditional values. See page 198 for more information on ideological outlooks.

18. The correct answer is (D). The Senate must approve ambassadors, the attorney general, and Supreme Court justice appointments. Replacements of governors are determined by the states. The White House Chief of Staff is a member of the president's staff and is not subject to Senate approval. See pages 392–94 for more information.

19. The correct answer is (A). Groups such as the ACLU rely on lawsuits to address unpopular issues that Congress won't act on but that might be ruled on favorably in the courts. Other examples of groups that might file lawsuits are the Sierra Club and the Natural Resources Defense Council. See pages 291–92 for more information.

20. The correct answer is (C). A legislative veto is an oversight tool used by Congress that requires Congress's approval before an executive agency or the president acts. See page 366 for more information.

21. The correct answer is (E). The "revolving door" refers to people in government taking jobs with lobbying groups and vice versa. Former government workers can use contacts in

government to help their lobbying group, while former lobbyists have knowledge about policies and how the policy process works, which can help them in government positions. See the box on page 290 for more information.

22. The correct answer is (C). Madison asserted in *Federalist* No. 10 that factions are natural and their potential damage can be controlled by spreading power. When one faction gains control, an oppressive government can result. See page 53 for more discussion of *Federalist* No. 10 and the appendix for the text of Madison's essay, originally published in a New York newspaper.

23. The correct answer is (C). The Tenth Amendment granted states specific powers. Recall that the Anti-Federalists did not want a national government with too much power. See page 78 for more information.

24. The correct answer is (A). Most cases start in district courts, and losing parties do not often successfully appeal to higher courts, thus ending the case. See pages 451–52 for more information.

25. The correct answer is (E). Without knowing the distribution of the popular vote, you cannot tell who won the election. There are no runoffs in presidential elections. It is unclear how voters who chose third-party candidates would have voted—or if they would have voted—had they chosen different candidates. Although the candidates of more than two parties received votes, the vast majority of the votes went to the Democratic and Republican candidates, indicating that this is a two-party system.

26. The correct answer is (E). Recall from the "Take Note" section of the Chapter 10 review that "horse-race journalism" is a concept that has appeared on the test. Although Patterson does not refer to it specifically, you need to remember that the media use polls to report who is ahead and who is behind in voter preferences. This contributes to candidates' momentum, which is discussed on page 385.

27. The correct answer is (A). Members of the United States House of Representatives have always been elected every two years by direct (popular) vote. The ways in which both senators and the president have been chosen has changed over time. See Chapter 2 for more information.

28. The correct answer is (C). Primaries and control of campaign funds have strengthened the control of candidates over party organizations in elections. Choice (A) is accurate but not an indication of the weakening of political parties. Choices (B), (D), and (E) are not accurate. See pages 256–57 for more information.

29. The correct answer is (D). Filibusters take place in the Senate when a minority of senators prevents a vote on a bill by holding the floor and talking until the majority withdraws the bill from consideration. See page 357 for more information.

30. The correct answer is (D). *Brown v. Board of Education* required government mandated school segregation to end but did not require integration of schools. Racial integration of schools occurred infrequently because of existing neighborhood segregation. See pages 146 and 172 for more information.

31. The correct answer is (D). Interest groups usually lobby members of Congress who are likely to support their preferred legislation because it is difficult to change long-held opinions, and it is to the groups' advantage to have allies in Congress to promote the groups' interests. See page 289 for more information.

32. The correct answer is (E). Although the press is responsible after the fact for what is reported or said, the government cannot prohibit freedom of expression before the fact unless it can prove that national security could be harmed, as, for example in the censorship of reports from the battlefront. See Chapter 3 and pages 111–12 and 315 for more information on the concept of "no prior restraint."

33. The correct answer is (B). Franklin D. Roosevelt's term in office was marked by a dramatic increase in presidential authority. See page 377 for more information.

34. The correct answer is (E). Alienated voters are less likely to vote. See pages 221–22 for more information on civic attitudes.

35. The correct answer is (D). Vetoes are a sign of presidential weakness because the president failed to persuade Congress and is using his "last resort." See pages 402–3.

36. The correct answer is (D). This type of delegate selection is done through open primaries or open party caucuses and was instituted by Democrats after the 1968 elections. (As the states adopted presidential primaries to comply with the Democrats' new rules, most also required Republicans to select delegates in the same way). See pages 381–84 for more information on nominating presidential candidates and page 384 for more information on open party caucuses.

37. The correct answer is (D). Gays and lesbians have received little legal protection from the federal government. This group's rights have been determined at the state and local level. See pages 158–61 for more information.

38. The correct answer is (D). Grassroots lobbying organizes the public to influence policy. One way is by having a group's members contact government officials to show that the group's interests have popular support. See page 294 for more information.

39. The correct answer is (D). Although the First Amendment applies to all these answers, this clause prohibits government from interfering with people's expression of religious views. See pages 117–21 for more information.

40. The correct answer is (D). The Constitution, not the Declaration of Independence, detailed the form of government and the checks and balances that make it difficult for one group to hold too much power. See pages 42–43 for a discussion of the Declaration of Independence.

41. The correct answer is (A). Midterm elections are held every four years, the same as presidential elections, so (B) is wrong. (C) describes primary elections, not midterm elections. Voter-registration laws do not differentiate by election, so (D) is wrong. Senators and governors are sometimes on the midterm ballots, and members of the House of Representatives are up for election every two years; therefore, local candidates are not the only ones to appear on the ballot in midterm elections, and thus (E) is wrong. Media attention is greater for presidential elections than for midterm elections.

42. The correct answer is (C). Most, but not all, federal agencies have clientele groups, groups that directly benefit from actions of the agency. These groups receive support, and they in turn support the agencies. Because of this, choices (A), (B), (D), and (E) are false. See page 429 for more information.

43. The correct answer is (E). The idea of equality in America has evolved to mean that all individuals are entitled to equal treatment under the law. Government-funded schools are the best answer, as they apply to all children. The other four choices apply only to select groups. See page 10 for a fuller discussion of the notion of equality.

44. The correct answer is (B). The General Accounting Office was created by Congress to assist in its oversight functions. See page 435 for more information.

45. The correct answer is (A). The Pendleton Act was passed in 1883, and it established the civil service system. See page 423 for more information.

46. The correct answer is (A). Dual federalism is based on the idea that national and state powers should be separated along strict lines. This is no longer the form of federalism used in the United States. Today, cooperative federalism exists, in which state and federal governments share power and work together to solve problems. See page 82 for more information on dual federalism and page 90 for more information on cooperative federalism.

47. The correct answer is (C). A simple majority of the House of Representatives is needed to impeach the president. The Senate then holds a trial, and a two-thirds majority in that chamber is needed to remove the president from office. See the box on page 405 for the steps Congress takes to remove the president from office.

48. The correct answer is (B). Iron triangles are informal groups consisting of government agencies, members of Congress, and lobbyists that form to promote policies helpful to a specific interest. Factions are groups, and though checks and balances are in place to control factions in a federalist system, iron triangles are one way that factions short-circuit these mechanisms and gain power under this form of government. See pages 292–93 for more information and Chapter 3 for more information on federalism.

49. The correct answer is (C). While precedents promote consistency in case law application, the Supreme Court can reverse them. Such an example was *Plessy v. Ferguson*, which was reversed by *Brown v. Board of Education*. See page 146 and pages 463–64 for more information.

50. The correct answer is (C). Single-member districts, news media coverage that tends to ignore third-party candidates, and rules for federal funds that favor the two major parties all make it difficult for third-party candidates to win. In addition, more than two-thirds of the public identifies with the Democratic and Republican parties. Split-ticket voting could benefit third-party candidates. See page 247 for more information on split-ticket voting, pages 248–49 for information on single-member districts, page 267 for the way news media cover campaigns, page 385 for more information on federal matching funds, and page 387 for the public's identification with political parties.

51. The correct answer is (D). Political parties in the United States tend to be less ideologically polarized and less class-based. The United States has fewer major political parties—two— than other European democracies, all of which have three or more. Voter turnout, discussed

in Chapter 7, is lower in the United States. See the box on page 249, the box on page 217, and pages 215–21 for more information.

52. The correct answer is (B). The Supreme Court usually acts as an appellate court, in which it reviews cases that have been heard in lower courts. Most cases that make it to the Supreme Court proceed through the court system in an orderly fashion, from district courts to the U.S. courts of appeals and finally to the Supreme Court. See pages 448–53 for more information.

53. The correct answer is (A). Although states were prohibited by the Fourteenth Amendment from depriving people of life, liberty, or property without due process of law, it wasn't until the 1960s that the Supreme Court used selective incorporation to require states to apply these rights to persons accused of crimes by states. See Table 4-2 on page 126 for a list of cases that the Court selectively incorporated into the Fourteenth Amendment.

54. The correct answer is (A). More than 40 percent of political action committees are associated with businesses. See pages 297–98 for more information.

55. The correct answer is (D). Party identification, which is the loyalty someone may feel towards a political party, tends to be a lifelong association traced back to childhood influences. See pages 204–5 for more information.

56. The correct answer is (A). Block grants give states broad authority in how to spend federal money, as opposed to categorical grants, which limit states' spending authority by placing limits on how the money can be spent. The 1996 Welfare Act authorized a system of block grants to the states, which were given the responsibility for reducing long-term welfare dependency. See page 522 for more information.

57. The correct answer is (C). Civil liberties refer to the rights of individuals that are protected from government interference by the Constitution, while civil rights, or equal rights, refer to whether the rights of groups (racial or sexual groups, for example) are treated equally under the law or require government intervention. See page 144 for more information.

58. The correct answer is (C). More than 95 percent of political activists work for local party organizations. See pages 257–61 for more information on national, state, and local party organizations.

59. The correct answer is (A). White Protestants, men, and people who live in the West and Midwest and suburbs are central to the Republican party coalition. The Northeast is more Democratic because of increasing minority populations, and women are slightly more likely than men to vote Democratic. See pages 246–47 and pages 251–52 for more information. See also Figure 8-4 on page 252.

60. The correct answer is (D). The cartoon illustrates bipartisan logrolling and its negative consequences.

Answer Guidelines for Section II

Question 1 is worth seven points.

Part "A" is worth three points. One point is earned for identifying the major trend as being that popularity goes down during the course of a presidency. Answers can note that there is variability (that for some periods of time popularity goes up), but variability does not earn the point for "major trend." The second point is earned by identifying a factor that contributes to this trend. The third point is for explaining how or why it contributes. Acceptable factors include: president's getting blamed for economic downturns but not usually rewarded for good economic news; cumulative effect of critical news coverage because the media are attracted to negative news, scandals, conflict; public impatience with problems not being solved or wars continuing; the public's unrealistic expectation for president's power; "coalition of minorities," in which the opponents to a variety of policies add up; momentum of election and comparisons to a less-popular opponent fade; and decrease in political resources (influence over Congress; lame duck).

Part "B" is worth two points. One point is for identifying either Fall 2001 (or September 2001 or September 11, 2001), when terrorists attacked the United States, or Spring 2003 (March or April 2003), when the United States attacked Iraq. The turning point can be described in terms more specific to the president, such as his response to September 11 or his decision to confront Iraq militarily. The second point is for describing this turning point as an example of the "rally 'round the flag" effect, in which presidential popularity goes up temporarily when the nation is threatened from abroad or foreign policy crises begin. Answers do not have to include the term "rally 'round the flag" to get points, but references to "wars increase popularity" do not get credit.

Part "C" is worth two points. One point is for identifying a factor about public opinion that contributes to the public's limited effectiveness. Acceptable factors include: public opinion is not well informed, public does not pay close attention to politics, public opinion is inconsistent or erratic, public opinion is more easily led than leading, there is not one clear public opinion (there are "many publics"), public opinion is difficult to measure (for example, because of non-attitudes or leading questions), and public opinions not often followed by public action. No points are given to factors that have to do with the president or the limited power of the president. Acceptable criticism of polls does not include "only interviews a sample."

Question 2 is worth nine points.

Part "A" is worth three points. One point is for explaining how the linkage institution connects the mass public to politicians. One point is given for identifying a specific technique used by this institution and describing how it facilitates the connection. One point is given for explaining how or why this institution is limited in its ability to connect the mass public to politicians. The easiest case to make is for political parties.

Acceptable answers for political parties are: parties bring together majorities to elect public officials under the party label, representing the issues and a broad coalition of supporters. Techniques are: nominating and running candidates for election, creating party platforms that appeal to diverse set of interests, realignments, organizing and informing coalitions in government that reflect public interests, and "going to where the public is" ideologically to win elections. Limitations include: lack and weakness of party affiliations in the public (dealignment), candidate-centered campaigns, lack of difference between parties (no real choice, both too moderate or too conservative to represent diverse opinions), and lack of party discipline in government.

For the choice of interest groups to get any points, the answer must discuss the collection of interest groups representing the mass public. It cannot simply talk about interest groups representing people. Acceptable techniques are: providing information about the public's will to politicians directly (through lobbying) or indirectly (through organizing grassroots efforts and influencing the mass media). It could also talk about how interest groups promote certain candidates in campaigns. Limitations include: the class bias of interest groups preventing them from "adding up" to a representation of the general public, interest groups not representing their own followers' interests, and lack of interest groups' effectiveness (such as their inability to oust incumbents, opposing groups winning out).

Acceptable answers for mass media include the media as a representation of the public or the media as containing the public's voice. Techniques include: civic journalism, public forums, call-in shows, people-on-the-street interviews, letters to the editor, watchdog journalism, and polls. Limitations include discussions of the inability of the media to detect the public's will or their inability to convey it. These can include: lack of substantive attention in the press, top-down nature of the information (covering politicians rather than the people), beat system, and objectivity norm prohibiting the use of the media as a forum.

Part "B" is worth three points. One point is awarded for explaining how the linkage institution connects particular groups to politicians. One point is given for identifying a specific technique used by this institution and describing how it facilitates the connection. One point is given for explaining how or why this institution is limited in its ability to connect the groups to politicians. The easiest case to make is for interest groups.

Acceptable answers for interest groups need to convey the idea that small groups organize to convey their interests to government. Acceptable techniques are: providing information about the group interests to politicians directly (through lobbying) or indirectly (through organizing grass roots efforts and influencing the mass media). It could also talk about how interest groups promote certain candidates in campaigns through contributions to political action committees or through 527 advertising. Limitations include: the class bias of interest groups preventing them from representing some groups well, interest groups not representing their own followers' interests, and lack of interest groups' effectiveness (such as their inability to oust incumbents, opposing groups winning out).

For an answer focusing on political parties to get any points, the answer needs to convey the idea that parties try to be effective without winning majority votes. This entails a discussion of parties influencing agendas of campaigns and government or serving as opposition within government.

For an answer focusing on mass media to get any points, the answer needs to convey the idea that the media includes voices of groups within the public but not the public generally. Techniques include: interest-group advertising, letters to the editor, and people-on-the-street interviews. Limitations include: inability of groups to compel media attention, lack of substantive attention in the press, top-down nature of the information (covering politicians rather than the people), beat system, and objectivity norm prohibiting the use of the media as a forum.

Part "C" is worth three points. One point is for explaining how the linkage institution connects politicians to the mass public. One point is given for identifying a specific technique used by this institution and describing how it facilitates the connection. One point is given for explaining how or why this institution is limited in its ability to connect politicians to the mass public. The easiest case to make is for the mass media.

Acceptable answers for the media include the idea that politicians communicate with the public through the media. Techniques include: coverage of presidential speeches such as the State of the Union address, interviews with politicians, beat system organized around centers of political power, coverage of campaign speeches and events such as the conventions, coverage of campaign debates, and news about government actions or proposals. Limitations include: lack of substantive attention in the press, priority on entertaining rather than informing the public, skepticism of the press toward politicians resulting in failure to communicate their messages or heavy negative spin, feeding frenzy, distrust of public in media, and public's lack of attention to news.

Acceptable answers for political parties include the idea that politicians communicate with the public through parties.

Acceptable answers for interest groups include the idea that politicians communicate.

Question 3 is worth six points.

Part "A" is worth one point. The answer needs to convey the idea that incumbent representatives—those already holding a seat—are likely to win reelection.

Part "B" is worth three points. One point is earned for identifying two factors that contribute to the advantage. Identifying only one factor results in no first point, but a good explanation for the factor can earn the second point. The second point is earned for explaining how the first factor contributes to the advantage. The third point is earned by explaining how the second one contributes to the advantage. Acceptable factors include: higher name recognition, ability to bring benefits to the district or its members such as pork-barrel projects or case work, staff that works year-round on helping the member (no point if the answer says that this staff campaigns for the member), franking privilege (free mailings—letters, surveys, newsletters—to district and press releases to newspapers in the district), campaign funding (more contributions from political action committees, party support, or individual contributions), generally positive year-round news coverage, more media attention during campaign, trust developed over years of visits to the district paid for from a publicly funded or interest-group-funded travel budget (successful "home style"), and House facilities to enhance news coverage such as recording studios. To get the explanation points, the answers need to explain how or why these factors contribute to advantages over challengers. Because gerrymandering can jeopardize the incumbency advantage of individual members by pitting them against other incumbents, an answer is acceptable only when it describes creating a system of safe seats.

Part "C" is worth two points. The first is for identifying a policymaking consequence of the incumbency advantage. The second is for explaining how the incumbency advantage results in this consequence. Acceptable consequences include: status-quo oriented (same interests win out), fewer new ideas, policies are less responsive to changes in public opinion and national conditions, fewer "clean government" reforms because members seek to maintain or increase spending on things that help them win (such as franking privilege, institutional resources, pork-barrel legislation, campaign finance system), and policies continue to reflect the point of view of a demographically unrepresentative body because the largely white, male, lawyer membership stays in office.

Question 4 is worth eight points.

Part "A" is worth two points. The first is for describing a reform that the group seeks. Acceptable reforms include: same-sex marriage, outlawing private discrimination based on sexual orientation, replacing the "don't ask, don't tell" military policy with acceptance, full legal rights and employee benefits for civil unions, strengthening hate crime legislation. No points are given for "making homosexuality legal," as the Court has already invalidated laws against sexual relations between consenting adults and reversed laws that imposed employment discrimination. The second is for explaining how a value is evoked to oppose this reform. Acceptable answers need to include core American values (unity, national security, freedom, self-reliance, patriotism) and explain how they are used to oppose the reform identified.

Part "B" is worth two points. An explanation that indicates an understanding of federalism and generally how it would be an opportunity is worth one point. An explanation that indicates an understanding of federalism and provides a clear explanation for how or why federalism provides an opportunity is worth two points. Acceptable explanations include: ability to appeal to the federal government against discrimination at state level (this might include references to judicial review, national supremacy, or rights recognized in the Constitution), ability to win in specific states or regions (perhaps through referendum or legislatures), states as laboratories to test out policies that can serve as examples for other states or the nation, and fiscal federalism (interdependency allows federal government to influence the states through funding programs that relate to GLBT's goals).

Part "C" is worth two points. An explanation that indicates an understanding of federalism and generally how it would be an obstacle is worth one point. An explanation that indicates an understanding of federalism and provides a clear explanation for how or why federalism provides an obstacle is worth two points. Acceptable explanations include: states, perhaps through initiatives and referendums, restrict the rights of the group; having these restrictions upheld by state courts and legislatures; and state power over education and public safety.

Part "D" is worth two points. One point is awarded for correctly identifying another group that the selected test applies to. These are: race and ethnicity for strict; gender or sex for intermediate; and age or income for reasonable. One point is awarded for correctly identifying the implications the test has for decisions. These are: discrimination is assumed to be "suspect" and unconstitutional in the absence of overwhelming justification for strict; it is assumed to be "almost suspect" and unconstitutional unless there is a clearly compelling and justified purpose for intermediate scrutiny and it is assumed "not suspect" unless no sound rationale can be provided for "reasonable." Students do not get the point if they simply use the words "suspect," "almost suspect," or "not suspect." They can earn the point without using the words if the description is correct.